A Reporter's Guide to the EU

A Reporter's Guide to the EU addresses a pressing need for an effective, in-depth guide to reporting on this major governing body, offering practical advice on writing and reporting on the EU and a clear, concise breakdown of its complex inner-workings.

Sigrid Melchior, an experienced Brussels-based journalist, gives a detailed overview of the main EU institutions and explains the procedures for passing EU law. Interviews with professionals working for the EU, from areas including lobbying, public relations, diplomacy and journalism, are featured throughout the book.

Building on this, the second half of the book provides useful journalistic tools and tips on how to approach EU reporting. It identifies common mistakes in reporting on the EU and how to avoid them, as well as offering guidance on investigative reporting. Melchior also details how to work with information gathered and maintained by EU institutions, including their audiovisual archives, the Eurostat and Eurobarometer, which are invaluable resources for journalists and journalism students.

With few aspects of political life that remain untouched by EU decision-making the book demystifies the EU system and its sources, enabling professional journalists and students of journalism to approach EU reporting with clarity and confidence.

For updated resources related to *A Reporter's Guide to the EU*, please visit www.areportersguidetotheeu.com

Sigrid Melchior is a Brussels-based freelance journalist. Since 2007 she has covered EU politics and European politics for Swedish written press. She has previously published *Handbok i EU-journalistik* (2013) and *EU-handboken* (2016) in Sweden.

A Reporter's Guide to the EU

Sigrid Melchior
Edited by Stephen Gardner

LONDON AND NEW YORK

First published 2017
by Routledge
2 Park Square, Milton Park, Abingdon, Oxon OX14 4RN

and by Routledge
605 Third Avenue, New York, NY 10017

Routledge is an imprint of the Taylor & Francis Group, an informa business

© 2017 Sigrid Melchior

The right of Sigrid Melchior to be identified as author of this work has been asserted by her in accordance with sections 77 and 78 of the Copyright, Designs and Patents Act 1988.

All rights reserved. No part of this book may be reprinted or reproduced or utilised in any form or by any electronic, mechanical, or other means, now known or hereafter invented, including photocopying and recording, or in any information storage or retrieval system, without permission in writing from the publishers.

Trademark notice: Product or corporate names may be trademarks or registered trademarks, and are used only for identification and explanation without intent to infringe.

British Library Cataloguing in Publication Data
A catalogue record for this book is available from the British Library

Library of Congress Cataloging in Publication Data
Names: Melchior, Sigrid, 1981– author.
Title: A reporter's guide to the EU / Sigrid Melchior ; edited by Stephen Gardner.
Other titles: Reporter's guide to the European Union
Description: London ; New York : Routledge, 2017. | Includes index.
Identifiers: LCCN 2016047680| ISBN 9781138678637 (pbk. : alk. paper) | ISBN 9781138678620 (hardback : alk. paper) | ISBN 9781315558820 (ebook)
Subjects: LCSH: European Unon. | European Union–Press coverage. | Reporters and reporting–European Union countries. | Press and politics–European Union countries.
Classification: LCC JN30 .M443 2017 | DDC 341.242/2–dc23
LC record available at https://lccn.loc.gov/2016047680

ISBN: 978-1-138-67862-0 (hbk)
ISBN: 978-1-138-67863-7 (pbk)
ISBN: 978-1-315-55882-0 (ebk)

Typeset in Goudy
by Cenveo Publisher Services

Contents

Preface ix
Acknowledgements xi

PART I
Introduction 1

1 Introduction to EU reporting 3

2 A few tips and tricks to get started 8

3 What, really, is the EU? 15

PART II
The three main EU institutions 27

4 The European Commission 29

 The commissioners and their portfolios 30
 The European Commission as a source 36
 What the European Commission does 47

5 The European Parliament 56

 The MEPs 57
 Party groups 60
 Committees 72
 Plenary sessions 76
 MEPs' performances 81
 What the European Parliament does 84

6 The Council of Ministers and the European Council   95

The council formations 96
The permanent representations: the national governments in Brussels 100
The rotating presidency of the council 102
Council of Ministers press office and website 105
The decision-making process in the Council of Ministers 108
The European Council 116

PART III
Decision-making in the EU   125

7 The legislative process part I: The European Commission proposes a new law   127

8 The legislative process part II: The European Parliament and the Council of Ministers amend and adopt the law   137

Special legislative procedures 138
The ordinary legislative procedure 141

9 Tools for following the legislative process   152

10 Delegated decision-making   157

PART IV
Other EU sources   163

11 Other EU institutions   165

European External Action Service, EEAS 165
Court of Justice of the European Union 168
The European Central Bank 170
Court of Auditors 171
OLAF: the EU's counter-corruption agency 171
The European Economic and Social Committee and the Committee of the Regions 172
Decentralized EU agencies 173

12 Statistics, opinion polls, sound, photo and video   180

Eurostat 180
Eurobarometer 181
Photo, audio and video from the EU institutions 183

Contents vii

13	Lobbying	185
14	Think tanks and research	197
15	Media	202

PART V
Practical EU reporting 211

16 Bringing the EU home 213

Making the connection between Brussels and home 213
Holding your politicians accountable 217
Specialist journalist? Integrate the EU into your reporting 221
Consumer journalism 221
Men and women – who are your sources? 223

17 Common mistakes in EU reporting and how to avoid them 225

18 Investigative EU reporting 237

The state of investigative EU reporting 237
Investigating EU spending 241
Investigating lobbying, conflicts of interests and corruption in the EU 245
Access to documents in the EU 252
Whistleblowers 259

19 Practical help in Brussels 263

Accreditation to the European institutions 263
When in Brussels 265
Journalist organizations 266

20 Writing about the EU 268

Glossary 273
Index 283

Preface

The book you are holding in your hands is what it's called: a reporter's guide to covering the European Union. I wrote this book to give both professional reporters and students of journalism, from any EU country, some concrete tools for following any story that emanates from, or leads to, Brussels. Most European reporters will at one point stumble across a story that has its roots in the EU; this is inevitable when so many of our national rules are decided at the EU level.

My aim and hope is that we will all raise our standards when we write about the EU. By that I mean that we should be more careful with facts, skip the stereotypes about the EU institutions and EU countries other than our own and explain to our readers what effect EU policies have on their lives and not simply repeat our national politicians' versions of what goes on behind closed doors in Brussels. I hope that we can dig up our own stories about the EU institutions and ignore their pre-packaged 'news', i.e. propaganda, and that we publish without considering whether our story will influence EU opinion in any way. In short, that we treat the EU as other political institutions are treated: seriously and critically.

Because whether we take the EU seriously, ignore it or make fun of it, laws continue to be made in Brussels and Strasbourg. The gap between how much the EU influences your life and mine and how little we are aware of it and try to influence it is growing every day. That gap is, in my opinion, the EU's biggest democratic deficit.

This book was originally published in Swedish in 2013. It was updated, translated and re-written in 2016, in large part before the United Kingdom's referendum on leaving the EU. At the time of writing, there are still 28 EU countries. The negotiations about the coming UK–EU divorce have not yet started and what the future relationship will look like is unknown, which is why I leave speculation about this out of the book.

Ahead of the Brexit vote, many false claims were made about the EU by British politicians and the debate became superficial in some parts of the British media. This proves the main point that I want to make in this book: that it is important to talk about the EU and explain what it is and how it works so that people can make informed decisions.

There is some factual information in this book that will be outdated and inaccurate in a few years, so please do not copy-paste facts without double checking if they still hold true. At the end of each chapter, there are links to all websites mentioned in the text. Some of these links will also become outdated, but you can find the correct ones, updated on a regular basis, here: www.areportersguidetotheeu.com.

If you have any questions or remarks about the book or about EU journalism, please get in touch.

Brussels, September 2016
Sigrid Melchior

Acknowledgements

This book is to a large extent based on background interviews. Thank you to all the unnamed civil servants, politicians and press people in the EU institutions, political scientists, lobbyists and other EU people who have helped me with facts, cases, ideas and anecdotes.

Thank you friends in the Brussels bubble and fellow EU reporters – longtime colleagues and new acquaintances – for big and small tips that have been useful for this book: Brigitte Alfter, Staffan Dahllöf, Jan Werts, Andreas Liljeheden, Rikard Jozwiak, Rikke Albrechtsen, Meabh McMahon, Gareth Harding, Ryan Heath, Jon Worth, Carina Folkesson Lillo, David Lundy, Andreas Müllerleile and Aleksandra Eriksson Pogorzelska. Thank you Elin Hellström and Becky Sear for explaining the publishing business to me and thank you Stephen Gardner for editing the text.

Especially thank you friends and family who have read parts of the book and whose comments have made it so much better: Fredrik Haglund, Charlotta Asplund Catot, Teresa Küchler, Sara Ahnborg, Helena de Groot, Agnes Wold and Lars Melchior. And finally, thank you to my husband and partner David Jauzion-Graverolles for love and support.

Part I
Introduction

1   Introduction to EU reporting

A few years ago, I was covering a late-night EU summit. Just ahead of my print deadline, at midnight, the EU leaders agreed a compromise and presented a new set of figures. I compared the numbers to those I already had from an earlier stage of the negotiations and, in the rush, I miscounted. The headline of my article was something along the lines of 'EU backs out on earlier promises', while the midnight compromise had actually meant a bigger commitment.

The next day, I woke up to five missed calls from the Swedish prime minister's press secretary. I called my editor at one of Sweden's biggest dailies, prepared to get fired from my just-started assignment as their freelance correspondent. But he did not understand the gravity of my mistake. There had been no reactions from readers or anyone at the newspaper. Not a single person among tens of thousands of readers had picked up on the blatant error.

That is when I realized how lonely we Brussels correspondents are. Our articles fly off into space and never really land anywhere. If a journalist misplaces a comma in an article about national politics, he or she can expect to get a bunch of angry emails from people who claim to know better. This is rarely or never the case with EU stories.

All Brussels correspondents have these kinds of anecdotes. There was the experienced EU reporter who wrote about a government inquiry that had showed huge gaps in knowledge about the EU. Sixty per cent of Swedish political science master students could not name the two legislative bodies of the EU. The reporter wrote the right answer – 'the parliament and the council' – in brackets. Ironically and embarrassingly for her, someone at the news desk changed that to the factually wrong 'the parliament and the European Council'. (The European Council is the EU countries' presidents and prime ministers while the council consists of the EU countries' ministers from the different policy areas.)

And there was the public service TV journalist from a non-EU country who called his editor from the Maastricht summit, in December 1991, telling him that the EU countries had plans for a common currency. OK, the plans were ten years into the future, but it was still huge news – this would become the single biggest transfer yet of national sovereignty to the EU, the power over the money printing presses. The feature the reporter made never got aired because the editor told him that it was 'incomprehensible'.

Does it have to be boring and complicated?

EU journalism is caught in a vicious circle. Reporters and editors do not report from Brussels because people do not want to read about news from Brussels. The EU is considered boring and difficult. The most read articles about the EU are the jokey articles that are often far from the truth, such as Brussels bureaucrats conspiring to ban a popular sausage somewhere.

National politicians are not keen on shining a light on the EU. Talking seriously about EU politics does not win them many votes. In many countries, there is still controversy about the country's relationship with the EU, and within some political parties the EU issue causes painful divisions. If the media does not report about the EU, and politicians don't talk about the EU, how can the general public think that the EU is important and interesting? Chances are small.

Our readers consume news every day about our own national political systems and know the necessary basics. But when we write an article describing a precise moment in the EU decision-making process, we have to start from zero and first describe the fundamentals of how the EU institutions work. If the public had some basic knowledge about how the EU works, we could skip this admittedly boring part and write more about what *is* interesting: the power dynamics and the political values, for instance.

Since journalists do not write about the EU in a way that grabs the attention of readers, there is little public awareness about everyday EU matters. No TV series depicts the political power struggles in the EU; no hip hop song has ever been sung about the European Commission. Many European citizens know much more about the political life at the White House in the US than they do about Brussels. Only in the EU capital Brussels is there a critical mass of people who know enough about the EU to enjoy cultural representations of its political life. The Brussels opera house *la Monnaie*, for example, located the Mozart opera *Mitridate, re di Ponto* at an EU summit, in a representation in spring 2016.

'The EU has decided'

Newspaper texts about the EU are often bone dry and full of legal and political jargon. Another, even worse, fault is that they are often simplified to the point of inaccuracy. All too often we write that 'an EU report says', 'according to an EU proposal' or 'the EU has decided', without explaining what this mysterious 'EU' is, without showing what role our national politicians are playing and without explaining whether the decision is final or if it can still be changed. Neither our editors nor our readers would accept such a lack of precision if we were writing about national politics.

This imprecise news contributes to the feeling that the EU is not part of 'normal' politics, that is, national, regional and local politics. Laws made at EU level are depicted as different and less important than those made at national level and the EU political process is shown as distant, cold and strange, even hostile.

I personally think that the 'the EU has decided to' line is often the result of the reporter's own insecurity about how the EU functions. Rather than taking the risk of making a mistake, we use the all-inclusive concept 'EU'. We cover our backs but we haven't made our readers any wiser.

A large portion of what becomes national law in the EU member states has first been decided at EU level. We will cover how this is done in subsequent chapters, but a general, simplified outline is given here.

The three major EU institutions that take part in the law-making process are:

- The European Commission, which is the only EU institution that has the right to propose new laws (see chapters 4 and 7).
- The Council of Ministers, which is composed of the ministers from the 28 member states' governments – if the proposed EU law has to do with agriculture, it will be the ministers of agriculture who negotiate the issue; if it is an energy matter, it will be the energy ministers (see chapters 6 and 8).
- The European Parliament, directly elected by the European citizens every fifth year (see chapters 5 and 8). The council and the parliament amend the commission proposal and, in the end, adopt the law.

One of my main points in this book is that it is seldom an adequate description to say: 'The EU has decided ...' or 'The EU wants to ...'. It is only the European Commission that bears any resemblance to the mythological picture of the 'EU elite' in Brussels. The European Parliament consists of British as well as Polish, Portuguese and Finnish politicians, for instance, put on electoral lists by their national political parties and elected by their fellow citizens. The Council of Ministers is nothing more and nothing less than the sum of 28 countries' governments.

Your politicians like to blame 'the EU' for decisions they have made

Politicians in all EU countries take credit for popular EU actions and blame the unpopular ones on 'the EU'. But if we look at the general scheme of decision-making at the EU level, we see that no EU law can pass if the Council of Ministers says no. And in the Council of Ministers, each national minister has a seat at the table.

For some decisions, every country has the right of veto (see chapter 6). In those cases, it is technically impossible for 'the EU' to have decided something that your national government has not also agreed to. In other cases, the decision requires a majority vote. But even then, almost all votes are still taken with unanimity. Of course, nobody loves every detail of the law – it is after all a compromise between 28 governments' different positions – but in most cases all countries' governments agree that the compromise is better than the status quo.

The information jungle

National politicians can be blamed for passing the buck on unpopular decisions to 'the EU', but the EU institutions are, unfortunately, also unhelpful in making the EU understandable to the wide public. The EU institutions as a whole are miserably poor at communication, with the exception of some designated press people.

Web-wise, the EU institutions are a nightmare. When you research a story, you can often find all the background information you need on the different websites, but it tends to disappear in a flood of reports from the early 2000s, sections called 'highlights' or 'news' that are guaranteed to be the least interesting thing on the site, educational games to teach high school students how the EU works, and search functions that just don't work. The worst is that nothing ever seems to be removed, not even information that with the passage of time and treaty changes has actually become inaccurate.

People working in the European Commission can seriously be heard saying, with pride, that www.europa.eu is 'the world's largest website', not meaning the site with the most visitors, but the most crammed one.

The cumbersome communication set-up is in large part a reflection of the very construction of the EU. Every EU country guards its national interest. The EU institutions never compromise on diplomacy for communicative or aesthetic values, so anything that might be sensitive to one EU country is erased. And since there are 28 countries in the club, that means a lot of erasing. All the fun is glossed out. There are too many cooks in the communication kitchen.

Every EU country wants to make a cultural and linguistic mark in the union, and begrudges other countries choosing a name for new EU terminology. Therefore, the currency euro – pronounced with difficulty in several European languages – is not called the more beautiful and interesting acronym écu (European Currency Unit), which sounded too French for the British. In order not to upset anyone, most things are called something that starts with 'EU' or 'Euro', and everything that has ever passed through an EU institution comes out with yellow letters against a blue background.

Just compare the bland EU terminology to American political concepts such as the 'Patriot Act', 'Fiscal cliff' or 'Budget Super Committees'. These are catchy terms that stay in the memory and that become popular cultural references. Many Europeans could explain the meaning of those American political terms. But how many of us can offhand explain the – to us at least much more important – difference between the European Commission and the Council of Ministers?

The EU institutions do not adapt their communication to what people outside the Brussels bubble know. For a start, they only communicate what their respective institution is doing. There is actually nobody who speaks on behalf of 'the EU'.

Most people cannot tell the different EU institutions apart. They think of 'the EU' as one thing and their own country as another thing. But the way the people working in the EU institutions, including the press people, see the world is like this: the commission, the parliament and 'the member states'.

Why is EU journalism important?

The fact that so few reporters scrutinize decisions taken at the EU level is dangerous to our democracies. For democracy to function, we all need to understand how, when and why political decisions are taken. How otherwise could we debate the political alternatives and hold our representatives to account for their actions?

The media is a crucial link between political power and the citizen, with the power and responsibility to investigate, explain, put news into context and expose. At the EU level, this unfortunately does not work. Citizens are severely under-informed about political issues that are decided at the EU level and that affect their lives much more than many of the issues decided nationally that get much more reporting.

In 2009, the Lisbon Treaty came into force, transferring a sizeable chunk of political power from national governments and parliaments to the EU level. Around the same time, the financial crisis and the euro crisis led to a series of quick decisions that in combination created a new economic–political architecture in which Brussels wields ever more influence over national economic policies. That the EU is important is not an opinion, it is a fact.

During the same period the newspaper crisis also reached new peaks. Many media let go of their expensive correspondents in Brussels. Their shoes were filled – if at all – by freelance journalists.

Brussels-based reporters tend to cover the big stories: the EU summits; major votes in the European Parliament and the Council of Ministers; and big decisions and legislative proposals from the European Commission. On top of that, they often serve as a sort of Europe correspondent, rushing to Paris to cover a terrorist attack and to Italy or Greece for the latest refugee tragedy. They often do not have time to cover the many steps of the EU legislative process to give the readers the same level of coverage as they would for an equivalent law passed within their home country – this would not be possible even if there were two or three times as many EU correspondents. The only solution to giving EU questions the attention they deserve is for both generalist and specialist reporters to start incorporating the EU into their everyday reporting, because there is hardly any part of political life today that does not have an EU dimension to it.

2 A few tips and tricks to get started

Subsequent chapters deal with how to find information and sources in the different EU institutions and how to write about the EU. But first, let us begin with some general tips to get started with EU reporting.

There is no central EU press office – keep track of three EU institutions plus your government

If you want to be sure not to miss any important EU news, you need to keep an eye on the three main EU institutions: the European Commission, the European Parliament and the Council of Ministers. You also need to keep track of your national government through its permanent EU representation in Brussels (and maybe those of the other main EU countries too).

There is a common website for press releases and calendars for all the EU institutions, including those that are tiny and almost completely unknown: **the EU's online newsroom**. It is a good starting point to get an overview of what is going on in the different EU institutions. The EU TV channel **Europe by Satellite**, EbS, is also good for keeping track of major events. Many Brussels-based correspondents use the TV schedule as a calendar.

The EU institutions represent different aspects of EU cooperation: the commission represents the EU as a whole, the Council of Ministers the EU governments and the European Parliament the people. These three institutions are involved in all EU action to various degrees depending on the policy area and the purpose of the action. Whatever EU issue you are covering, and whatever the actual procedure is, there is value in talking to all three institutions to not miss out on one of these perspectives. Call the commission when you need to understand the idea behind some EU initiative and get background information that puts it into perspective. Talk to the Council of Ministers to understand the different national interests on the issue. And finally, turn to the European Parliament if you want to know what politicians to the left, right and centre think about it.

Sign up to the EU institutions' email lists

A good story often begins in your inbox. Make sure you are on the mailing lists of the EU institutions, European Parliament committees and political groups, the commission's directorates-general (policy departments), lobbyists and think tanks – anything and anyone that you think might be of interest to you.

Once you have mapped who you want information from, get in touch with the press people from these institutions directly, rather than signing up to their email lists on the websites. Use the initial contact to get to know the press people a little and explain to them what information you want from them. The better they know you, the easier it will be to get the information you want next time you call.

Get yourself a separate email account for these general EU emails because they can easily exceed a hundred a day.

When something big that you have been waiting for happens, like a final deal in the tripartite legislative negotiations (see chapter 8) or a final vote in the European Parliament, many of those involved will be quick to send out their comments. You get a quick overview of the different positions and reactions in your inbox, along with their contact details, which will save you a great deal of research time.

Always select English or French on the institutions' websites

When you go to **the home page of the EU institutions**, you are first asked to choose which of the EU's 24 official languages you want to continue in. If you understand English reasonably well (and you do; you are reading this book), you should always choose English. In second place, choose French and in third place German.

All texts that come from the European Commission have been written in one of these three languages and then translated to the others. The language quality is therefore always better in English or French than in the less prevalent languages. But most importantly, translation takes time and new documents are often only available in English and French, maybe German, to start with.

Also, there are still some forgotten texts lurking in the dark corners of the EU institutions' websites that have become factually wrong after treaty changes, but still have not been changed. This is more often the case for information in less spoken languages.

If you click Czech or Portuguese or another less spoken EU language, you will get a really irritating language mix. The static content (background information) will be in Czech and Portuguese, while most of the changing information (that is, virtually everything of interest) will be in English and French.

It is easy to lose the overall picture when you mix languages. Therefore, it is safer to do all your research on the EU websites in English or French and then, once you have found the text or the site you want, change the language setting. Sometimes it will be available in your language, sometimes not. Look for a language menu in the upper right corner, or check the URL (website's address). Somewhere in the long line of characters there is 'en' for English. Change that to the language code of your choosing.

Once the UK has left the EU, the language balance in the EU institutions will probably shift towards more French and German. But even without the UK in the EU, English is the main second language for most Europeans, especially in Northern and Eastern Europe, and will probably still be used as a major working language in the institutions.

Better google than use the search engines of the EU institutions

Do not waste time using the EU institutions' search engines to find specific documents, or trying to find them on the institutions' websites based on logical thinking. If you know a few key words in English, or if you have a paragraph from a text, it is often easier to just google that, and then jump to the right website.

Narrow your searches to the EU institutions by typing 'site:europa.eu' in the Google search field. Or restrict by file type, by typing 'file type:XLS' or 'file type:pdf' or whatever file type you are looking for.

Be aware that the '.eu' top-level domain is not only used by the EU institutions. Organizations and companies that lobby the EU, and news outlets and think tanks, use it as well. All EU institutions are called something + 'europa.eu'.

Call the press people in Brussels

The EU press people are in general very competent – both on policy and procedure. You will always save time by calling them directly, instead of looking around the institutions' websites for background information.

There is one thing you cannot get around: in order to know who to call, you need to have some idea of which EU institution is dealing with the issue you are writing about. But if you know that, it gets you a long way. If you do not know, start by calling the European Parliament's press service rather than the European Commission or the Council of Ministers. In my experience, they are more open and answer more quickly. The European Commission and the European Parliament have **representation/information offices** in all European capitals, with a couple of press people. You can always call them if you want to speak your own language and talk to someone from your own country who might be easier to communicate with than someone in Brussels.

Most EU issues are dealt with by all three main EU institutions, so they will be in the loop. If you are looking for background information rather than reactions to a specific event, you can often find someone in any institution who can help you. If you have been in contact with a nice press person who explains things in a way that you found helpful, call him or her back with all sorts of questions.

All press people I have talked to say the same thing: it is so rare for people from outside the Brussels bubble to call, that we always make sure to find the answer for them, even if it is a question we are technically not in charge of.

EU politicians are your reader's politicians. Call them

Many EU myths in newspaper articles could easily be killed off with just one phone call. Yet many of us do not make that call. Some reporters might be a bit scared of making the international call, and not really knowing how to phrase the question. But even if the EU feels distant and weird, EU politics is *not* foreign politics; most of the time it is domestic politics. Pretend the EU people are in your national capital and call them.

The laws that are adopted by the EU institutions will eventually become binding national laws that will affect your readers in your country. You need to make a mental shift and think of the MEPs in the European Parliament and the ministers and civil servants in the Council of Ministers – even the politicians from other EU countries – as part of your country's political system. They have an influence on your national politics through the EU decisions. Your readers have the right to know and you have the right to gather the relevant information.

EU policy is always a compromise between all the EU countries. No single country feels completely at ease with the compromise position. But there is no homogeneous, united EU on one side and your country on the other side. This is only a myth kept alive by national politicians who want to have 'the EU' to blame when they feel like it.

Let go of prestige. Just ask

To most reporters, the EU means a bad conscience. Many journalists feel embarrassed because they know too little about how the EU works and think that everyone else knows more.

There is nothing inherently difficult about the EU; it is no more complicated than national or local politics. EU issues, however, often tend to be quite technical, so you really need to be sure about the procedure, i.e. which EU institutions decide in the matter and in what way they take the decisions, before you can get on with your story.

The Brussels correspondents ask simple questions every day in the commission's daily press conference, like: What institution is dealing with the issue, and can the EU really decide this? Ask those questions too.

Be culturally sensitive

Your EU sources will come from 27 other countries. The more languages you know and the more cultures you have some understanding of, the more easily you will find the information and sources you are after. This does not mean that you should feel hampered if you, like most of us, only speak English, or your native language and some English. What is important is that you actually dare to contact sources other than those from your country, and that you try to look beyond your national frame of reference.

People in the EU institutions speak EU jargon: an international and basic form of English, mixed with technical EU terms. For Scandinavians, just be a notch politer than you would be back home, saying 'Good morning' instead of 'Hi'. For French and Germans, do not be offended by people using the informal rather than the formal 'you'.

A lobbyist once told me that EU lobbying was so much fun because the range of the positions you could morally defend in Brussels was much wider than in any EU country, because everything that is politically correct in *one* EU country will also be accepted in the EU context, and that justifies a great range of opinions and causes. It is kind of the same thing about behaviour: what is normal behaviour as a journalist in your country will also be OK in Brussels, ranging from the extremely polite and submissive to the extremely informal and critical.

Read the actual texts

The devil is in the details and when it comes to EU laws, you need to read the actual legal texts. This is the only way you can be independent from the politicians and do your job as a reporter.

Too often we quote politicians with different views on a text, without actually explaining what the text says. Also, too often we rely on other people's journalism and re-write their EU stories. It will not take much more time to read the texts yourself.

Read the proposal from the commission, the impact assessment, the conclusions from the EU summit, the report that is being voted in the parliament committee, the amendment that all the fuss is about and the final adopted text – whatever it is you are writing about.

Catch the EU people in the European Parliament

Some of the EU institutions are not very open with media. But representatives from all EU institutions will at one point visit the European Parliament, in Brussels or Strasbourg. Make your trips coincide with theirs.

In the European Parliament, all plenary sessions and committee meetings are open for journalists and streamed online. The MEPs are outspoken and prone to debate and the culture is less respectful and diplomatic than in the other EU institutions.

You can try to set up an interview in the margin of whatever meeting your target interviewee is going to. If he or she is trying to dodge your questions, you can always approach him or her in the hallway outside the meeting room.

Catch your national politicians off guard in Brussels

The same tip also works for national politicians who come to Brussels for a meeting in the Council of Ministers or an EU summit. It can be easier to set up an interview with busy politicians in Brussels, in between meetings, when they are away from home and all other obligations. The cost: a low cost airline ticket to Brussels from your capital.

This is especially useful if there is a big scandal back home and your minister or prime minister refuses to answer questions. The press conferences after council meetings or EU summits are often small affairs. After a Foreign Affairs Council, for example, the press conference with the foreign minister from a medium or small country attracts the attention of a maximum of ten reporters. It is an intimate setting around a small table, where it is almost impossible for the minister to avoid questions.

Come over for a study visit

If you are planning to write about the EU more than once a year, it will probably be worthwhile to make a short trip to Brussels. You need to walk between the institutions yourself and see where the politicians have coffee to get a feeling of how things work. The abstract EU will become concrete more quickly that way; 'the faceless eurocrat' will get an actual face.

Walking around the EU quarter, you will get a feeling for the real size of abstract institutions or organizations and for the way the different interests are connected. For instance, you will see that the watchdogs the European Ombudsman, the Court of Auditors and the European Data Protection Supervisor share the same office building. And that some 50 NGOs that work with environmental, social and transparency issues share a building in Brussels' Congolese quarter, close to the EU centre, where they network in their common cafeteria.

The European Commission and the European Parliament organize study visits for journalists. Check their representation offices in your country to see if you can join.

Use the term 'EU' sparsely. Tell us who the decision-makers are

Headlines need to be short. 'The European Parliament's Committee on Women's Rights and Gender Equality', for example, is not fit for a headline. It is not surprising that editors and reporters often use the catchier but often meaningless term 'EU'.

However, to shorten all kinds of committee or other names to the admittedly snappier 'EU' is unnecessarily vague. Often, it is also wrong. To call a European Parliament committee, a consultative body or an individual MEP 'the EU' is as wrong as saying that 'Spain' wants something when you write about what one specific Spanish political party or politician wants.

Only refer to 'the EU' when you are talking about the institution that has the actual power in the issue, for example the European Commission when it executes EU policy, or when all EU countries, at the end of a long legislative process, have finally signed the dotted line on a deal. It is also vague to the point of inaccuracy to write 'EU report' or 'EU proposal' if the report or proposal comes from an institution that does not have the power to decide anything about the current issue. This is why it is so important to know at all times which institution has this power.

Let go of the mysticism

Many perceive EU decision-making as complicated and a bit mysterious. Often we think dealings are secret when they are actually not. A great deal of mystery derives from the simple fact that there is so little media coverage of the legislative process. We do not write about the many discussions and negotiations prior to a final decision; we simply report on the end result. People get the (wrong) message that 'everything is already decided'.

Many documents can be difficult to find because of the EU institutions' bad websites, but they are not secret. For example, online newspaper *Politico* wrote that a 'leaked draft report fears robots could herald the end of humanity'[1], referring to a draft report from the European Parliament's Committee on Legal Affairs, that was not 'leaked' at all, but had actually been published on the committee's own, public website two days earlier.

Do not overuse phrases such as 'secret EU report', 'leaks' and 'disclosure'. Be honest: was the report really secret? Or was it you who did not know where to find it?

Links

EU's online newsroom
europa.eu/newsroom/index_en.htm

EU TV channel Europe by Satellite, EbS
ec.europa.eu/avservices/ebs/schedule.cfm

The home page for the EU institutions
www.europa.eu

The European Commission's representation offices in all the EU countries
ec.europa.eu/represent_en.htm

The European Parliament's information offices in all the EU countries
www.europarl.europa.eu/atyourservice/en/information_offices.html

Notes

1 *Politico*, Brussels Playbook [newsletter], 3 June 2016

3   What, really, is the EU?

The EU cannot be compared to any other international organization. There is nothing like it, neither internationally nor historically. 'Sui generis' is the term political scientists use to denote such an entity: one of a kind.

Two different EUs

The EU is a mix of two types of political organization that we are familiar with: an intergovernmental organization (like the UN, OECD or WTO) and a federal state. The EU has characteristics of both models. How much of each depends on the area we are talking about – trade, foreign policy or social matters, for example.

It might be useful to think that there are two different EUs: the supranational EU and the intergovernmental EU. The supranational EU can force a member state to do something. The intergovernmental EU cannot, it can only recommend that EU countries do something. Before I start digging into a new topic, I ask myself which EU we are we actually talking about in this case.

In the intergovernmental EU, the power always resides with the 28 national governments. Their representatives who meet in the Council of Ministers and the European Council have the right to veto each decision, which means that no country can be forced to do something it does not want to do.

In foreign policy, for example, the EU functions according to the intergovernmental model. When 'the EU' decides to impose economic sanctions on Russia after the annexation of Crimea, it is in fact the 28 EU countries that have decided this together and no individual country decided to put in a veto and block the deal – but it could have done.

In the supranational EU, the national governments share power with the European Parliament, the European Commission and the Court of Justice of the EU. The national governments in the Council of Ministers legislate together with the European Parliament and when they take decisions in the council, they do so by a majority vote. This is the decision-making model when it comes, for example, to environmental policy.

The distinction between the intergovernmental and supranational EUs is not just a matter for law students to write essays on. It is crucial for journalists writing about the EU to keep these two entirely different models for decision-making in mind. Which type of EU is acting determines whether a decision is newsworthy or not, who is accountable and what the decision actually means to the readers.

The ever closer union

In 1957, six states signed the Treaty of Rome, creating the European Economic Community, which would later evolve into the EU. In the preamble, the signatories state that they are 'determined to lay the foundations of an ever closer union among the peoples of Europe'. One of the goals from the start was a federal European state, although many EU countries have since changed their minds.

Since the beginning of the European cooperation and until now, the direction has always been the same: EU cooperation has deepened. The EU acts more and more as a bloc and less and less as a collection of countries. In other words, the EU becomes more like a federal state and less like an international organization.

Two factors contribute to the EU becoming an ever closer union. First, the national governments have throughout the years placed new policy areas under EU jurisdiction/power. Second, decisions over an increasing proportion of the policy areas under EU power are taken supranationally rather than intergovernmentally, i.e. more often by majority vote in the Council of Ministers and with more power given to the European Parliament, as opposed to the intergovernmental model in which the 28 countries have one vote each and each country has the right of veto.

The first factor – putting ever more policy areas and decisions on the EU's table – is inherent in the construction of the EU. A common market creates the need for common product standards, which create the need for environmental and social rules. Free movement of people in the EU creates the need for a passport-free zone, which creates the need for police cooperation and a common asylum system. And so on.

The second factor – EU decision-making becoming increasingly supranational – is in part a result of the EU club growing. The more EU countries, the more difficult it is to reach an agreement if every country maintains its veto right. At the beginning, there were six member countries. At the time of writing, the EU has 28 member states, which may increase to 30 or 35 in the not so distant future. Turkey, Albania, Macedonia, Serbia and Montenegro are so called candidate countries. They have started to negotiate with the European Commission, to implement reforms requested by the EU and to allow the commission to evaluate these reforms. When the whole process is completed, these countries can become EU members. Bosnia and Kosovo are so called potential candidates, waiting in line to start negotiations about future membership.

The movement towards closer EU cooperation does not happen in secret; it happens through revision of the EU treaties. The treaties are agreements between the EU countries. When they are negotiated, each country's government can veto changes that it does not like. Moreover, every treaty has to be ratified by all the national parliaments. So far, with every new EU treaty, all EU countries' governments have decided to cede some national sovereignty in exchange for closer cooperation at the EU level, because it has been in the individual countries' interest to do so. The fact that the EU's power increases is because the EU countries' governments have decided that this is what they want. Keep this in mind when national governments complain about the EU meddling in some national affair. The EU is nothing more than what its member countries have decided that it is. It cannot and has never attempted to grab power from the member states.

National politicians are not keen on admitting that the scope of their power is much more limited today than before, because many policy areas are now dealt with at EU level.

When European cooperation was only about negotiating the price of coal and steel, journalists could be forgiven for not covering it in detail. But today, more and more politically sensitive issues are decided at the EU level, such as how our personal data should be handled and how to deal with climate change and terrorism. This means that journalists must follow their stories to where the power has been transferred, i.e. to the EU.

Which areas are under the EU's jurisdiction and which are not?

If you open a national newspaper you will read articles with headlines such as 'The EU wants to ban porn' and 'The EU wants to ban bullfighting' (see chapter 17 on typical mistakes in EU reporting) and you will hear politicians say that 'the EU should make sure abortion is legal everywhere'. But several of these areas of political life are completely outside the EU's jurisdiction, or scope.

One could divide all policy areas into:

- Areas in which the EU decides everything
- Areas in which the EU and the national governments both decide
- Areas that are the responsibilities of the national governments but where the EU plays a coordinating role
- Areas in which the EU has no say

Articles 2–6 in the Treaty of the Functioning of the European Union (TFEU) list all these policy areas. The articles are called 'the competence catalogue'. Policy areas that are not mentioned in this list are not within 'EU competency', or 'EU power', i.e. the EU does not have the mandate to act in these fields.

The competence catalogue is not a neat list with clear boundaries. The catalogue was merely an attempt, when drafting the Lisbon Treaty, to create some overview of and order in what the EU could decide and in what way.

For example, under 'shared competencies' we find both agriculture and energy. While almost everything that concerns agriculture is decided at the EU level – from production quotas and subsidies to rules – only part of an EU country's energy policy is decided in Brussels. The most important, a country's choice of energy source – its 'energy mix' – is not decided at EU level.

Fact box: 'The competence catalogue' – which decisions are taken at EU level and which at national level?

The EU has exclusive right to decide in these areas:

- customs union
- internal market competition rules
- monetary policy for the euro countries
- fishing quotas
- common commercial policy (trade agreements)

In these areas, both the EU and the member countries make decisions, but EU law has primacy. Member states may only regulate matters that have not been regulated by the EU.

- internal market
- social policy, the parts covered by the treaty (see Articles 151–161 TFEU, which are about coordination of employment policies, taking into account national practices)
- 'economic, social and territorial cohesion' (regional development)
- agriculture and fisheries (with the exception of fishing quotas)
- environment
- consumer protection
- transport
- trans-European networks (EU infrastructure such as transport, energy and telecommunications networks)
- energy
- 'area of freedom, security and justice' (asylum and refugee policy, police and judicial cooperation and Schengen cooperation)
- common safety concerns in matters of public health, for aspects covered by the treaty (see Article 168 TFEU. These aspects include safety standards for drugs)

In these areas, the EU member states have exclusive right to decide. The EU can only coordinate, support or supplement the EU countries' actions.

- public health
- industry
- culture
- tourism
- education, vocational training, youth and sport
- civil protection (prevention and protection against man-made or natural disasters)
- administrative cooperation

In these areas, both the EU and the member countries decide. But EU decisions cannot restrict member states' decision-making.

- research and technological development
- space
- development cooperation and humanitarian aid

In some areas, the EU can coordinate national policies.

- economic policies
- employment policies
- social policies

The policy areas under the same heading are also not necessarily decided in the same way. For a more detailed insight into what powers the EU has in a policy area, you need to look at the treaty articles that concern the particular area. All policy areas correspond to a heading in the treaty. For example, Articles 191–193 in the TFEU concern environmental policies. Here you can read what the objectives of the EU policy are, on which underlying principles they are based, and which type of legislative procedure applies when the EU makes new laws in that area.

All this can appear random and illogical, because the EU has grown to its current form organically. An EU official once explained it like this: You first decide to build a wooden shed in your garden. Then you think that you might protect it from rain, so you tile the roof. And then, you think it might look good with a terrace, so you build that too. And then a kitchen and another floor, and yet another one. The EU house would never have looked like this if the 28 governments sat down today and created the EU from scratch.

Areas in which the EU decides everything

In a few policy areas, the EU countries have handed all power over to the EU. This is for example the case with competition rules for the internal market, trade agreements with countries outside the EU, monetary policy for the countries that have the euro and fishing quotas.

The common internal market is the cornerstone of the EU. For this market to function, competition rules need to be the same for all companies on the European market. This is also an 'exclusive competence' of the EU. If two German companies want to merge, and the merger risks creating a company that will become too dominant on the EU market, it is the European Commission, not the German competition authority, that has the power to stop the merger.

In terms of trade, the EU behaves like a single country. From the beginning, the EU was a customs union, and this is a policy area in which the EU has exclusive power. The EU sets the same tariffs on trade with countries outside the EU; the tariffs on imported products from China are the same in Italy and Finland.

Because of the single customs policy, the EU also needs common trade policies relating to countries outside the EU. This policy, termed the EU's 'common commercial policy', is exclusively decided at EU level. It is the EU as a bloc, not individual EU countries, that strikes trade agreements with other countries, such as the EU–Canada trade agreement (CETA) or the EU–South Korea free trade agreement.

When it comes to these decisions, it makes sense to think of the EU as a federal state, and the European Commission as its government. Beware though that when we talk about 'the EU' having exclusive power, this does not mean that there is no one from your country who is responsible. Quite to the contrary: as stated earlier, EU law is hammered out by the European Commission, the European Parliament and the Council of Ministers. That means no EU laws are adopted without your country's government having had its say. But once the law is adopted, its execution is the responsibility of the European Commission. For example, in 2013 the European Commission introduced anti-dumping duties on Chinese solar panels, even though a majority of EU countries were against it.

Areas in which the EU and the member countries share the responsibility

In most policy areas, and certainly most of those that are of importance for the general citizen, the power to take decisions and write new laws is shared between the EU level and the national level. Within these areas, national governments are free to act where and whenever the EU has not done so already. These areas include, for example, transport, environment, regional development, police cooperation and asylum and refugee policy. For a complete list, see the fact box above.

The EU's main task is to create and maintain a single market with free movement for people, goods, services and capital. Most of the areas of 'shared competence' are at the intersection between what is needed to uphold the common market, to open borders between the EU countries and to stimulate mobility.

The EU for example sets out minimum standards in environmental or social policy, so that countries should not engage in unfair competition through social or environmental dumping on the internal market. There are also minimum standards for asylum reception centres, so that EU countries should not try to make asylum seekers leave their territory by creating centres with horrible living conditions. For these types of EU laws, EU countries can always set higher standards at home if they want to.

National politicians determine where exactly the border is between the EU's power and that of the member states in policy areas over which competence is shared. When there is no EU action, countries decide themselves. And when 'the EU' acts, by making new laws in this policy area, the national governments in the Council of Ministers decide how far these EU policies should go.

Every country decides for itself, but the EU coordinates and supports

On issues that are politically sensitive or closely connected to the idea of the nation – taxes, healthcare, schools, social services, culture, foreign policy and defence – the EU countries have chosen to keep all power to themselves. That does not mean that they do not cooperate at EU level, but the cooperation is not manifested as rules or laws that are binding on the national governments.

For example, welfare policy is decided by national governments. At the same time, EU countries use the EU structures to collect statistical data, compare themselves and, if they so wish, adjust their national policies. This is based on an idea of voluntary consensus that will eventually emerge as a consequence of the free trade and movement of individuals within the EU. It is practical for the EU countries that they do not differ too much in certain aspects of their economic and social policies.

This type of integration process happens when the countries agree on common goals, prepare action plans and report progress to the European Commission. The EU institutions and EU structures are involved, but only as a form of support. The real decision-making power remains in the hands of the national governments of each country. It is important to understand this, because this is where some EU stories go wrong – when EU countries use the EU structures for simply talking about and comparing data, this is sometimes mistaken for 'EU decisions' imposed by Brussels.

Areas in which the EU has nothing to say and there appears to be no movement towards harmonization

The EU started out as, and still mainly is, a motor for facilitating trade between the EU countries. On issues of values that have nothing to do with the internal market or with mobility, there is no movement to harmonize policies if the EU countries disagree.

For example, EU countries have different laws and policies on abortion or gay marriage. But since these differences have little bearing on trade, the EU countries have no interest in harmonizing their laws.

One must bear in mind that the division of power between the national and the European levels can change if the EU countries choose to change it in new EU treaties. Areas that are not under EU power today can be put under the EU's umbrella in the future. That is why Ireland, a country in which restrictive abortion laws are important for many national politicians, required a written guarantee before ratifying the EU's latest rulebook, the Lisbon Treaty, that the country's abortion laws, along with its military neutrality and taxes, would not be affected, ever.

The objective determines whether it is the EU or the member states that have the power

It is not possible to simply write a list of policies that belong to the 'intergovernmental EU' and policies that belong to the 'supranational EU', even though the 'competence catalogue' and the corresponding articles in the treaties give some guidance. Whether an EU action is decided on in a supranational or an intergovernmental way, or not at all by the EU, can depend on what the goal of the action is.

Take education for example. Education is mostly a matter decided by the national or even regional governments, e.g. what the pupils should learn in school. This does not prevent the EU countries' education ministers from occasionally discussing school politics and even sometimes agreeing on common goals, most often of the fluffy sort, such as the goal that no more than ten per cent of schoolchildren should quit school before graduation (the EU's growth strategy Europe 2020). Since there is no law and no sanctions connected to this, this is, at the most, a common wish.

At the same time, part of education policy is decided by the EU. University degrees have been standardized across the EU, in the so-called Bologna process. That a university degree should mean the same thing in all EU countries is considered an important prerequisite for truly functional free movement of the workforce. With degrees that mean the same in all countries, young Europeans can look for jobs across the EU and a Spanish employer, for instance, will not automatically hire Spaniards because he or she cannot evaluate, say, a Polish diploma. These rules are binding for EU countries.

Another, somewhat awkward, example: the EU forbids trade in furs from cats and dogs. Our attitudes towards animals as pets or as sources of fur or food are products of culture and customs. Why should the EU interfere in something like that? Because before the EU ban, buying and selling cat and dog fur was explicitly prohibited in some EU countries while other countries did not prohibit it, probably because there had never been a need for such a law. The single market – in this case the fur market – was not functioning perfectly. From the European Commission's perspective, it was a problem that European fur companies were governed by different rules within the single market, not that cats or dogs are killed for their furs.

News values and source criticism

The importance of knowing what power the EU has in the area that you, as a journalist, are writing about cannot be emphasized enough. It is essential in determining whether an EU event is newsworthy or not.

Ask yourself:

- Does the EU have any power in the matter?
- If yes: which EU institutions have the power?

This relates to the importance of not taking sources at face value. If a national politician ahead of the elections to the European Parliament says 'Vote for me and I will go to Brussels and stop the travelling circus to Strasbourg', then you as a journalist need to know that the European Parliament does not have the power to decide whether to abandon the French second seat of the parliament and simply stay in Brussels. This electoral promise is empty. The seats of the European Parliament are written into the EU treaties. Neither the European Parliament nor the European Commission can change the treaties. Only the member states' governments can do so. Fundamental changes to the EU cooperation that would require treaty changes are often debated ahead of the European Parliament elections, when in fact they should be issues of debate ahead of *national* elections.

Social legislation is the task of national governments, and not of EU policymakers. Even so, national politicians sometimes talk as if these issues were decided by the EU. Scandinavians are sometimes horrified by what they consider as old-fashioned and sexist social structures in other EU countries, and want them to be more like Scandinavia. Eastern and Central Europeans can be equally shocked by the too liberal West. National politicians sometimes exploit these feelings.

Anyone who wants the EU institutions to make sure that prostitution is prohibited throughout the EU or that marriage should be defined as the union between a man and a woman, also has to argue that the EU should get to legislate on these matters. Because for now, these areas are not part of what the EU has power to decide on. But does any national government want to give that power to the EU? I have never heard that opinion expressed.

If the EU were to get the power to decide on abortion, the likely outcome would be a law that would be an approximate average of all the EU countries' laws. EU countries with very liberal or very strict laws on abortion would lose equally from a common law. Therefore, if you interview a national politician who says, 'The EU should ensure that abortion is permitted in all EU countries', your follow-up question must be, 'Do you want *our* national abortion law to be decided at EU level?' It is too easy for national politicians to score political points on topics beyond their power.

Take your readers by the hand – be clear about what power the EU has

Speaking of social laws: former Swedish liberal minister for European affairs Birgitta Ohlsson wrote in an opinion piece that no EU country should allow corporal punishment: 'eleven EU countries still allow parents to hit their children for educational purposes. Allowing violence against children is in contrast to the common values that all EU countries have chosen to stand behind. The goal should be that all countries soon incorporate national legislation against corporal punishment.'[1]

Throughout the article, she writes that the *national* rules should change in the countries where corporal punishment is permitted. Ohlsson at no point argues that there should be *EU legislation* on the matter. But when you read the article a little fast and carelessly, you are still left with the impression that she is calling on the EU to act, not least because she was at the time minister for European affairs. A glance at the comments section below the online version of the op-ed clearly proves that some readers also thought that the minister was proposing EU action.

The EU that Birgitta Ohlsson is talking about is the intergovernmental EU: the EU as a forum for discussion and comparisons between 28 developed countries in the same region of the world, which have all signed the same fundamental charter of human rights. She could just as well have written 'the OECD countries' or 'the G20 countries' or any other club for rich countries. The commenting readers are clearly thinking of the supranational EU, the EU that makes binding laws for its member countries. Misunderstandings like these cause potentially interesting debates to become stuck and remain superficial.

As a journalist, you need to guide the reader through the whole article and be very clear about what powers the EU has in the area on which you are reporting. If you write that somebody thinks that 'the EU' should do this or that, many of your readers will assume that the EU has decision-making powers in the matter. If this is not the case, you need to explain that. It is not enough to mention it; you need to make a point of it. Write 'this is a matter for individual EU countries', 'the EU countries have decided that they want to achieve x, but the goal is not binding', or something along those lines.

How much does the EU decide?

What share of national law is decided at EU level? There are many different figures around, depending on country, time period and the method used to answer the question. Most studies come to the conclusion that somewhere between 10 and 50 per cent of all new national laws originate in the EU. Whichever way you count it, it is safe to say that a substantial part of all national legislation, in all EU countries, has been decided by the EU institutions – including the national governments in the council – and not by the national parliaments.

The most ambitious study dates from 2012. Political scientists from several European universities studied the share of national laws in eight EU countries that originated from the EU, between 1986 and 2008. The study covered Austria, Finland, France, Germany, Italy, Luxembourg, Netherlands and Spain. Non-EU European country Switzerland was included as comparison. The share ranged from 10 to 30 per cent. This included binding EU laws (regulations), binding EU framework laws (directives) and national laws that were a direct response to an EU decision. The study also shows that the share of laws stemming from the EU increases over time, and that the share varies significantly between policy areas. In agriculture, banking and finance and environment, a large share of national laws actually come from the EU. In the policy areas defence, housing and social welfare, the national laws are less often a product of EU laws.[2]

A figure often cited in media across Europe is that 80 per cent of national laws derive from the EU. That number, used by politicians across the field to make both pro- and anti-EU arguments, stems from a speech by then-president of the European Commission, Jacques Delors, in 1988. He predicted that within ten years, 80 per cent of all economic legislation would come from the EU. History proved him wrong.

The EU in local politics

The EU also affects local and regional politics. Local reporters should keep in mind that a substantial part of what appears to be decided in the town hall is directly or indirectly influenced by prior decisions at the EU level.

'What does the EU have to do with the decision to build a sports arena in Vetlanda?' begins the report 'Europe in local politics', commissioned by the Swedish Association of Local Authorities and Regions. Of course, the decision to build the arena in the small town Vetlanda was not taken in Brussels. Nor does the EU have any opinion on what the arena should look like or where it should be placed. But the local politicians who want to build the arena need to take a number of EU laws into account, including, for example, environmental protection rules of relevance to construction projects. Maybe most importantly, the decision about which company gets to build the arena will be subject to a public procurement exercise. The local politicians are not allowed to give the construction job to friends or relatives, or to choose national companies over foreign ones. These procurement rules have been decided at EU level and are the same across the union.

The Swedish report examined how many items on a typical municipal and regional council agenda were, directly or indirectly, affected by EU rules. The answer was 60 per cent for the municipalities and 50 per cent in the regions.[3] A report by Danish municipal organization KL, using the same methodology, concluded that 47 per cent of decisions in Danish municipal councils were affected by EU policy.[4]

The definition of EU influence in these two studies is quite broad and takes into account both legal and 'political/cultural' influences. Legal influences are directives, regulations and fundamental principles of the treaties and they account for around half of the EU influence at the municipal level. One example is that all municipalities with more than 100,000 inhabitants must publish noise management action plans every five years (the Environmental Noise Directive).

Around half of the 'EU effect' on local/regional council agendas was political/cultural. That could be that the municipality wants to live up to a non-binding EU strategy of some kind, for example in the field of employment or healthcare, over which the EU has limited legislative powers. An example of this could be a municipal project to promote female entrepreneurship (the EU's strategy for equality between women and men 2010–2015).

The exact figure here is not what is important. What is important is to understand that your local and regional politicians are taking decisions within a

26 What, really, is the EU?

European framework. Many stories might start local but turn European when you take a closer look.

Notes

1 Ohlsson, Birgitta, Ingen europé ska tillåtas slå sina barn, *Newsmill*, 9 May 2011
2 Brouard, Sylvain, Costa, Olivier and König, Thomas (eds), *The Europeanization of Domestic Legislatures: The Empirical Implications of the Delors' Myth in Nine Countries*, New York: Springer, 2012
3 Nyberg, Linda and SKL's international section, *EU i lokalpolitiken – En undersökning av dagordningar från kommuner, landsting och regioner*, Sveriges kommuner och landsting, 2010
4 KL, *The relation between the EU and the Danish municipalities*, 2015

Part II
The three main EU institutions

4 The European Commission

What does the European Commission really do? When can I use the commission as a source? Who do I call? Who speaks on the record? How do I describe the commissioners?

Whenever you wonder what is going on in the EU, **the European Commission** is a good place to start. All EU laws and rules emanate from the commission, because the commission is the only EU institution that has the right to propose legislation. It is also the commission that checks that the EU countries follow the rules that they have decided on together and takes the countries that do not follow the rules to court – a task summarized in the commission's somewhat pompous job title: 'guardian of the treaties'.

The commission is the EU's executive. Therefore, the commission often represents the whole EU in engagements with the rest of the world, such as in international climate or trade negotiations.

The European Commission is the most 'European' of the EU institutions. Its task is to promote the union's common interest and – this is important – to push the integration forward: to advocate common European solutions to perceived common European problems. Therefore, you should turn to the commission when you look for an EU-wide perspective on whatever you are writing about, as opposed to a national perspective or a left–right one.

If the EU were a fully fledged federal state, the commission would be its government and civil service. But the commission is a completely unique institution, like no other in national or international political systems. Therefore, the comparison is far from perfect.

What does the term European Commission actually mean?

The term European Commission, or commission, is used in two ways, to refer to:

- The college. That is the 28 commissioners, one from each EU country. This is the political commission.
- The bureaucracy. That is the roughly 30,000 civil servants, secretaries and translators who work in the 33 directorates-general (broadly equivalent to governmental ministries). This is the administrative commission.

The commissioners and their portfolios

The individual commissioners represent the whole commission and the whole EU, never their own countries. This is an important point that cannot be overstated. The commissioners even swear an oath, by which they solemnly promise to respect the EU treaties, to work for the union's common interest and never to take instructions from a (their own) national government.

The college consists of one commissioner from each member state. Every commissioner, apart from the commission's president, is responsible for a specific policy portfolio. These portfolios differ enormously in importance. Prestigious portfolios are trade, competition, economy, internal market and agriculture – areas over which the EU has extensive powers. Less important portfolios are social affairs, education and culture – policy areas where most of the power remains with the individual EU countries.

With every new commission, new portfolios are created, others scrapped, some merged and some split up, just like national ministry posts. As new member states join the EU, some sometimes illogical portfolios are created to accommodate new commissioners.

The commission is appointed

The political commission – the college – is replaced every five years. The process starts when the EU countries' heads of state and government (the European Council), at an EU summit, suggest who should be the next commission president. Then the European Parliament elects him or her (so far it has always been him), by a vote that requires an absolute majority (that is, a majority of all MEPs, rather than all MEPs present, or 376 out of 751).

According to the treaties, the European Council should propose a candidate for commission president 'taking into account the elections to the European Parliament'. This has been interpreted to mean that if the centre-right party group EPP (European People's Party) becomes the biggest party group in the European Parliament election, the EU countries should propose a politician from a party that belongs to the centre-right for the job as president of the commission, and if the S&D (Socialists and Democrats) becomes the biggest party group, the candidate for commission president should come from a centre-left party.

Previously, presidents and prime ministers picked their candidates in behind-closed-doors discussions, with little information about the reasons for their choice reaching the outside world. But in the European Parliament elections in 2014, the parliament pushed through a profound change. Ahead of the election, the European political families, for the first time, rallied behind common candidates for commission president, quickly dubbed 'Spitzenkandidaten', a German word that roughly translates to 'top candidates'. These candidates held debates that were broadcast via national media across the EU, and had proper campaigns at the EU level.

When the centre-right EPP eventually became the largest party group in the parliament election 2014, the European Council reluctantly proposed the EPP candidate Jean-Claude Juncker for the commission's top job, thus creating for the first time a direct link between the European Parliament election and the president of the European Commission, the EU executive.

Critics of the Spitzenkandidaten procedure say that this creates a sort of EU prime minister backed by a parliament and that this had never been put to vote by the union's 500 million citizens. Its proponents see the procedure as a way to make the EU more democratic and the commission more accountable.

For journalists, this change in procedure – if it is confirmed in the next parliament election in 2019, which is far from certain – matters a great deal, because it politicizes the appointment of the commission president. Once Jean-Claude Juncker became president, the promises he had made during the Spitzenkandidaten campaign eventually became a document with political priorities for the commission. Political reporters often compare politicians' electoral promises with what they actually achieve once in office. Only now has this become possible with the European Commission.

After the commission president has been appointed, the other commissioners – one from each country – are nominated by their respective national governments. Then the commission president decides which policy portfolios should go to whom. This becomes a tug-of-war between the countries, and the bigger countries usually secure the heavier portfolios.

Competition, industry, trade, internal market, economy and finance are widely sought after. Other portfolios might be strategically important for specific countries. Energy is interesting for Germany, agriculture for France, financial services for the UK and fisheries for Spain, for example.

The European Parliament accepts or rejects the commission

When the scramble between the countries is over and all the portfolios have been distributed, the European Parliament has to approve the whole college of commissioners. But before the MEPs vote, each commission candidate is interrogated – the session is usually referred to as a 'grilling' – in the parliamentary committee or committees that are in charge of the candidate's future policy area.

These hearings are the closest you will get to public campaigning and electoral promises from the individual commissioners. The MEPs question the candidates about issues related to their portfolio and to the EU in general, in order to ascertain whether or not the candidate is competent. It is not unusual that the candidates are also held accountable for their private morals and previous statements. Most commission candidates have spent most of their political life in their capitals and can be newcomers on the Brussels scene, so scandals that might already be long forgotten in the candidates' home countries are once again dragged into the light for thorough examination.

The hearings are open to the public and there are usually plenty of media in the room. The hearings are also streamed on the parliament's website.

The parliament cannot cherry pick the commissioners; it can only accept or reject the whole college. But on a few occasions, individual candidates have withdrawn their candidacies because they would otherwise endanger the whole set. This was the case in 2004, when Italian Rocco Buttiglione was nominated for the post of justice commissioner – a job that the MEPs did not see fit for a politician who had earlier said that homosexuality is a sin. In 2010, Rumiana Jeleva, the Bulgarian foreign minister who was proposed as emergency aid commissioner, withdrew her candidacy after MEPs had found her knowledge of development politics too shallow and after accusations of conflicts of interest. In these cases, the governments in question nominated another candidate, who then went through the same procedure in the European Parliament.

In 2014, the Hungarian candidate Tibor Navracsics, from the ruling right-wing party Fidesz, who was one of the architects behind a contested new Hungarian media law, was proposed as commissioner for culture, education and citizenship. After criticism, his portfolio was stripped of the responsibility of citizenship, a topic deemed inappropriate for a man and a country at the time accused of breaching citizens' rights with a media law that compromised free speech. He instead became commissioner for culture, education and sport.

Is the commission ideological?

Every commissioner is nominated by his or her national government and normally, but not always, has the same political colour as it. Since there are always some EU countries with right-wing governments and some with left-wing governments, the college is always a mix of politicians from the centre-right and the centre-left. In that sense the European Commission differs from many national governments. Left–right ideology plays a lesser role in the commission than many think.

The Jean-Claude Juncker commission that was appointed in 2014 is predominantly centre-right. Among the 28 commissioners, nineteen come from right-wing and centre-right parties, and nine from left-wing and centre-left parties. At the top layer, there is a left–right parity: While Juncker comes from the EPP, Vice President Frans Timmermans is a social democrat. Among the other vice presidents there are three each from the centre-right and centre-left political families.

What should I call the commissioner?

It is not always easy to know how to describe the commissioners. The first thing to bear in mind is that a commissioner is primarily defined by his or her policy area, not nationality. The commissioner's portfolio needs to be mentioned in your article at least once. Or, if you have already established what issues are concerned, you can write 'the responsible commissioner'.

It can look like this: 'Kristalina Georgieva, the commission's budget tsar'[1], 'Margrethe Vestager, the European Union competition chief'[2], or 'Günther

Oettinger, the telecoms and IT commissioner'.[3] For German media to call the commissioner for the digital agenda, Günther Oettinger, the 'German commissioner' or just 'commissioner' is as unnecessarily vague as calling your finance minister or culture minister 'minister'.

Most of your countrymen will have a rough idea of what your government ministers do. Fewer people have a clear idea of what is included in the EU commissioners' job descriptions. When you write about the commissioners, you will probably need to explain and highlight different parts of their portfolios depending on the topic you write about.

Many commissioners have combination portfolios, such as Tibor Navracsics, mentioned above. When he talks about culture affairs, call him 'culture commissioner'; if the topic is education, call him 'education commissioner'. It can look something like this, from an article in *EUobserver* about a commission proposal on targeting radicalization through, for example, educational programmes: 'The attackers, the education commissioner Tibor Navracsics added, were "young people who have been raised in our society and taught in our schools".'[4]

Try to use terms that more or less correspond to those used by your national government, to make it easier for your readers to grasp. For example, some countries might not have a minister for home affairs. Those policies are instead dealt with by the migration minister and the justice minister. Journalists writing for that audience are better off calling the home affairs commissioner 'justice commissioner' or 'migration commissioner', depending on the topic.

Many countries and international organizations have job titles that sound very much like EU titles. Be careful not to confuse them. For instance, the Swedish news agency TT quoted the 'German commissioner for data protection and freedom of information Peter Schaar' – a civil servant in Germany – in an article that also mentioned the European Commission.[5] Although there were no errors in the article, most readers would probably, wrongly, assume that Schaar works for the European Commission, and not for a German national data protection body.

If there is any room for misinterpretation, ensure you make a point of saying what institution or country the commissioner in question represents.

Vice presidents

The European Commission, like the other EU institutions, is obsessed with titles and hierarchy. As a journalist, do not let the institutions' own meaningless titles slip into your text. If a title is relevant to the article, then spell it out. But never do so just because the institutions want you to.

Take for example the commission's vice presidents. From a journalistic point of view, that particular title has only mattered since 2014, when the title was actually filled with content, a job description. Before that, a commission vice president was just an ordinary commissioner but with a slightly fancier title than the rest of them.

Interview: Vytenis Andriukaitis, European Commissioner for health and food safety

What does it mean to be a commissioner?

[Norway's former prime minister] Gro Harlem Brundtland was once asked what it means to be a politician. She said: I don't know what it means. There are people in parliament, people in government, people in municipalities. They are just people who represent people.

I don't understand what it means to be a politician either. I know that I am a medical doctor, a historian, a member of society who knows the difficulties of everyday life [he was born in a Stalinist gulag and was involved in the underground social democratic movement during the Soviet years]. I was a Lithuanian member of parliament, chairman of the European affairs committee, minister of health. I am now a European commissioner, responsible for health and food safety. But I am the same Vytenis Andriukaitis. I'm not alienated from society. I'm here because I know that I'm one of 520 million Europeans, all with their nationalities, differences, cultural heritages, languages, who have decided to do something together.

The European institutions do not represent something different, as autonomous European bodies. No. They represent a summary of 28 societies and 28 government bodies. Some people blame 'Brussels'. I don't know what that means. Brussels as the Belgian capital – yes. Brussels as a place where 28 member states act together – yes. But Brussels as something separate, as a European bureaucracy – that is misleading. In my cabinet I have Tuuli from Finland, Vilija from Lithuania, Paula from Portugal, Annika from Germany, Nathalie from France, Arūnas from Lithuania and Marco from Italy. Please show me the Brussels bureaucracy. The commission is a composition of all the member states.

The European Commission plays different roles. It initiates new laws for all 28 EU countries, it controls that the EU countries live up to its obligations, it implements the commonly decided policy and it represents the whole EU internationally.

Vytenis Andriukaitis on executing EU policy:

For example, the African swine fever virus has no understanding of the Schengen Area, passports, borders and nations. It is spreading across borders today, and we have four affected countries: Estonia, Latvia, Lithuania and Poland. We have introduced common measures in these countries. These measures will help us stop the virus before it spreads around the Baltic Sea, and crosses into Finland, Sweden and Denmark. [he knocks on the wooden table in his office]

Representing the EU internationally:

Of course my obligation is to represent the EU in different international forums. On Sunday I will go to New York to the United Nations general assembly to present the European Commission's position on antimicrobial resistance. Last week I was in the G7 meeting in Kobe [Japan]. I also attended different meetings about lumpy skin disease in Sofia, and next month I will go to Warsaw to attend a high-level meeting on African swine fever.

Initiating new laws:

The member states have decided that there should be some laws at the European level. All commissioners have the right to initiate legislation. But we know very well that we have the right only to initiate. We provide the initiatives to the parliament and the council. And your prime minister, or the prime minister of Spain or Portugal, then assesses the initiative at home and presents their opinion and votes in the council. If it's a good pan-European initiative, it's good for Sweden, for Spain and Portugal.

We 28 commissioners are from all the member states, but we have no right to present national initiatives. We try to understand the national interests and see what the common denominator is, to help to solve problems that arise because of the common single market. I communicate with all 28 health ministers, all 28 agriculture ministers, as well as with all the 28 different parliaments' committees involved in health and food safety issues and, finally, with health experts from all 28 member states. When there is a common view, we will start an initiative, a common one. I see the EU as a big orchestra. The commission is the conductor. I have 28 different instruments and my obligation is to create a symphony.

The college of commissioners takes decisions in the weekly college meeting. Tell me about the meeting.

Every week on Wednesday we have a college meeting. If something happens we can have more meetings. [In addition to the 28 commissioners,] there is also the legal service, the secretary-general and commission president Jean-Claude Juncker's head of cabinet. If I can't attend the meeting because of some international obligation, my head of cabinet has the right to attend in my place, but without the possibility to intervene or vote, but only listen and report back to me what went on.

The president of the commission presents the agenda of the meeting. Of course he collects all the ideas, proposals and issues beforehand. Sometimes we have many hot potatoes on the table.

We use French, German and English. We have translators to and from those languages. Jean-Claude Juncker and [first vice president] Frans Timmermans speak all three languages, some commissioners use two languages, but most only use English. I try to develop my English skills so I mainly use English, but sometimes I use German, my first foreign language in school.

Before the college meeting, my head of cabinet has the 'Hebdo' [French slang for 'weekly'] – a weekly meeting with all the other heads of cabinets.

> There they discuss in more detail the questions which will be on the college table. The legal service and experts from different units in all the DGs [directorates-general] present solutions to the Hebdo and the Hebdo agrees. Then this is presented at the college level.
> *How often do you vote in the college?*
> The vote is a last resort. Generally, we only have one way of taking decisions, to build a broad consensus. I can't remember that we have voted once in my one year and nine months as commissioner.
> *What does a typical week look like for you?*
> My week looks like this: [he holds up a piece of paper with a daily agenda] Every day on my agenda, I see the proposals from my cabinet for meetings with DG Sante [short for Directorate-General for Health and Food Safety], NGOs, national ministers, the council, the parliament. Sometimes there are eight meetings a day, sometimes eleven, sometimes four. And sometimes we only have meetings within my cabinet, because we need to discuss something very thoroughly amongst ourselves.

In the current commission, Frans Timmermans is 'first vice president'. He is the commission president's right-hand man, with a right to veto any initiatives from his commissioner colleagues. There are also six other vice presidents, who coordinate clusters of other commissioners who work on related portfolios. These vice presidents are the filter for all legislative initiatives from the commissioners in their cluster and they can stop any initiative from being proposed to the college.

In the 2010–2014 commission, there were eight vice presidents. Their only extra power was that they could chair college meetings if the then-president José Manuel Barroso was at home sick or busy elsewhere. Still, media from the vice presidents' home countries often spelled out the title, and didn't mention that there were eight vice presidents in total, which gave the reader the false impression that the commissioner in question was the second most important person in the commission.

The European Commission as a source

The European Commission is a supranational institution that is supposed to work for the EU's common interests. Media often have a hard time portraying that. It can be difficult to grasp an institution that represents the whole EU – what is that really and who are the people with such a pretentious mission?

It is often easier to understand and portray the left–right divide in the European Parliament or the diplomatic fights between EU countries in the Council of Ministers and at EU summits.

All communication from the European Commission is top-down and impersonal, which contributes to the feeling that the institution is anonymous and somewhat opaque.

Talk to the commission

The European Commission is often portrayed as the bad guy: bureaucratic, undemocratic, oversized, inefficient and always trying to grab more power at the expense of member countries. It is easy to blame the commission and it has few defenders.

Remember to let the commission be heard if you write about something that concerns it. And remember that almost all EU policies concern the commission in some way.

When an MEP or a national politician says that a commission proposal will have some horrendous consequences, do not settle for simply reporting this. Give the commission a chance to comment. It is much too easy for national politicians to blame 'the EU' or 'Brussels', which is often shorthand for the commission, for unpopular decisions that they have taken themselves. Too few journalists check the facts in these situations.

Make the commission's different roles clear

The commission has different roles, which we will see later in this chapter. When you write about proposed legislation from the commission, it is of course the commission that should answer questions about it and be criticized if the proposal is bad. But when the commission is executing EU decisions or supervising the correct implementation of EU rules in the member states, it only carries out what the legislatures – the European Parliament and the Council of Ministers – have decided. If the commission does so in a bad way, then yes, the commission should be held accountable. But if it is the policies that are bad, you should instead get to the bottom of it with the people who made those decisions. Do not shoot the messenger.

When it comes to legislative proposals from the commission, check if the proposal was an in-house product or if it was in fact ordered by the European Council (which will be mentioned in the proposal). At EU summits, the leaders of the EU countries often ask the commission to put forward specific proposals. Check the summit conclusions to see what your government agreed to.

Who to talk to in the commission

The only people who are allowed to speak 'on the record' to journalists on behalf of the European Commission are:

- The commissioners themselves;
- The commission spokespersons;
- The directors general (the highest official in each directorate-general).

Commission spokespersons

Do you want to know when the commission proposal for a mid-term review of the long-term budget will be presented? Or how far the EU–US free trade negotiations have got? Or where to find statistics on freshwater acidification in Europe? Start by calling the **commission spokesperson's service**.

You should also turn to the commission whenever you ask yourself: can a country really do this? Is there really no EU law that Spain is breaking when it allows bullfighting? The commission is the 'guardian of the treaties', making sure that EU countries follow the EU law, and will know the answer.

The commission spokespersons never speculate or deliver fun quotes. But they can always give you an official comment, refer you to the right legal text, explain if other EU countries have been in a similar situation before and provide some context. Quite a few of them used to be EU correspondents and will understand what kind of information you need.

It is only the spokespersons who will speak on the record; it is him or her you need to talk to in order to quote someone from the commission. The press officers in the spokesperson's team can give you background information and tips, but will not let you quote them.

There are about twenty spokespersons, some of whom are responsible for several portfolios. It goes without saying that they are extremely busy. When something big is going on that is of Europe-wide or international importance, there will be many dozens of journalists calling the same person to get a quote.

Therefore, the spokespersons are not always very accessible and, because their number has reduced in the Juncker commission, are becoming even less so. But they understand tight deadlines and will most of the time give you a comment the same day, if not directly then after one or two reminders.

Some tips to get a quick response from the commission's spokesperson service:

- The press people will respond more quickly and in more detail if they know who is calling. So if you know that in the future you will often be contacting the trade commissioner's press people, it is worth calling to introduce yourself, and tell them about the issues you cover. If you visit Brussels, get a one-day-accreditation to the commission HQ, go to the spokesperson's offices and knock on the door. That is what Brussels-based journalists do.
- Email your questions. If you call, they will probably ask you to send an email anyway, so you might as well start there. They will send your email around until they find the right person who can answer the question, or cut and paste the same response if it is the twenty-fifth time they have been asked the same question that day.
- Email the spokesperson and cc the press officer, or vice versa. Often one of them is out travelling, sometimes in a different time zone.
- As in all administrations, there are varying levels of competence among the spokespersons. You might get busy, snooty replies from some of them, giving

you the feeling that your question is stupid or insignificant. Then send a polite reminder, ask if he or she has a colleague who does have the time, and cc another spokesperson and some more press officers. That normally does the trick.
- Be sure to write in the email when your deadline is and when by the latest you need an answer (day, hour). Journalists from across the EU will email them, and the filing time for (paper) articles varies quite a lot in different countries. This allows the spokespersons to organize themselves better.
- Explain in as much detail as you feel comfortable the background to your question, so that they understand what you are actually after. Bear in mind that the commission's press people probably do not know your country's national context.
- State clearly whether you need a quote, or just background information.
- If you haven't received a response within a couple of hours, call them.

When should you call your country's commissioner?

The easy answer is: only call 'your' commissioner on topics that he or she is actually responsible for. You would not ask your home country's culture minister questions about public transport just because you happen to be from the same town as he or she, would you?

That said, most commissioners have a closer relationship with their national media. And they are often interviewed in national media about the EU or the European Commission on a general level – but then that is more an issue of general education rather than real news.

Even though the commissioners represent the entire EU and not their home countries, they have been nominated by their home governments and most of them are planning to continue their careers in their capitals after a few years in Brussels. So they are not completely independent. For any commissioner, it is clearly more important to get good press in his or her own country than elsewhere.

National media and EU correspondents from the commissioner's own country often have a VIP lane to 'their' commissioner. They are invited for informal sessions, like breakfast or afternoon coffee, with the commissioner. They can get the news before other EU correspondents and it is easier for them to get interviews. Because of this, there tend to be many more articles written about the topics of the national commissioner than on other EU topics.

Questions that concern your country should not be directed to the commissioner from your country. If, for example, the commission has decided to take your country to the EU court because it is late implementing an environmental directive, it is the environmental commissioner that should answer questions about this, not the commissioner from your country.

The commission representation offices in the EU countries

The European Commission has a **representation office** in every EU country capital. You can always call their press people as a starting point; they know the national context and they can help you in your own language.

These offices and the equivalent offices for the European Parliament are good sources for political journalists in the national capitals. The information they have is rarely exciting, but it is an easy source – they tend to want to communicate a great deal.

The commissioners' communications advisors

The commission spokesperson has to be of a different nationality from the commissioner who is in charge of the same portfolio. For example, the agriculture commissioner is Irish and the commission spokesperson for agriculture is Portuguese. But the commissioners also have personal press secretaries in their cabinets, called 'communications advisors'. This person is almost always from the commissioner's own country.

The communications advisors travel and attend meetings with the commissioner, so they are closer to the commissioner than the spokespersons are. They are the ones who manage interview requests for the commissioner. They are not supposed to speak on the record, but some of them do anyway. They are a little freer than their spokesperson colleagues and so they tend to be more personal and nicer to deal with.

These personal press secretaries are not listed in one place on the commission's website. Instead, you can find them on the commissioners' respective websites. Google the commissioner's name and 'cabinet' or 'team'. Somewhere in the staff list, you will find the communications advisor. Or, if you know an EU reporter from the commissioner's home country, ask him or her for the number.

Interview: Aura Salla, communications advisor for Jyrki Katainen, commissioner for jobs, growth, investments and competitiveness

Explain how your role differs from that of the spokesperson for jobs, growth and investment.

The spokespersons speak on the record. I only speak off the record. I meet a lot of journalists to give them updates. I can explain the story and then give you on-the-record quotes from the commissioner.

I write speaking points for Katainen and confirm his quotes for press materials. I also work as his speechwriter. Basically I should know everything he communicates. Maybe spin doctor is a better description of my job.

What about interview requests for the commissioner?

If you want an interview with Katainen, you can contact me. You can contact the spokesperson service too, but then they will ask me. The spokespersons can only give you the commission line, not Katainen's lines.

If you want a quote from Katainen, you can text me and I will text you back a line or two. But I prefer to set up a phone interview rather than send written information. As a journalist, I would not accept a written interview. But this varies between commissioners' cabinets.

Is it difficult to get an interview with him?

If you want to talk about something that is related to his portfolio – the investment plan, Europe 2020, circular economy – then you will get an interview for sure. Especially if you mention the magic words 'jobs, growth, investments' in your email.

How many interviews does he do every week?

We get approximately five requests a week. Then we try to do at least two to three interviews, but often it is three or four. Last week we were in the US, and there was a press conference and a few interviews.

Who asks for interviews?

We get most requests from Finnish journalists, so most interviews are with the Finnish press.

Do Finnish media write more about Katainen's portfolio because he is 'their' commissioner?

Yes, definitely. We used to have the economy portfolio before. [Finn Olli Rehn was the economy commissioner between 2009 and 2014.] Now Katainen is responsible for investments. Sometimes I have to explain that he cannot talk about the Finnish budget or the Greek budget. I tell them to call the budget commissioner or the economy commissioner.

What if I work at a local newspaper somewhere in Europe, can I still give you a call?

I think it is very important to do interviews with local newspapers. There is no point in only talking to journalists in the Brussels bubble or in national capitals. I am from a small village; I know how important the local paper is. But small newspapers never make any requests. Instead we try to reach out to them.

And what if I just want to check an EU story but I don't know where to start. Can I call you with some random EU question?

Yes. I would be happy to explain. It is our communication mission to talk to people about anything. I would ask for your email address and get back to you with some information. If you want quotes, then I would refer you to someone else.

Like most commissioners Katainen is on Twitter. Are the tweets his own and does he reply to questions on Twitter?

Not all tweets, no. Maybe half are from him personally. I also tweet. But from my side it's information, from his side it's more personal, what he is feeling. The press officer also has access to the account.

We never write tweets in a language that Katainen doesn't speak himself. He likes to interact and does so whenever he has the time.

How to get an interview with a commissioner

For your own commissioner, it is rarely a problem to set up an interview. But what about the others? Every week, the commissioners are interviewed in European and international media. When you ask for an interview, you are competing with giants like the *Financial Times* and *Le Monde*, so if you are not writing for them, you need some leverage.

- First, make sure you get in touch directly with the communications advisor and not the commission spokesperson. As they are a bit hidden, they get fewer calls and then mostly from their own countries' media. If he or she already knows you, you have a better chance than if it is the first time they hear from you.
- Play the national card. Everything in the EU is based on an underlying idea of national quotas. If you are Greek and no Greek media has interviewed the transport commissioner this year, you will have a much greater chance of getting an interview. Point out to the commissioner's people that Greek readers do not know who she is.
- The clearer you are about the angle of your article, the greater the chance you have of getting an interview, because the commissioner can prepare better and feel safer. This is of course a journalistic trade-off. Only give as much information as you feel comfortable with.
- Give the communications advisor arguments to persuade the commissioner to meet you. For example, are your readers/listeners/viewers a group that is strategically important to the commissioner, for example dairy farmers or teachers?
- Take the opportunity when a commissioner wants to 'do press' in your home country. If the environment commissioner goes to Germany to participate in a seminar on wind turbines, his press people will give priority to German media in Brussels before the trip and to local and national German media when he is in Germany. The commission's representation bureau in your country will know which commissioners are planning to visit. Give them a call now and then, and make sure you are on their mailing list.
- Your own country's commissioner will probably be in your country now and again, and will usually be available for interviews with national media.
- Join forces with colleagues. A Swedish colleague of mine from a relatively big newspaper made interview requests together with colleagues from Danish and Finnish newspapers, of roughly the same size. That way, they managed to get interviews with otherwise inaccessible commissioners. They could show that the commissioner would reach millions of readers all over the Nordic sphere, and were able to trump the largest newspapers from their respective countries, whose journalists approached the commissioner singly with interview requests. There are many informal journalist cooperations of this kind in Brussels.
- If you get your hands on the commissioner's mobile number, save it and contact him or her directly without going through the spokespersons or communications advisors. Text first and ask if it's OK to call.

Sources in the administrative commission

The administrative commission is made up of policy departments – **directorates-general** – that are comparable to government ministries. The commissioners are politically responsible for one or several departments and the director general is the administrative boss of the DG. The director generals are the only ones in the DGs who are allowed to speak on the record. They can also be interesting interviewees, and might be easier to access than the commissioners.

Each DG is divided into a handful of directorates, which all deal with specific policy areas. The managers of the directorates are called directors. The directorates are in turn divided into units, which work with specific issues within those policy areas. This manager is called the head of unit. Within the unit, there are desk officers, who deal with policy development and implementation.

The DG's press service

Every directorate-general has its own website, its own newsletter and its own routines for dealing with press contacts. The websites are different in appearance and content. Some are easy to use and have good background information accessible. Others seem never to be updated.

If, for example, you want to find the unemployment rates for young people in Spain, you can start on the website of the Directorate-General for Employment, Social Affairs and Inclusion. Then, have a look on the EU's statistical office Eurostat.

And if you are a specialist reporter and often write about a particular topic, such as cars or food, contact the relevant DGs and make sure that you are on their mailing lists.

Every DG has a handful of press secretaries. The division of work between the directorate-general press service and the commission spokesperson service is not crystal clear. If you email a technical question to a commission spokesperson, he or she will probably send the email on to the DG's press people, who will identify the civil servant who can best answer the question, and then email the answer back. If you instead call the DG's press people directly, they will probably check with the spokespersons (at least if it is a politically sensitive issue) before they respond to you.

Generally speaking, the more political an issue, the better it is to turn to the spokespersons. And again, for official statements, it is only the spokespersons who are allowed to give them. But for more technical questions on a background basis, it is sometimes better to call the DG, as they often have more time.

Civil servants

Of course, often you want to talk to the people who actually work hands-on on a specific policy area. The real expert is often the head of unit or the desk officer. Contact him or her directly; do not go through the spokespersons service or the DG's press people.

44   *The European Commission*

The commission civil servants only speak on the basis of anonymity, unless they have received explicit permission from their superiors to comment on the record. They are not supposed to talk to the media, and if they are caught doing so, they risk punishment, ultimately losing their jobs (read more about the protection of whistleblowers in chapter 18). Often they will not take the risk and will instead refer you to the official spokespersons. But try anyway.

Be sure not to use information that can be traced back to them and check with them how you can ensure they are not identifiable. When you make your initial contact, make sure they know that you know about the commission on/off the record rules.

How to find your EU civil servant source

- Go to the DG's website. Google 'European Commission', 'DG' and 'Environment' for example. Somewhere on the website, there is some kind of organizational chart. Look for a tab labelled 'who are we', 'organizational chart' or 'organigram'. In the chart you can see the different subsections (directorates and units). Check to see which section seems most relevant to you. In the chart, you can see the names of the heads of unit.
- You can find the phone numbers of directors general, directors and heads of unit in the EU institutions' own Yellow Pages, **'Who is who'**.
- Construct commission email addresses as follows: firstname.lastname@ec.europa.eu.
- Call the head of unit and ask her or his assistants which official in the unit is working on the issue that you are interested in.
- As we will see in later chapters, the commission DGs consult stakeholders (or lobbyists, if you will) to a great extent when drafting legislative proposals. Call the main European lobby group in the field that you are interested in and ask them who their counterpart in the DG is.

Fact box: On the record/off the record

These rules and definitions apply to all EU institutions, but especially the commission. The rules of the game are fixed and everyone knows about them and respects them. If you are an outsider, you might want to point out, in the initial contact with people in the EU institutions, that you understand these rules, to show them that they can safely speak with you off the record or on background.

Most press conferences/meetings/phone chats begin by establishing the status of the information that will follow. 'This is on background' or 'From now on I'm off the record' are typical phrases. If nothing is said, then 'on the record' of course applies.

> *On the record* means you can quote the person speaking and refer to him or her by name.
> *Off the record* means you can quote the person, but without naming him or her. He or she is often referred to as an 'EU source', 'senior official' or similar, depending on the topic.
> *Background* means that you can neither quote nor attribute the information to a person or an institution. You can only use the information to explain something yourself.

Midday briefing: the commission's daily press conference

Every weekday at noon, there is a press conference, the midday briefing, in the commission headquarters Berlaymont. The commission spokespersons are present during the briefing, ready to answer any question and give an on-the-record statement. A typical midday briefing lasts between half an hour and an hour. The press conference is broadcast live on the EU's TV channel **EbS**.

The press conference is led by the European Commission chief spokesperson. He or she starts by listing the other press conferences with commissioners, background briefings with civil servants or other events that will take place later in the day or the next day, and reads out commission statements. Then questions are taken from the floor.

Since the midday briefing is the only daily press conference in the EU institutions, it is often the commission spokespersons who comment on all questions that relate to the EU in general. They are also often asked to react to events that have happened in other EU institutions, or even world events that have nothing to do with the EU, say the death of Michael Jackson or Nelson Mandela.

Wednesday's press conference is usually the week's best attended. Each Wednesday morning, the 28 commissioners (the college) meet and take decisions.

The midday briefing is often a cat-and-mouse game between Brussels correspondents and the spokespersons. The spokespersons only give the commission's official position and the journalists try to trick or provoke them into saying more than they should. It is impressive how quickly the spokespersons can throw up facts and figures and also a bit intimidating how they seem to have predicted almost all coming questions and prepared monologue answers. I once witnessed a journalist, on the occasion of an announcement of EU climate targets, ironically ask how many of the commissioners cycled to work. A spokesperson strode up to the podium and began to rattle off in a monotone how many bicycles and cars were available in the commission fleet.

The midday briefings are in English and French and are translated simultaneously between the two languages. If a journalist asks a question in English, the reply will be in English and then the spokespersons typically go on in English until someone asks something in French, when it passes to French. If you watch the briefing online, you can choose between the two languages or the original. The Wednesday press conference is interpreted into all official EU languages.

Because everything that is said at the midday briefing is on the record, the statements are often completely stripped of any human touch, and are boring, unnecessarily vague and complicated. Most Brussels reporters therefore prefer to take the lift up from the press room to the spokespersons' offices, or call or email them afterwards. When you are in direct contact with the spokespersons, you get much more information, on background. At the press conference, you only get the official statement.

Even so, the midday briefing is a daily ritual for many EU reporters, perhaps most of all to glean what other journalists are working on. Based on the questions, rather than the answers, you get an idea of what EU issues are talked about in the EU countries other than your own. When all Spanish journalists ask really detailed questions about a bank scandal that you have never heard of and you see the spokesperson break out in a sweat, you realize that the bank scandal is probably worth checking out. Being at the midday briefing, or watching it online, is a bit like skimming through tomorrow's newspaper in every EU country. And it is one of the best ways to get ideas for EU stories!

Press conferences with commissioners and background briefings

When commissioners present a new initiative or decision of some sort, they usually hold a press conference in connection with the midday briefing. These press conferences are interpreted into more languages than English and French, but often not all the official languages. If a commission decision specifically concerns Spain and the Netherlands, for example, there will probably be interpretation in English, French, German, Dutch and Spanish.

After press conferences on specific topics there are often 'technical briefings', in which the DG officials and experts walk the journalists through the text and explain the legal details. These briefings are always on background, and are not filmed. You can only take part if you are in Brussels.

Outside the commission pressroom, there are paper copies of all press releases and background materials of the day. The same information is released via the 'commission press room' online within an hour. The press material is in most cases in English and is quickly translated into French and German.

Rapid

The **EU online pressroom** is a good one-stop-shop for EU news. But when there is a lot of activity in the other EU institutions – for example during the European Parliament plenary week – the online pressroom is flooded with those press releases. Then the commission's own press site, **Rapid**, is preferable if you are looking for something from the commission.

All written material from the commission's press department ends up here. Rapid actually has a really good search engine. Unfortunately, it is only in

English and French. Here you can find the press releases, always in English and depending on the subject in other EU languages. You will find the news, the background and the contact details to the spokesperson in charge.

On Rapid you can also see the 'Daily news', which is a list of all major events in the commission that day. This document is sent out to accredited reporters at midday Brussels time. You can also find statements by commissioners, new figures from Eurostat and factsheets.

As soon as the commission wants to communicate something, it sends an email to all accredited journalists. The information is also posted on the Rapid website, so accredited journalists don't really have an advantage. But if you still want to receive the emails and be sure not to miss anything, you need to call the commission's accreditation office (see chapter 19) and ask them to add you to the email list, despite not being accredited or residing in Brussels. They might grumble a bit, but will probably go along with it.

Embargoed information from the commission

Some of the information that the European Commission produces might have a direct market effect, such as on the euro's value, a company's stock price or a euro-area country's borrowing rates. News agencies that are accredited to the commission will get this information in advance on condition that they promise not to publish it until the end of an embargo period.

Material of this sort could be statistics such as the economic forecasts for the euro area. It could also be a commission decision, for example to publicly criticize a euro-area country that has allowed its budget deficit to soar, or to initiate an investigation into a suspected company cartel.

Depending on the topic, this information is emailed to accredited news agencies between half an hour and an hour before the official publication. They have the time to produce an article, ready to be published once the embargo is lifted and the information is made public.

You cannot work your way around this embargo – either send down your own correspondent to Brussels or contact an accredited journalist and humbly ask them to share the information. Media organizations that violate the embargo and publish the information in advance are thrown out of the system for one month. If it is repeated within a two-year period, the shut-out lasts for four months. This does not happen often – only a couple of times in recent years have media organizations been excluded.

What the European Commission does

As stated earlier in this chapter, the European Commission has three main tasks:

- to submit legislative proposals
- to manage and implement – execute – EU policies
- to ensure that EU law is enforced in the member states

How the commission drafts and adopts legislative proposals will be explained in detail in chapter 7.

Implementing EU policies

The commission is the EU's executive. Like a national government it executes the policy that the legislative power has decided.

The commission is responsible for implementing the EU budget. The bulk of the money is awarded to the member states, which in turn dole it out to different projects. A small portion is paid out by DGs and independent EU agencies.

Most often, it is only when the commission implements the EU competition policy that it becomes big news (see later in this chapter).

The European Commission represents the EU internationally (sometimes)

When it comes to foreign policy, both the commission and the EU member states are the EU executive. 'Who do I call if I want to talk to Europe?' is an expression attributed apocryphally to Henry Kissinger. Nevertheless, the question remains relevant and still has no answer, despite the EU nowadays having both a foreign affairs chief (see chapter 11) and a permanent president of the European Council (see chapter 6).

It is difficult for journalists to know which EU institution represents the EU in different international forums. Sometimes the institutions themselves disagree. This was painfully obvious when the EU won the Nobel Peace Prize in 2012. Should then-commission president José Manuel Barroso pick up the prize? After all, the commission is the most European of the institutions. Or should it be the European Council president, at the time Belgian Herman Van Rompuy? He was, after all, chair of the supreme governing body of the EU. In the end it was agreed that Barroso and Van Rompuy together would receive the prize in Oslo and both give speeches. European Parliament President Martin Schulz also came to Oslo but was not allowed to make a speech. As a consolation prize, he got to keep the Nobel Prize medal in the parliament building.

For events more mundane than Nobel Prize award ceremonies, the rule can be summarized as follows: where the EU has exclusive power (see chapter 3), the commission speaks for the whole EU. This for example applies to negotiating fisheries agreements with African countries, where the EU as a bloc pays for the right of European fishermen to fish in those countries' coastal waters.

In international trade negotiations, for example in the WTO framework, the commission gets a negotiating mandate from the Council of Ministers. It is the commission, not the individual member states, that negotiates trade agreements with countries or regions outside the EU, such as the EU–US free trade agreement. The same goes for the international climate negotiations. The EU countries in the Council of Ministers and the European Parliament agree on a common position ahead of UN climate negotiations. The commission then speaks for the whole EU in these negotiations. If new things are put on the table and there is as yet no common EU position, the member states' representatives, in the margins of the meeting, decide on a new position that the commission then represents in the negotiations. Even so, national media tend to focus more on 'their' own negotiators, for example in the UN-led climate talks in Copenhagen or Paris, and interview these compatriot officials rather than the commission negotiators.

In foreign policy, in the politically sensitive questions about war and peace, the member states have all the decision-making power. But when they choose to act together they use the EU structures for this, especially the EU's foreign policy chief.

The commission implements the EU's competition policy

The point of the EU's internal market is that European companies should be able to compete freely with each other, even in countries other than their own, and that the same rules should apply to all. Competition is one of the policy areas over which the EU has the most power. When the European Commission is implementing EU competition policy, the best comparison is with the US competition authorities.

The competition directorate-general does its own research and makes binding decisions. It has very broad powers, for example to carry out raids. It is actually EU officials who go from Brussels to Dublin, for example, and knock on doors of the headquarters of a company at nine o'clock on Monday morning, to seize their documents and computers. The DG receives anonymous tip-offs about anti-competitive behaviour from the public and from affected companies and national authorities.

All decisions that the commission takes relating to competition policy are communicated to the press through emails and via the commission online press service, Rapid. Because these decisions can have a direct effect on the stock market, they are published without prior warning.

Key competition policy decisions are always followed by a press conference with the competition commissioner, which can be watched on EbS. For planning reasons, the commission usually announces on the midday briefing a few days in advance if a commissioner will hold a press conference. Reporters who closely follow competition policy and know what cases are in the pipeline can often make an educated guess what the case in question is and get a few days' head start.

Cartels

Companies that have formed a cartel can be fined up to ten per cent of their turnover. The money is paid into the EU budget. In 2012, seven television companies were fined a total of 1.4 billion euros. In July 2016, the commission handed out a record 2.9 billion-euro fine to five of Europe's biggest truck producers, including Volvo/Renault and Daimler, who for more than 14 years had illegally teamed up and agreed on prices for trucks.

Cartel cases are not very common; there is only a handful every year. For media in the countries where the companies operate or have their headquarters, the commission decisions are always big news.

As long as the commission is investigating a suspected cartel, it will not mention the names of the companies concerned. These names become public when the commission adopts a decision on whether to fine them or not. The size of the fines tends to be significant, and can be found in a press release published the very moment the decision is made.

If there is a specific company on the list that, surprisingly, has not been fined, this probably means that that company was the one that revealed the cartel and as a reward had its fine written off. The vast majority of cartel cases come to the commission's knowledge through one of the companies telling on the others. The other companies in the cartel can get reduced fines if they cooperate with the commission.

Abuse of dominant position

Companies that have a dominant market position and abuse it can also be fined by the European Commission. An example of abuse is when a company artificially cuts its prices to get rid of competitors.

When it comes to clamping down on illegal anti-competitive behaviour, the commission can go after all entities that operate on the European market, and not only European companies. In 2012 for example, the commission opened an investigation into Russian energy giant Gazprom, accused of abusing its dominant position on the EU energy market through unfair pricing.

A company that connects a product with the sale of another product in a way that reduces consumer choice can also be found guilty of abuse of a dominant position. That was the case when the commission decided that Microsoft abused its position by including Windows Media Player in its bestselling operating system Microsoft Windows.

Commission investigations into Gazprom and Microsoft are of course world news, and not only interesting for European media.

The procedure in cases of cartels and abuse of dominant position

When it comes to cartels or abuse of dominant position, the commission acts according to a strict procedure. A case can take years. Between the various stages, the commission does not communicate at all about how the investigation is progressing.

The following three stages are interesting for journalists:

- When the commission decides to open a formal investigation if one or many companies are suspected of illegal anti-competitive behaviour. This decision is communicated to both the concerned companies and the media.

- The next step is the argumentation, or the 'statement of objectives'. The commission presents its reasons for starting an investigation to the company or companies – why their behaviour seems illegal. The concerned companies then, in turn, are given a chance to justify their actions.
- The commission makes its final decision.

Mergers

The European Commission can veto company mergers if it considers that the merger will give the new company a dominant position on the European market or strengthen an already dominant position. Companies that plan to merge must notify the commission, which has 25 working days to either give the deal its go-ahead or open a formal investigation into it. The commission then has 90 working days to investigate the matter.

Again, these rules apply not only to European companies, but to all companies that operate on the European market. In 2001 for example, the European Commission vetoed the merger of the two US companies Honeywell and General Electric, although the US antitrust authorities had approved the merger. The commission concluded that the merger would reduce competition in the aviation and aerospace sector in Europe, and lead to higher prices for consumers, in this case the airlines. Rather than risk being excluded from the European market, the American companies abandoned their planned merger.

The commission agrees to hundreds of mergers every year, so this is usually not big news. But when the companies get a no, which happens once or a few times a year, it usually leads to big headlines, especially when it is a matter of national giants. In Sweden, the highest profile case was when the commission, in 2000, stopped the planned merger between Volvo and Scania, because it foresaw that it would distort competition in the truck and bus market. Another case that attracted a great deal of media attention was the thrice rejected merger between Ireland's Ryanair and Aer Lingus. The commission believed the merger would create a de facto monopoly on certain flights.

The legal text that is in play is the EC Merger Regulation 139/2004. Look it up in the EU law database, **EUR-Lex** (see chapter 9), if you often write about mergers and need to check the exact rules.

When the commission decides whether to allow or stop a merger, it justifies its move thoroughly. A press release is sent to journalists on the mailing list. You find the same information on Rapid, along with background material and contact information for the spokesperson and the press secretary responsible for the issue. In cases of major media interest, the competition commissioner holds a press conference, which can be watched on EbS.

State aid

The European Commission can also stop EU countries from supporting their own businesses. Here the commission is walking on eggshells. State aid is much more politically sensitive than other parts of the EU competition policy, because it is the member states' governments, not the private sector, that are officially reprimanded by the commission.

If a public authority (state, regional or local) subsidizes the private sector, this might constitute unlawful state aid. The state aid can be in the form of direct grants, low interest loans, interest subsidies or tax breaks and loan guarantees. All these forms of subsidies should be notified to the commission, although this does not always happen.

A general principle is that state aid is prohibited. But there are many exceptions, and governments can in certain circumstances be granted the right to hand out state money, such as to reconstruction projects after a natural disaster has struck, or to programmes for regional development. Furthermore, the commission normally accepts state aid once a decade, and per company, but then in return requires a plan for how the company should get back on its feet in the future without government help, and proof that the subsidies do not distort competition.

If the commission decides that there has been a breach of EU state aid rules, it does not levy a fine; it requires the company to pay the money back to the state. In September 2016, the commission concluded that Ireland had granted undue tax benefits to the American company Apple. The tech giant had paid substantially less tax than other businesses operating in the same country. Ireland must now recover a whopping 13 billion euros from Apple. Irish journalist Jonathan Healy tweeted: 'Based on a population of 4,595,000, that's about 2800 euros each. I'd take cheque or cash'.

Commission decisions on state aid are very common: some twenty cases every month, on average. State aid cases get a great deal of media attention when they touch on sensitive issues for the country involved, like Ireland's tax deals, or when failing companies, such as big banks or airlines, are rescued with state funds.

Spanish newspaper *El País*, for example, reported in 2013 that for several years the European Commission had examined Spanish football and eventually started an investigation into alleged illicit state aid to the clubs Valencia and Hércules Elche. The newspaper wrote that many of the clubs were likely to be forced to repay the state money and thus go bankrupt.[6]

The European Commission monitors the EU member states

The European Commission is sometimes called 'the guardian of the treaties'. That means that the commission checks that member states respect their obligations under the treaties and punishes those that do not. Whether it is a national, regional or local authority that has violated EU laws, it is the country itself – the government – that is brought before the European Court of Justice.

The procedure to find out if a country has in fact violated the EU rules is called an infringement procedure. Around the 20th of every month, the commission takes all these kinds of decisions in an 'infringement package', with that month's harvest.

Every year, the commission has around three or four thousand open investigations into infringement of EU laws. That illustrates just how much of the commission's work is actually about ensuring that the EU countries stick to the rules that they themselves have adopted.

Many infringement cases deal with EU countries that have not implemented directives before a certain deadline. Every directive (an EU framework law) has a deadline by which it must be incorporated into national legislation, for example a year and a half after the directive has been published in the Official Journal. So, when a year and a half has passed, the commission typically does a first check-up.

The officials in the relevant DG do these investigations. The environment DG and the environment commissioner are responsible for infringement decisions relating to EU environment policy. Call the spokesperson for environment with questions about those infringement procedures.

Infringement proceedings: the three steps

When the commission sees a problem in an EU country, it does not immediately take the country to court. Before the formal infringement process, the commission tries to solve the problem with the EU country through informal talks. This is called an 'early settlement'.

If there is no early settlement, the infringement proceedings start:

- First, the commission sends a letter, called a 'letter of formal notice', in which it points out a problem in a country and asks for an explanation. The country must respond within a specified period, usually two months.
- If the commission is not satisfied with the answer, the next step is a so-called 'reasoned opinion'. The commission explains how it sees the problem and tells the country to correct it. The country is then given a new deadline, usually another two months, to show that it has taken the necessary measures to comply with the rules.
- Finally, the last step is for the commission to send the case to the European Court of Justice. This happens in around 15 per cent of the initiated infringement cases. Most of the time, the national governments go along with the commission's requirements before cases reach this point – it is embarrassing for any government to be dragged to court by Brussels bureaucrats. When EU countries haven't implemented a directive in time, the commission can ask the court to impose a fine.

Is it news?

It may sound serious that a country does not comply with EU rules, but it is very common. In a typical month, the commission will take perhaps two hundred infringement decisions. Most involve letters of formal notice, about fifty or so are reasoned opinions, and about a dozen cases are sent to the European Court of Justice.

The first step of the infringement procedure is therefore rarely exciting. But when the commission actually takes a country to court, this is often news for the media in the country concerned. Especially if you can stick a price tag on it and tell your readers that they, the taxpayers, will have to pay unless the government changes this or that to comply with EU rules.

When the conflict is about issues of national culture, for example when the commission says that the traditional bird-hunting in Malta is in breach of EU rules, the matter also tends to become big news in other EU countries and can trigger a debate about whether or not the EU apparatus should stay out of the business of individual countries altogether. If the commission chooses not to start infringement procedures, even though a country is in obvious breach of EU rules, this choice can also make big news, for example when big and powerful EU countries clearly violate the budget rules without the commission acting.

Links

The European Commission's website
ec.europa.eu

The European Commission's spokespersons' service
ec.europa.eu/dgs/communication/about/contact_us/ec_spokespersons/index_en.htm

The European Commission's representation offices in all the EU countries
ec.europa.eu/represent_en.htm

List of the European Commission's directorates-general
ec.europa.eu/about/ds_en.htm

'Who is who' – the EU institution's Yellow Pages
europa.eu/whoiswho/public

Europe by Satellite, EbS
ec.europa.eu/avservices/ebs/schedule.cfm

EU newsroom
europa.eu/newsroom/home_en

Rapid – press releases from the European Commission
europa.eu/rapid/search.htm

EU law database EUR-Lex
eur-lex.europa.eu/homepage.html

Notes

1 *Politico*, Brussels Playbook [newsletter], 7 September 2016
2 *Bloomberg*, EU's Vestager sees 'Clash of understanding' with US over Apple, 21 September 2016
3 *The Times*, Germans attack Cameron's EU campaign, 27 September 2016
4 *EUobserver*, EU proposes new steps against radicalization, 14 June 2016
5 *TT*, Jakt på dem som läckte i USA, 8 June 2013
6 *El País*, Bruselas investiga al fútbol español, 8 March 2013

5 The European Parliament

What can and can't the European Parliament decide? Who should I talk to in the parliament? How are my country's MEPs doing? Where can I find the committee and plenary votes? What is on the parliament's agenda?

Since the beginning of what would become the European Union, there has been a European parliamentary assembly. In the 1950s, this assembly was made up of delegations from the member states' national parliaments. The European parliamentary assembly was not a parliament in the true sense of the word, meaning an elected legislative body. But it is today.

In the early days, the way the EU made new laws was as follows: the European Commission put forward proposed legislation and the Council of Ministers amended and adopted the legislation. End of process. The parliamentary assembly could comment on the legislative proposals and it could also dismiss the commission. Beyond that, it had little power.

Much has happened since then. The European Parliament has been directly elected since 1979. MEPs themselves like to emphasize that the European Parliament is the only directly elected EU institution. During the 1980s, 1990s and 2000s the parliament was progressively granted greater powers – with every new EU treaty, the power balance between the two legislatures, the parliament and the council, changed in the parliament's favour. The Lisbon Treaty, which came into force in 2009, puts the parliament on an even footing with the council when it comes to adopting the annual EU budget and almost all new EU laws. Nevertheless, one can still read articles (and hear politicians) describing the European Parliament as a powerless talking shop. Journalists who write such articles have somehow overlooked the developments of recent years.

The greater powers of the parliament are reflected in the politicians who stand for election. Previously, Brussels and Strasbourg were graveyards for national politicians who had passed their sell-by dates or a temporary exile for politicians who had got into trouble in their capitals. Now, the parliament is increasingly a political springboard. Former prime minister of Finland, Alexander Stubb, began his career as an MEP; so did former Danish prime minister Helle Thorning-Schmidt.

Media coverage of the European Parliament has not kept up with this development. National and local journalists tend to turn MEPs into general EU spokespersons – 'our guy explains what is going on in the EU' – instead of interviewing them about the actual issues being decided in the European Parliament. Brussels-based reporters tend to cover the commission and the council – the EU's traditional centres of power – more than the parliament. This is also because the European Parliament takes most of its formal decisions in plenary in Strasbourg, 350 kilometres from Brussels, leaving behind the freelance journalists who cannot afford trains and hotels, and the EU correspondents who must cover meetings in Brussels on the same days.

The different roles of the European Parliament

The European Parliament's main task is to make laws for the EU as a whole. Since the Lisbon Treaty, the rule of thumb has been that the European Parliament and the Council of Ministers adopt EU laws together. This is called the ordinary legislative procedure. The two institutions adopt amendments to the legislative proposal from the commission, negotiate where there are differences of opinion and finally adopt a common text. This process is described in detail in chapter 8. Law-making aside, the parliament's main task is to scrutinize the executive power, the European Commission.

What makes covering the European Parliament a bit tricky is that the institution has *both* real legislative and investigative powers *and* has kept its habit from the old powerless days of talking about matters over which it has no powers whatsoever.

The MEPs will not help you as a journalist to make the distinction. On the contrary, they often have an interest in confusing the parliament's roles in order to maximize their significance. MEPs, like all politicians, love to talk about their pet projects, even when it concerns something that the European Parliament, or even the EU, has no power over. It is therefore important to be critical when MEPs offer news tips. We will come back to these different tasks later in this chapter, but first a bit about the MEPs themselves.

The MEPs

The MEPs are directly elected every five years, according to more or less the same procedure in all EU countries. Every EU citizen has the right to vote and run for election regardless of which country he or she lives in.

There are currently 751 MEPs. How many there are from each country depends on the population, but smaller countries have more MEPs per capita than larger countries. Germany has the biggest delegation with 96 MEPs. Estonia, Luxembourg, Malta and Cyprus have the smallest: only 6 MEPs each. On **the European Parliament's website,** you can click through to each MEP's own page. There you find contact details for the MEP and information about which committees and delegations he or she is a member of.

There is also the MEP's CV and a PDF file called 'declaration of financial interests', where the MEP has declared income from jobs and assignments during the last three years before the parliamentary term, as well as extra jobs while serving as MEP. The same information has been transformed to a searchable format by global anti-corruption organization Transparency International, and can be found on the designated website **Integritywatch**.

Other information you can find on the MEPs' own websites are compilations of each MEP's business in parliament: drafted reports, speeches in plenary and questions posed to the commission. By skimming through these statistics, you fairly quickly get an idea of what issues the MEP is most interested in and whether or not he or she is an important player.

Next to the MEP's name is a little audio symbol. Click on it to hear how his or her name is pronounced. This might be a good idea if you are a TV or radio reporter about to interview Beatriz Becerra Basterrechea, Ildikó Gáll-Pelcz or Tadeusz Zwiefka, for example.

Contact MEPs directly by phone or email. They are generally open and happy to talk to journalists. Do not forget their assistants, who often have key information. On the MEPs website, you can find a list of his or her staff. What the assistants' functions are really depends on the MEPs. Some assistants are secretaries – they book hotel rooms and keep the calendar – while others are senior policy advisors. Some of the assistants know more about the substance and procedure than the MEP him- or herself does, have been around longer in the parliament than the MEP and take part in negotiations on behalf of the MEP. So, talk to the assistants to get all the background and then interview the politician to get the quotes.

Which MEP should I interview?

Is it substance or nationality that should determine which MEP to interview? That is a judgement you must make on a case-by-case basis. Are you writing about the issue at stake, or are you examining your country's MEPs?

It is often most interesting to interview the real experts about an issue. They are the MEPs who are responsible for drafting the report, 'the rapporteur', and the responsible MEPs from the other party groups, 'the shadow rapporteurs', in the designated committee. At the same time, nationality cannot be ignored. In the future, there might be EU parties running for elections with common programmes and electoral lists. Then, Germans could vote for a Spanish Green MEP or a Finnish Social Democrat. But this is not yet the case and because MEPs are elected on national lists, it is obviously important for national media to keep track and examine what their national MEPs are doing. Your readers should know what their representatives are doing in Brussels and Strasbourg, in order to be able to re-elect them or elect someone else.

That said, for small EU countries there are not enough MEPs for there to be experts on every newsworthy event, or even MEPs who are members of all the committees that deal with the issues. Of course, just because there is no fellow countryman there to explain the issues in your own language, it is not a valid reason for you not to write about it.

The national media from the rapporteur's country tend to write more about this specific piece of legislation than about other EU laws that are being dealt with in the parliament. The same thing goes for the commission – the portfolio of 'our' commissioner gets more press than the other policy areas.

Use the parliament's law database, the Legislative Observatory (see chapter 9), to find out what committee is dealing with the issue that you are interested in and who the rapporteur and shadow rapporteurs are. Or call or email the committee press officers and ask them.

The European Parliament press service

Out of the three major EU institutions, the European Parliament is the most open. All committee meetings and plenary sessions are open to the public (i.e. journalists). And most MEPs are very accessible.

Every committee has one or a few **press officers** attached to it. They are veritable experts on the policy and the procedure of the committee. For each of the official EU languages, there is also at least one press officer. These groups overlap. For instance, one of the press officers for the LIBE committee is Spanish. So all reporters who want to ask questions in Spanish about anything concerning the European Parliament will call her, as well as reporters from everywhere, asking questions about justice and home affairs, which are dealt with in the LIBE committee.

These press people are employed by the European Parliament and remain at their jobs regardless of which politicians are elected for the next term. They are 'politically neutral' in the sense that they are not affiliated with either a party or a country.

There are also political press people. Each party group has its own press service (see the interview with Richard More O'Ferrall). Often the national parties and the individual MEPs have their own press people. They are not listed in one single place, like the parliament press service. Instead you can find them on their respective websites.

Just like the commission, the European Parliament has an **information office** in every EU country capital, as well as some large European cities. If you do not know where to start, you can always call this office in your country, and they will guide you to the right place.

As in the other EU institutions, the parliament's civil servants are not supposed to speak on the record, but the control in parliament is weak, so those who want to do so anyway. Formally, only two of the parliament's press people can be quoted: the parliament spokesperson and the deputy spokesperson. They can be interviewed on overall issues concerning the entire parliament, the management and internal rules, but they do not comment on political issues. Also, the press persons at the parliament's information offices in the member states can be cited, but also only on matters related to the institution itself, not the politics.

But most of the time, you will probably not be interested in quoting the press people – it is the MEPs that are interesting and they are happy to talk to the media.

Because there are so many potential sources in the European Parliament, there is less pressure on the press service in comparison with the commission's spokesperson service. The parliament's press people get fewer calls from journalists, so they get back to you more quickly and are in general more helpful. If they know the answers to your questions, they tend to answer straight away and not run it through the layers of the internal hierarchy. It is therefore easier to call them on the phone, instead of emailing like you often need to do with the commission's spokespeople.

EP TV: parliament debates, polls and press conferences online

The European Parliament's own TV channel EP TV broadcasts live from plenary sessions, committee meetings and most press conferences. Major events in the European Parliament are also broadcast on EbS, the common TV channel for all the EU institutions, but if you cover a parliament debate that is a little obscure, the EP TV works better.

Also, EP TV stores everything, unlike EbS. For example, all speeches in the chamber since 2006 are in the archives.

Party groups

Work in the European Parliament is organized according to two different structures: political ideologies in the party groups and policy areas in the parliament committees.

Political parties from across the EU come together in transnational political groups. Currently (September 2016), there are eight party groups in the European Parliament. In plenary and in the committees, MEPs sit with their party group friends, not with their countrymen. Right-wing politicians sit on the right-hand side and left-wing politicians sit on the left, seen from the position of the president, as they should.

The most important thing to know about the party groups is that MEPs most of the time vote according to their party group's positions, even though the national parties that constitute the party group might be very different from each other. In the political groups in the centre, the EPP, S&D and ALDE, the MEPs follow the party group line nine times out of ten, according to research from the parliament monitoring organization Votewatch.[1]

Why is that? Well, it would simply be impossible for an individual MEP to keep track of the huge flow of highly technical issues that the parliament deals with, so they tend to follow the party group line in all matters that they are not experts in themselves.

The leaders of the party groups meet in the Conference of Presidents. In their formal meetings, twice a month, they do much of the planning of the legislative work of the parliament. In informal meetings, the leaders of the party groups horse-trade over important posts, such as chairs and vice chairs of committees. And in each committee, the coordinators for each party group meet in coordinators' meetings. There they divide the reports between the party groups, according to a points system according to which the bigger the group, the more reports and the more important reports it gets to be in charge of.

To create a party group, there needs to be at least 25 MEPs from at least a quarter of all the EU countries (which currently means seven countries). In the European Parliament, there is a handful of MEPs who do not belong to any group. They are called non-attached. In the lists of speakers in plenary and other official documents, it says 'NI' from the French term 'non-inscrits'.

The three centre party groups – EPP, S&D and ALDE – have been more or less unchanged since the birth of the European Parliament, and correspond to traditional political parties that can be found in almost all EU countries. The Greens and the left group GUE-NGL have been stable elements in the European Parliament since the late 1980s/early 1990s. Other party groups appear and disappear often. Especially on the extreme right, the political groups are small and unstable, and are typically created and recreated at the beginning of every new parliamentary term.

For MEPs from small parties that do not have an equivalent in many other member states, there is a choice to be made between ideology and influence. Julia Reda from the Pirate Party Germany, for example, sits with the Greens in the European Parliament, voting along the party group line in exchange for key reports. Polish far-right politician Janusz Korwin-Mikke and three other MEPs who were elected with him in 2014 first became members of the Eurosceptic EFDD party group. After internal fighting and the party splitting up, one of the four MEPs remains in the EFDD group, two have changed to the ENF group and Korwin-Mikke himself is non-attached.

Compared with national parties, the European Parliament's party groups sprawl in all directions. They can include parties that are sometimes very distant from one another ideologically or on specific policy issues. Keep this in mind when MEPs make a guilt-by-association argument about their political opponents, which they often do. In every political group you will find parties very different from each other and every national party can be shown to have more or less strange bedfellows in Brussels and Strasbourg.

The eight party groups, in order of size (September 2016)

Centre-right group EPP (Group of the European People's Party)

The EPP originally consisted of classic continental Christian democratic parties. Today, the EPP is the large right-wing option that brings together both social conservative and liberal parties. Since the UK Tories left the group in 2009, in protest against what they considered to be overly federalist politics, the internal cohesion of the EPP is stronger. The group is generally positive about the EU.

Centre-left group S&D (Group of the Progressive Alliance of Socialists and Democrats in the European Parliament)

Along with the EPP, the social democratic S&D group is the power group of the European Parliament. It is also one of the party groups with the most cohesion; their MEPs tend to vote as a bloc on most issues. Like the EPP, the socialist group is mainly EU-positive, with a few exceptions.

Eurosceptic centre-right ECR (European Conservatives and Reformists Group)

ECR was formed by the Tories in 2009, when they left the EPP group. The Tories and the Polish Law and Justice Party (PiS) dominate the group. Apart from its EU scepticism, the ECR ideology is rather classic market liberal right-wing.

Since the 2014 election, the ECR group has grown in numbers and has replaced ALDE as the third largest party group. But the fact that the group mainly consists of two parties of almost the same size has made it harder to find a common position within the group. In 2015, its MEPs voted as a bloc 76 per cent of the time, compared to the two main groups with around 90 per cent cohesion.[2]

Liberal ALDE (Group of the Alliance of Liberals and Democrats for Europe)

ALDE is economically and socially liberal. It votes about as often with the left as with the right. On economic issues, it tends to vote with the EPP and on environmental issues or issues connected with personal integrity, it tends to vote with S&D. ALDE is the most pro-EU party group.

Left group GUE-NGL (Confederal Group of the European United Left – Nordic Green Left)

This party group gathers left-wing and former communist parties from across the EU. The internal cohesion is weaker than that of the larger party groups, perhaps because the attitude to the EU divides the group. GUE-NGL is clearly less pro-EU than the left-wing alternatives S&D and the Greens.

The Green Group-EFA (Group of the Greens – European Free Alliance)

Some European parties jump between the Greens and the left GUE-NGL group, such as the Danish Socialist People's Party. The Greens also have a high level of internal cohesion and are one of the most pro-EU party groups, with a few exceptions.

The 'EFA' in the Greens-EFA consists of representatives from regional independence parties, for example from Scotland, Catalonia and Wales.

Eurosceptic nationalist group EFDD (Europe of Freedom and Direct Democracy Group)

The party group contains EU sceptical nationalist parties from both left and right. The group is dominated by the UK Independence party and the Italian left-wing populist Five Star Movement. The EFDD party group has a weak whip. As the ideology of the group is to promote national interests, the MEPs are free to vote as they see fit. Its MEPs vote as a bloc in only about half of votes, effectively eliminating the group's potential influence over EU legislation.

Eurosceptic right-wing populist ENF (Europe of Nations and Freedom)

The party group ENF came about only in June 2015, more than a year after the election, after a British UKIP MEP defected from EFDD to ENF, and the ENF thereby obtained the seven nationalities necessary to create a party group. The group is dominated by the French Front National and the Dutch Freedom Party.

Non-attached MEPs

There are currently 16 unattached MEPs (the number changes all the time) who do not sit with any party group. A handful of them belong to neo-Nazi or Fascist parties. A couple of extreme-right politicians, such as Jean-Marie Le Pen (the father of Marine Le Pen), are not allowed to join the other National Front MEPs in the party group ENF, because of previous anti-Semitic statements. Among the non-attached, there is also a guy from a satire party.

Not being part of a political group basically means a complete lack of political influence in the European Parliament, and just being a highly paid troublemaker.

The party groups after Brexit

Even if there is no time-table for the UK leaving the EU (at the time of writing in September 2016), most EU analysts believe that the British MEPs will stay on until the end of the parliamentary term and that the next parliament, after 2019, will not have any British MEPs.

Currently, the UK has 73 MEPs, which accounts for a little less than ten per cent of the total. But not all party groups will feel the same effect from Brexit. The largest party group, the conservative EPP, will not be directly affected since there are no British MEPs in the group. The second largest party group, S&D, however, will lose their 20 Labour MEPs, accounting for around ten per cent of all their members. S&D will be weakened relative to the EPP, and the loss of Labour will also shift the balance within the group, towards a Southern European version of social democracy which is less liberal in economic terms.[3]

ALDE, which traditionally has been the third largest party group and bridge-builder between the left and right, will lose their MEPs from the Liberal

Democrats. In the 2014–2019 parliament, this is actually only one person, but traditionally there have typically been a dozen UK parliamentarians in ALDE.

The major direct impact of Brexit will be on the party groups to the right of the EPP. Both the ECR and the EFDD are groups centred on British political parties: the ECR on the Tories and the EFDD on UKIP. At least one of these two party groups, maybe both, will disappear in a post-2019 European Parliament. The other party group could possibly absorb the remaining parties and become the less radical alternative for Eurosceptic parties. Or, instead, the ENF could be consolidated and become the main Eurosceptic party group, once the less radical party groups are gone.

When you write about the party groups

You can tell by the name what kind of political group the Greens are. But do your readers know what S&D, ALDE, EPP, ECR, GUE, EFDD and ENF are? Help the reader by writing 'centre-right EPP', 'conservative EPP', 'leftist GUE', 'liberal ALDE' and the like, as in this example from *Politico*: '"Respect for European values is not a choice but an obligation", said Guy Verhofstadt, leader of the centrist ALDE grouping'.[4]

Mention what parties (from your country) sit in the party group, to give the reader an idea of what the group is all about. Also, remember not to write 'EU parties'. They are not real parties. Instead write 'party groups' or 'political groups'.

Political platforms ahead of European Parliament elections

Because MEPs mostly follow the party group line, one of the most important journalistic tasks ahead of European Parliament elections should be to examine the European political families' stances on political issues, and the party group's parliamentary voting records, and not only to examine where individual MEPs or the national parties stand. This is very rarely done.

To the extent that media dive into party politics ahead of European elections, it is the national parties that are asked what they think about EU issues. But national parties rarely have concrete positions on the often technical questions that the European Parliament will deal with during the next term. To the extent that national parties debate EU topics, it is often in respect of the broad strokes, not concrete policy.

In some EU countries, the whole EU debate in national parties has stalled at 'do we like the EU or not', a debate that helps neither individual MEPs to know how to vote on specific EU laws, nor voters to decide on who to vote for. When the MEPs are in Brussels and Strasbourg, they do not get much guidance from home and so will follow the party group line. It is therefore more important for a voter to know where the party group stands on major political issues that are decided by the European Parliament, rather than where a national party stands on the EU in general.

In the 2009 European elections, the European Green party (technically not the same thing as the European Parliament party group the Greens; see the fact box below) was the first to have a common manifesto in all EU countries. And in the 2014 election, the European political families decided to rally behind common candidates for commission president (see chapter 4), called 'Spitzenkandidaten'. The future will probably see more election campaigns based on common platforms.

All the political groups are listed on the European Parliament's first page. Click on their respective websites to find their political programmes and contact information for their press people.

Fact box: European Parliament party groups and European parties – what is the difference?

A European party, or 'Europarty', is a European transnational party organization, a European political family. A party group in the European Parliament is a structure that organizes the MEPs during the legislative term.

The Europarties and the European Parliament's party groups are affiliated and they have the same ideology. For example, the German social democratic party SPD is a member of both the European Parliament party group Socialists & Democrats (S&D) and the Party of European Socialists (PES). You could say that the party group is the arm of the Europarty, giving it a political arena where it can act: the European Parliament.

But the two structures are not a perfect fit. Within a single party group in the European Parliament, MEPs can belong to different Europarties. And the members of the Europarties are national parties from across Europe, not only EU countries.

It is only the Europarties that have the right to campaign ahead of the election to the European Parliament; the party groups do not. It was also the Europarties that rallied behind commission president candidates in the run-up to the European Parliament elections in 2014. And it is the Europarties that meet up with 'their' EU leaders on the fringes of EU summits.

If you write about any of the above-mentioned topics, try to find a way to write about them without mentioning either Europarties or party groups, to avoid confusing your readers. For example, you could say that the Spitzenkandidaten were nominated by the major European political families.

Party groups in the European Parliament:

Group of the European People's Party (EPP)
Group of the Progressive Alliance of Socialists and Democrats in the European Parliament (S&D)
European Conservatives and Reformists Group (ECR)

Group of the Alliance of Liberals and Democrats for Europe (ALDE)
Confederal Group of the European United Left – Nordic Green Left (GUE-NGL)
Group of the Greens – European Free Alliance (Greens-EFA)
Europe of Freedom and Direct Democracy Group (EFDD)
Europe of Nations and Freedom (ENF)

Corresponding Europarties:

European Peoples Party (EPP)
Party of European Socialists (PES)
Alliance of European Conservatives and Reformists (AECR)
Alliance of Liberals and Democrats for Europe Party (ALDE)
Party of the European Left (EL)
European Green Party (EGP)
European Free Alliance (EFA)
Alliance for Direct Democracy in Europe (ADDE)
Movement for a Europe of Nations and Freedom (MENF)

Interview: Richard More O'Ferrall, press advisor for the Greens-EFA in the European Parliament

When should I call you and when should I call the European Parliament press service?
The parliament press service gives context and explains the procedure. The political groups have a political perspective on the legislative files and insights into how the negotiations are going.

We can help journalists find the right people in the party group to interview. We know which MEPs work on a specific file and which MEPs speak in a way that people can understand. We also know what languages our MEPs speak. For broadcast media that is of course important.

What are the typical questions you get?
When there is legislation taken in the ordinary procedure, journalists call to get details about the process, ahead of key votes and trialogues. It is sometimes harder to get that information from the bigger political groups. The Green group is very much in favour of transparency, so if we get documents, we tend to give them if someone wants them.

Who calls you and how often?
It is mainly the Brussels-based correspondents. A typical week, there are a couple of calls a day. And many more before an important vote where we have active MEPs who are good sources of information.

From your perspective, what stories are under-reported?
There are many cases of important legislation that will have a big impact, like if the herbicide glyphosate should be allowed or not. But because it is taking place at EU level, it is only the Brussels correspondents who write about it, not the health reporters in the national capitals.

What is the most common misconception that you deal with?
Sometimes I get questions about what the Greens' policy is on something. But the political group is only organizing the MEPs for the duration of the legislative term. We look ahead on upcoming issues and take a position on them. We are not a party with a manifesto. For example, if someone calls me and asks what the Greens think about smoking on a terrace, I can't answer. We don't have a position because this is not an issue that is dealt with on EU level.

Another political dimension: EU federalism or looser cooperation?

In the European Parliament there is a political dimension that is missing in national parliaments and that you as a journalist need to know about and account for: the attitude towards European integration, or 'more or less EU'.

In its nature, the European Parliament, like the European Commission, is mostly pro-EU or federalist. It is in the interest of the institution as a whole to advocate more common solutions at the EU level and to have a greater say over EU policies in relation to the Council of Ministers, which represents the member states' governments.

But even if a majority of the MEPs in the big power-groups are friends of the EU, there are individual MEPs in all party groups that have been elected precisely for taking a Eurosceptic stance, and this share has grown in recent years. The issue of whether to advocate more EU integration with federalism as the ultimate end point, or loose economic cooperation between sovereign nations, shatters many party groups. Sometimes, the division over the attitude towards the EU is so strong that MEPs cannot work together. The British Tories gave up a seat in the biggest party group, with all the attendant perks of influence, speaking time and money, over that issue.

The large party groups in the middle, EPP, ALDE, S&D, as well as the Greens, are mainly positive about the EU. ALDE and the Greens in particular want more power for Brussels. The left group GUE-NGL is more mixed. The truly Eurosceptic party groups are conservative ECR and the populist right.

Ideology or nationality?

Party group, not nationality, is the main determinant of how individual MEPs vote. And the trend is that the MEPs in the party groups vote more and more alike over time – perhaps because of a socializing effect.

There is one exception: agricultural subsidies. When the European Parliament votes on this issue – which is a major EU affair because it is a huge part of the EU budget – MEPs stop following the party group line and instead vote along the lines of their countries' governments. This is especially the case for French and Scandinavian MEPs, according to statistics from Votewatch. Agricultural policy is the only policy area where nationality consistently trumps ideology.

There are other particular issues that can be sensitive for specific countries and where national MEPs vote as a group, instead of according to political affiliation. For example, the four Irish MEPs from Fianna Fáil went against their party group, liberal ALDE, in a 2013 plenary vote on the 'Estrela report' – a non-binding resolution about sexual and reproductive rights for women, which among other things stated the importance of access to safe abortions.

Remember that at any given time, the two major party groups EPP and S&D, and to some extent ECR and ALDE, are made up of national parties that are either in government or are the largest opposition party back at home. Domestic politics always seep into the European Parliament. An MEP whose national party is in government back home may find it difficult to follow the party group line in Brussels and Strasbourg if it means going against the Council of Ministers, where a minister from his or her party has a seat. One phone call from the prime minister's office is often enough to get stubborn MEPs to vote against their party group. An example of domestic pressure on MEPs was when the parliament voted on the EU seven-year budget in spring 2013. The Council of Ministers had hammered out a compromise that was not liked in the European Parliament – all major party groups agreed. But a majority of the EU governments were formed by centre-right parties and many capitals persuaded 'their' EPP members to take a more conciliatory attitude.

When the European Parliament in 2013 voted on a non-binding resolution calling for an end to travel between Brussels and Strasbourg, and instead for the parliament to have a single seat, it was backed by 483 MEPs, with 141 voting against and 34 abstaining. However, only a handful of the 74 French MEPs voted for the report. Had it been a closed vote, there probably would have been many more French supporting the resolution.

Weaker whip

Compared with most national parliaments, the party group whip is weaker in the European Parliament. The EU party groups cannot punish a contrary MEP by knocking him or her off the electoral list, since it is the national parties that draw up the lists.

The party groups can sanction MEPs by assigning them to less popular committees or delegations in the distribution at the beginning of the term, or at mid-term. The MEP can also be punished by not getting to be a rapporteur or by getting less speaking time in plenary debates. In a few cases, MEPs have been expelled from their party groups, but in those rare cases expulsions were for unseemly behaviour, rather than for voting against the party line.

Since control of the party groups is weaker than it usually is in national parties, and since the issues that the European Parliament deals with often are highly technical, MEPs have the opportunity to carve out niches for themselves and become real experts on one specific issue.

More cooperation between the political blocs

Compared to most national parliaments, the European Parliament is less dominated by the left or the right. Since there is no EU government, there are no government or opposition parties in the parliament (although a step in this direction was taken in the 2014 election with the Spitzenkandidaten procedure).

No single party group has a majority in the European Parliament. Cooperation across the major political blocs in committees and in plenary is the rule rather than the exception.

The organization Votewatch has shown that the EPP and S&D vote alike in about 70 per cent of all votes. The most typical winning alliance in the European Parliament is a large majority that consists of the EPP, ALDE and S&D. When the EPP and the S&D do not agree, ALDE almost always holds the pivotal position. The winning majority then consists of an alliance in which ALDE backs either the EPP or S&D.

ALDE votes with the left about as often as it votes with the right. Coalitions shift depending on the topic. On economic policy, for example, EPP and ALDE tend to vote together, but quite often the three centre party groups vote together on economic issues and it is the smaller groups on the right and left that hold the minority position.

When it comes to matters of individual freedom, such as everything that relates to freedom on the internet, the most typical winning alliance is a centre-left alliance of ALDE, S&D, Greens and GUE.

Voting rules require large majorities

Cooperation between political blocs is in part a consequence of the European Parliament voting rules, which require very large majorities. In some votes, only a simple majority is required, i.e. more for than against among the MEPs who cast a vote. It can happen that the 'wrong' proposal wins – a proposal that does not have the support from a majority of all MEPs – because a party group was more successful in getting its MEPs to press the vote button.

Other votes require a majority of its component members, i.e. a majority of the 751 MEPs. An example of this type would be a vote for the European Parliament to reject the EU's seven-year budget. This requires very large coalitions to be sure to win the vote.

There is a constant power struggle between the three main EU institutions – the European Parliament, the European Commission and the Council of Ministers. Through big deals between the party groups, the parliament manages to show a united front and get what it wants in the negotiations with the council.

This is of especial importance when the European Parliament has an interest as an institution.

But all this is changing. While the parliament was previously more united against the council, today, since the Lisbon Treaty that gives the parliament a much greater say in legislative matters, the parliament is becoming more a venue for ideological battles. European Parliament politics is becoming more partisan and less about the institutional struggle.

More odd birds in the European Parliament

Members of the European Parliament are a motley crew: They are political superstars, celebrities and people elected on a protest vote. Michael Cashman, formerly an actor on *EastEnders*, the UK's most watched soap opera, was an MEP for 15 years up to 2014. Slovak hockey pro Peter Stastny and Finnish world champion in walking Sari Essayah were also MEPs. A number of former presidents and prime ministers are or have been MEPs, for example German Willy Brandt, Danish Poul Nyrup Rasmussen, Belgian Guy Verhofstadt and Finland's first female prime minister Anneli Jäätteenmäki. All four French presidents that preceded François Hollande – Nicolas Sarkozy, Jacques Chirac, François Mitterrand and Valéry Giscard D'Estaing – were MEPs at one time in their careers.

But if some MEPs have more star power than our national parliamentarians, the bottom is also lower. There are more strange people in the European Parliament and the weirdest ones are weirder than most national politicians.

Because the turnout for the European Parliament election is so low (43 per cent, and falling – inversely proportional to the parliament's growing powers) one-issue parties can more easily get elected. It is rare that the issues dealt with in the European Parliament are debated nationally, so voters lack clear, transparent alternatives. The cost of a dissatisfaction vote is perceived to be smaller in the EU elections than in national general elections.

It is important to keep this in mind when you evaluate news events. Individual MEPs sometimes say completely crazy things that have no chance of going anywhere. It is important never to write that 'the European parliament wants' or 'according to an EU proposal' when it is just an individual MEP's opinion.

Nigel Farage, co-leader of the Eurosceptic EFDD party group, and Marine Le Pen, co-leader of the right-wing populist ENF, are two MEPs who get enormous media attention whenever they open their mouths. They are well known across Europe and they are controversial quote machines who will make good headlines. But they both represent political groups that have little real influence in the European Parliament. Remember not to exaggerate the importance of what they say. The non-attached MEPs are the most extreme and shout the loudest, but their political influence is nil.

When you assess the news value of an individual MEP's statement, ask yourself:

- Does the MEP belong to a party group at all?
- Is the party group big or small?
- Does the MEP have an important position in a committee or in the party group, e.g. rapporteur for a report that relates to his or her statement?
- Does the European Parliament have any power in the field that the MEP is talking about?
- Does the EU in general have power to decide on the issue that the MEP is talking about?

Party group meetings

In the European Parliament's annual calendar, you can see when the party groups have their meetings in Brussels. During these meetings, the MEPs brief each other on what is going on in their respective committees and talk tactics ahead of plenary votes. The meetings are not open to journalists.

Since most MEPs follow the party group line in the committee and in plenary, the party group's position is important. It gives an indication of how the majority of MEPs will vote later on. Call the party group's press people or an MEP from the party group to ask about a party group's position.

Voting in the party group meetings is done by a show of hands. A simple majority of those present is needed to adopt a position.

The party groups also meet in Strasbourg during the plenary week, to recall how to vote and to fine-tune their positions.

Key players/sources in the party groups

- If you cover EU politics often, a good shortcut is to get to know at least one MEP and/or MEP assistant from every party group, from your own country. Use these sources as shortcuts to find out what is going on in the party groups.
- Party group chair and vice chairs.
- Party group coordinators in the committees. Every party group has a coordinator and sometimes a deputy coordinator in the committees. He or she reports to the party group about what happens in the committee and makes sure that the MEPs stick together in committee, turn up for the votes and follow the party group line. The coordinators also try to ensure that party group members are made rapporteurs for important reports, and dole out the reports among their members in the committee.
- Rapporteur (the MEP in charge) and shadow rapporteur (responsible for his or her party group's position) for important reports. The importance of these individuals depends on how big their party group is. A shadow rapporteur from the major party group EPP has much more real influence than a rapporteur from small party group EFDD, for example.
- Chairman/leader of the national delegations within the party group. National delegations in the party groups are not important for small EU

countries, which never have more than one or two, maybe four, MEPs in every party group. For large EU countries, though, it matters. For example, in the EPP, the 34 MEPs from the German CDU/CSU or the 20 MEPs from France's Les Républicains are a power to take into account. How the national parties stand on specific issues and whether the party is a government or opposition party on the national level are important when these parties dominate the party group.

- The party group secretariat. All political groups have a secretariat, headed by a secretary-general, consisting of very knowledgeable political advisors. Small party groups can have one advisor for several committees, and large party groups can have several advisors for every committee. The political advisors assist the party group MEPs in the committee, especially the ones who are rapporteurs. You can find the political groups' policy advisors on the party groups' respective websites. The secretariat also includes the party groups' press people. Find them on the party groups' websites via the website of the European Parliament.

Committees

Are you a reporter for a car magazine? Then you should probably follow the European Parliament's Transport Committee and the Environment Committee. Do you often write about gender, agriculture or trade? Then those parliament committees are important to follow.

It is in the parliamentary committees that most important debates and votes take place. The committees debate issues and amend and adopt legislative reports. The vote in the committee is a good indication of how the whole parliament will later vote in plenary.

There are 20 permanent committees in the European Parliament. There are also some temporary committees that are set up to examine a specific question or investigate a scandal. The committees are of varying levels of importance. The most important are those that deal with EU legislation in fields in which the EU has substantial power.

Typically, MEPs are regular members of one or two committees and substitute members of one or two other committees. Only ordinary members are allowed to vote in the committee. Substitute members can vote only when they replace an absent member. They can always speak, however.

In the committees, the party group whip is slightly weaker than in plenary – probably because the committee members are familiar with the issue and have formed their own opinions. Factors other than the party group line can prevail here.

Since EU policies often relate to technical issues – the specific rules on deposit guarantees for banks, for example – and MEPs tend to specialize on some issues, most MEPs have some sort of specialist competence. You can't find on any list who the unofficial expert on your topic is. But you get a good idea by looking at who has been rapporteur and shadow rapporteur on past and present reports that deal with the issue. Ask MEPs who are members of the committee, the committee press people or the party group press people.

The committee websites vary in quality and in the amount of information they make accessible. Certain information can always be found: a list of committee members, agendas, minutes from previous meetings, planned future meetings, reports and opinions from the committee, information about how the MEPs voted (unfortunately only in PDF format, making it impossible for transparency organizations to crunch the data and make it searchable) and webcasts from meetings.

The rapporteur

Much of the political work done in the European Parliament takes place in the committees. Every report (legislative report or own-initiative report) is handed to a responsible committee and a responsible MEP. This MEP is called the rapporteur. Big reports can sometimes have two rapporteurs.

Fact box: The 20 standing committees (abbreviations in brackets)

- Foreign Affairs (AFET). This committee has two subcommittees: Human Rights (DROI) and Security and Defence (SEDE)
- Development (DEVE)
- International Trade (INTA)
- Budget (BUDG)
- Budgetary Control (CONT)
- Economic and Monetary Affairs (ECON)
- Employment and Social Affairs (EMPL)
- Environment, Public Health and Food Safety (ENVI)
- Industry, Research and Energy (ITRE)
- Internal Market and Consumer Protection (IMCO)
- Transport and Tourism (TRAN)
- Regional Development (REGI)
- Agriculture and Rural Development (AGRI)
- Fisheries (PECH)
- Culture and Education (CULT)
- Legal Affairs (JURI)
- Civil Liberties, Justice and Home Affairs (LIBE)
- Constitutional Affairs (AFCO)
- Women's Rights and Gender Equality (FEMM)
- Petitions (PETI)

The European Parliament can treat the bill in two rounds – first and second reading – but most legislation passes in the first round. This is done through direct negotiations between the commission, the council and the parliament (see chapter 8). In these negotiations, the rapporteur represents the parliament and speaks for the whole institution. The rapporteur is therefore a key position.

Being the rapporteur for a big, important legislative report is an important post and causes scrambles between party groups. The politically sensitive reports usually go to the largest party groups, or to an MEP who is acknowledged to be an expert on the issue.

It is the rapporteur who writes the draft report. He or she proposes amendments, negotiates with other party groups in the committee, i.e. with the shadow rapporteurs, consults external stakeholders and finally presents the report in the committee. A deadline is set for when the other members of the committee can propose amendments. The most important amendments come from the shadow rapporteurs; they represent more MEPs.

The rapporteur leads the negotiations with the shadow rapporteurs about compromise amendments, which would replace the individual amendments. The rapporteur usually makes sure that the compromise amendments have the support of a majority, so looking at these amendments can give you a good idea of how the report will look after the committee vote. Some committees put the compromise amendments on their website. If you can't find them there, ask the committee press officer.

The rapporteur usually asks for expertise from the European Commission and the commission is always present at committee meetings to answer questions when the MEPs are dealing with commission proposals.

When the report has been adopted in the committee and is to be voted on by the full parliament in plenary, it is the rapporteur who opens the plenary debate. After a new round of amendments and votes, the whole parliament adopts the report. The rapporteur again is the main representative for the European Parliament, and is interviewed in the media about the issue.

Writing about the committee and the rapporteur

Just like the commissioners' official titles, the names of the European Parliament committees are often too long and complicated to be fit for a journalistic text. Printing the correct name often confuses more than it explains. Many committees have double or triple names, such as the Committee for Environment, Public Health and Food Safety (ENVI). Choose what is relevant in your specific case and call the committee that. If you write about car emissions, write the Environment Committee or perhaps the Environment and Health Committee. Are you writing about the Tobacco Products Directive? Then call the committee the Public Health Committee. You can always add the committee acronym, so that readers can find their way back to the right committee. Also, write

'European Parliament committee', never 'EU committee', which does not mean anything.

When you write about the rapporteur, it can look something like this: 'Jan Philipp Albrecht, the German Green MEP shepherding the proposal, said: "This will grow the digital market in Europe, perhaps even [allow it to] dominate the global digital market on this issue".'[5]

Sometimes, when an MEP is interviewed about a law for which he or she is responsible, his or her nationality is mentioned, but not the political affiliation. Party group affiliation is almost always more important than nationality; you need to mention that.

In an article from the *Irish Independent* about a banking reform, the caption underneath a picture of the parliament rapporteur Othmar Karas refers to him as the 'Austrian politician Othmar Karas'.[6] This gives the incorrect impression that Karas in some way represents the Austrian government, when he is in fact negotiating with the Austrian government and the other EU countries in his role as representative for the European Parliament. Better to mention his party group affiliation, like this: 'Othmar Karas, the Austrian Christian Democrat who negotiated the deal on behalf of the European Parliament'.

Delegations

Alongside the committees, the European Parliament also has 44 delegations that are in contact and exchange information with countries and organizations outside the EU. Often, MEPs are members of at least one delegation.

The European Parliament has delegations to countries such as Israel, Turkey, Canada, Belarus and South Africa, to regions such as the Arabian Peninsula or South Asia, or to international organizations such as NATO's parliamentary assembly or the Pan-African parliament.

Delegations usually travel during parliament's constituency weeks, when most MEPs are in their home countries anyway. Typical delegation activities during a constituency week might be that the EU–US parliamentary delegation meets members of the American Congress and environmental organizations to talk about climate change, MEPs travel to Afghanistan to study how EU-funded projects work, and a delegation meets Brazil's minister for agriculture and Brazilian parliamentarians, to talk about biofuels.

On each **delegation's website** you can find information about their activities and which MEPs are members. The delegations are organized in much the same way as the committees, with a chairperson, vice chairman and a secretariat.

The number of MEPs in every delegation ranges from 10 to 70. The chairman of the delegation submits an activity report to the Committee on Foreign Affairs.

Foreign policy is a policy area over which the European Parliament has basically no decision-making power. The delegations, however, are a very good example of the informal power that the parliament exercises in foreign affairs. The delegations do not adopt any formal decisions but they write reports and air opinions that are nevertheless listened to. In this way, they put issues on the agenda.

The delegations are a good place to look for MEPs who are interested in a specific region. Say you are writing something about Afghanistan–EU relations. Then check the Afghanistan delegation in the European Parliament to find MEPs from the left to the right who are interested and knowledgeable.

The delegations have no designated press people. The press people who cover the Foreign Affairs Committee have split between them responsibility for the delegations, one continent each. Call them to find out who keeps an eye on the delegation that you are interested in.

Intergroups

Intergroups are informal groups of MEPs from across the political spectrum, who are interested in a particular issue: from children's rights, climate change and anti-racism, to Western Sahara and LGBT issues.

These groups have often been initiated and are led by an outside organization. It is a way for companies and NGOs to connect with like-minded MEPs and get their attention. The point of the intergroup is precisely to strengthen contacts between MEPs of different political affiliations, and between the parliament and civil society. The intergroup does not take any decisions; it is only a forum for discussion.

The intergroups can be a good place to look for sources, as you will find only the parliamentarians who are particularly interested in an issue there, from the left to the right.

The intergroup has no formal powers but is a group that is formally recognized by parliament. In addition, there is a plethora of even more informal groups and clubs with different members.

Plenary sessions

First-time visitors to the European Parliament in Brussels tend to wonder about the large, grey plastic coffins that are scattered in the corridors. Into these coffins, the MEPs and their assistants throw work that is in progress (memos, reports), photos of the kids, notes, favourite pens – yes, all that stuff that you normally have on your desk. Some 1,500 coffins are transported by truck 350 kilometres between Brussels and Strasbourg.

The trip to Strasbourg is also made by the MEPs (but usually by train or plane). Add to that their assistants, some of the parliament civil servants, translators, interpreters, and also many lobbyists and journalists. Somewhere between 7,000 and 8,000 EU people invade the city of Strasbourg one week a month.

On the plus side is the enormous symbolic value of the fact that the EU's directly elected assembly meets in a city that for the last hundred and fifty years has been conquered in turn by France, Germany, France again, Germany again and finally France. It was when the sworn enemies laid down their arms and began to cooperate within the Coal and Steel Community that the seeds were sown for what today is the EU.

On the minus side is that the monthly move costs EU taxpayers 180 million euros every year and contributes 19,000 tons of CO_2 emissions.[7] The MEPs suffer from the constant travel to 'Stressbourg' and they are very aware that the reputation of their institution suffers a blow every time the uncomfortable arrangement is mentioned in the media.

A large majority of MEPs have voted that the European Parliament itself should get to decide when and where to have its plenary sessions.[8] However, this would require a treaty change, and when the EU changes its rulebook, every EU country has a veto. Any reform effort would be stopped by France and Luxembourg: France because the country would lose prestige and the city of Strasbourg would lose a lot of money; Luxembourg because the city-state is the host to all council meetings three months every year and because about half of the European Parliament's administration is based there, also according to the treaties. If France could be convinced to let go of the Strasbourg parliament, the pressure could increase on Luxembourg to do the same. The travelling will continue for the foreseeable future.

It is mainly during the plenary sessions in Strasbourg that the European Parliament takes decisions, that the politicians make their key speeches, and the full chamber debates. This is where the parliament votes on legislation that concerns 500 million people. A whole month's worth of debates and votes are concentrated into two or three days, so it is very intense. As a journalist, it is an exciting place to be: the air really smells and tastes of politics!

Quite often, however, the party groups have already agreed in principle in Brussels and the vote is only a formality. The speeches are written in advance and the debates feel stilted. Many MEPs read from notes and since they speak their native language, which most other MEPs need to have interpreted, the other MEPs sit with their headphones on and look the other way. A quick and witty word battle is rare.

Despite this, it is exciting in Strasbourg. What is special is that the corridors really are buzzing. Since everyone is there and everyone is away from home, family and everyday routines, the work day is much longer than normal. Nobody needs to rush off from a meeting to pick up kids at the crèche, so it is easier to steal an MEPs time for a coffee and a chat, or to schedule long interviews.

But despite the fact that it is during the Strasbourg session that the parliament takes the important decisions, few reporters are there. Of the correspondents in Brussels that continuously cover the EU, only a few go to Strasbourg – and then only if it is a matter of important votes and if this does not clash with other important meetings in Brussels. Freelance journalists and small media rarely if ever make the Strasbourg trip, for obvious economic reasons. This democratic problem is seldom heard as an argument when the Brussels–Strasbourg issue is discussed.

Monday: Introduction

The plenary session lasts for three and a half days, from Monday afternoon to Thursday evening. It opens on Monday at five o'clock. The parliament president begins by giving a short speech. Sometimes he takes the opportunity to congratulate a colleague who has a birthday, comment on a world event, condemn a terrorist attack or take note of an anniversary. After these opening words, the plenary session agenda is adopted. This is a technical point, but there is room for coups. Many MEPs drop in only on Tuesday morning and small party groups can take advantage of this and join *en masse* on Monday evening and get a controversial issue on the agenda.

After the agenda has been adopted, half an hour of 'one-minute speeches' follow. The speaking time can be used to talk about anything – but just for one minute. Here too, the small party groups that are awarded little speaking time in the real debates can seize the opportunity. The one-minute speeches vary enormously. Often they involve local issues that have nothing to do with the EU, and are mostly aimed at showing the constituency that the MEP is fighting for its interests everywhere. It is mostly grandstanding, although sometimes quite funny.

Tuesday to Thursday: Voting, debates and lofty speeches

During Tuesday, Wednesday and Thursday there are plenary debates and votes. Usually the votes are in the middle of the day – with the main votes on Tuesday and Wednesday – but the debates can go on until eleven pm. On Thursday after lunch, MEPs' attendance starts to drop again, as they head back to Brussels or home for the weekend.

Frequently, top European or international politicians visit the parliament and make a speech in the chamber. Under parliament president Martin Schulz, the European Parliament increasingly became an arena for debate about Europe. The German chancellor, Italian prime minister and the French president have all been there to expound their visions for the EU and Europe.

If there has been an EU summit during the month, the European Council president comes to Strasbourg to report on the summit for the MEPs and answer their questions. At the plenary sitting in January and June, the prime minister or president of the country that takes over, or leaves, the rotating presidency of the Council of Ministers (see chapter 6), usually reports to the parliament or presents his or her vision for the next six months.

A report goes from committee to plenary

Once a European Parliament committee has adopted a report, the report moves to plenary. Any party group, or at least 40 MEPs, can now table amendments to the report. The party groups negotiate with each other and propose compromise amendments. In this process, the non-attached members have zero influence.

The rapporteur and the shadow rapporteurs or committee coordinators now have the job of getting their party groups' MEPs to follow the compromises that were made in the committees. Normally, it is the shadow rapporteurs who lead the party group, but if it is a politically very sensitive issue, someone higher up in the party group hierarchy might take over.

The debate in plenary begins with the rapporteur or rapporteurs saying a few words about the report. The responsible commissioner is usually present to answer questions about how the commission reasoned in its initial legislative proposal, as well as a representative from the council presidency, explaining the council's view.

Before the final vote, the commissioner explains his or her views on the amendments that the parliament has tabled. It is important for the commission to maintain its right of initiative, so that the parliament amendments do not change the proposal beyond all recognition.

Voting

'Amendment 11. Votes in favour. Votes against. Abstain. The proposal is rejected. Amendment 13 by GUE. Votes in favour. Votes against …'. The parliament president reads from the list at a crazy speed. Voting in plenary can go on for hours. A large legislative package can have hundreds of amendments that are either accepted or rejected. Party group leaders show the thumbs up or thumbs down to signal to their party group colleagues how to vote.

The list with all the amendments that MEPs vote on is found on the designated **website for the plenary session**. The votes go very quickly, so it can be difficult to keep up if you do not have the list next to you. When you hear the rustling and humming, it is an indication that there is a big issue up for voting.

About an hour after the vote is done, the final text is out and the inbox is full of press releases and comments. Many MEPs also tweet from the chamber.

MEPs usually vote by a show of hands. The parliament president takes a quick glance at the sea of hands and decides where the majority lies. If it is unclear, or if an MEP requires accurate counting, the MEPs vote electronically, by pressing a button.

This electronic voting does not record who has voted for what. This is only done for roll-call votes, where the individual votes are recorded and a full voting list is published.

Voting by roll call is done for all final legislative votes, or if a party group or 40 MEPs require it. For practically all important votes, there is at least one party group that has an interest in making the voting record public – to show how they have voted, to check (and discipline) their own members, or to embarrass a fragmented opposition.

Roll-call votes are therefore standard for most votes that are of media interest. But there are exceptions. One of the most important votes in recent years was when the European Parliament rejected the Swift agreement, in 2010. The Swift agreement was a deal between the EU and the US to exchange information on banking transactions. The purpose was terror prevention but the parliament feared that the agreement would violate people's privacy. The vote was not done by roll call. It is therefore impossible to find out now how individual MEPs voted.

A few hours after the plenary vote, you can find the vote record on the parliament homepage. It is also posted on the website Votewatch, in a more easy-to-read format.

A few votes are closed votes. They are for example nominations, such as president of the European Parliament, or votes to accept or reject the college of commissioners.

Press conferences before and during the plenary session

Every Friday before the plenary week, there is a press briefing in Brussels at 11am. There, the party groups' press officers explain what issues their party group thinks are particularly important, how they intend to vote and why.

On Monday, at 4.30pm, half an hour before the plenary session opens, there is a last minute press conference in Strasbourg, with the committee press officers. You can follow both these press conferences on the European Parliament's TV channel, EP TV.

During the plenary, many press conferences go on as well: the party groups, the rapporteurs on important reports that have been adopted, the parliament president, invited guests, parliament delegations and commissioners ... Most of them can be watched on EP TV.

Small, informal press meetings also take place throughout the week. Many groups of MEPs take the chance to gather with 'their' national journalists in one of the many cafés and meeting rooms for a breakfast meeting or afternoon coffee.

A month in the life of the European Parliament

The work in the European Parliament is cyclical. Every month looks more or less like this:

- One or two weeks of committee work in Brussels.
- Two to three days of meetings with the party groups in Brussels.
- One week in plenary session in Strasbourg.

Twelve times a year, the European Parliament holds plenary sessions in Strasbourg. In addition to that, every year there are around six 'mini plenaries' in Brussels, between Wednesday and Thursday, so that the parliament can get all the votes and debates done. In August, the parliament is on vacation.

Since the parliament is required, by the treaties, to have 12 Strasbourg sessions every year, and since it closes down during one summer month, there will be one month with two Strasbourg sessions. This is usually September or October.

A few weeks every year are 'constituency weeks'. During these the MEPs go back to their constituencies to have meetings with their national political parties and meet voters. Other trips, such as parliament delegation trips to countries outside the EU, normally take place at the same time. These weeks are news-light times in the parliament. Committee weeks and plenary weeks are news-heavy.

The MEPs are constantly travelling between Brussels, Strasbourg and their home constituencies. Most MEPs still live in their home country, and commute to Brussels and Strasbourg every week, while others have settled in Brussels and instead go to their home country for work reasons.

For obvious reasons, it is rather difficult to know where an MEP is. Be sure to check the **parliamentary calendar** before you book your Brussels trip.

If you frequently contact MEPs, it's handy to have the yearly calendar close by. People working in the parliament have it printed on the back of their staff badges and constantly turn them around to check before making any arrangements more than a week ahead.

Weekly calendar

On the parliament's website you can also find a detailed **weekly calendar**. Check it by day or by type of event, to find out where the meeting will take place, in what room, if you can follow it on the internet or not, and the contact information for the responsible press people.

As many MEPs go to their home countries for the weekend, many are already away on Fridays and the parliament is calmer.

Votewatch: voting statistics

Votewatch was founded in 2009 and is an independent organization that wants more debate about the EU's legislative process, and EU institutions to be more transparent. The founders are transparency activists and political scientists, including Simon Hix who is one of the world's top authorities on the European Parliament.

Votewatch uses the parliament's own statistics, but presents them in a more user-friendly format, for anyone to use. You can use Votewatch as a shortcut to check how the MEPs voted on a certain topic, or to compare MEPs. Votewatch does its own analyses and writes reports, which are often newsworthy.

The following data is available for all MEPs: presence in plenary, how he or she has voted in plenary (roll-call votes), reports that the MEP has drafted (i.e. been the rapporteur for) and opinions that the MEP has drafted.

MEPs' performances

Ahead of the elections to the European Parliament, or half-way through the parliamentary term, an obvious news angle is to compare and rank your national MEPs by activity.

Attendance: a way to measure performance

A typical way to examine the MEPs is to check how often they are present and how active they are on the job. With a few clicks on the Votewatch website, you have a list of the 'participation in roll-call votes'. Be careful not to write 'presence' but 'presence in plenary' if you use the data from Votewatch.

You can also check attendance in committee meetings; it just takes more work than a simple search on the Votewatch site. You have to download the PDF files from all the committee meetings, or call the designated press person and ask him or her to send them to you, and manually go through them to see who has been present at the meeting.

Don't go blind staring at the attendance rankings. It is of course important for MEPs to be in their seats during the votes in plenary and in committees, but it should not be used as a blunt tool to determine which MEPs work the most.

If an MEP is the rapporteur for a big legislative report, then that is a huge job. If he or she is in the top level in the party group, that too takes up a lot of time. Those MEPs are probably missing from votes because they have other things they need to do, such as negotiate with other EU institutions in Brussels.

Other statistical noise in the attendance figures could be that MEPs are away because of illness, pregnancy or parental leave, or that an MEP started mid-term or quit before the end of the term. Before drawing conclusions and publishing a ranking, you need to check this. Call the MEPs or their assistants and ask.

Activities in parliament

In the Votewatch statistics, you can see how many reports and opinions the MEP has drafted. The watchdog **MEPranking** lists even more activities: drafted amendments, speeches made in plenary and written questions to the commission (see later in this chapter) and more. Comparing all these stats, you can get an idea of how much the MEPs work. But you need to weigh and explain the numbers, not simply present them as self-evidently meaningful in and of themselves. An MEP who is the rapporteur for an important report but asks no questions is working more than an MEP who is not a rapporteur but who asks thousands. One MEP can work on a single huge report for years, while another MEP can be in charge of many, small, technical reports.

As these rankings have come to be used by media and watchdog organizations more and more, some MEPs have started to bloat the statistics that they can impact directly. For example, some MEPs ask five different questions with more or less the same content, rather than just one. If you do your own activity ranking, either exclude the activities that can be bloated (which Votewatch does), or explain this to the readers. Or, maybe, do your own investigation into ranking abuse. Is there perhaps an MEP who has gone from the lower level of activity to the top in just a year? Is that not a bad use of taxpayers' money to have MEPs' assistants write meaningless questions, which poor commission interns are required politely to answer?

How did MEPs vote?

Comparing activity might be interesting, but it says nothing about to what extent an MEP actually has acted in their voters', your readers' or viewers', interest. For this, you need to look at how the MEP has voted on specific issues.

On Votewatch's site you can find all the roll-call votes. For votes in the committee, you again need to go through the PDF documents and count manually. Find them on the committee website or by calling the committee press secretary. MEPs have voted in the committee by roll-call only since March 2014, so individual MEPs' voting records are only accessible after that date.

If you write for an agricultural magazine, an obvious angle is to select the five most important votes about agricultural policy during the last parliamentary term and see how your country's MEPs have voted. Or choose five votes where there is a clear free trade perspective and compare how MEPs from your country voted, to determine who the most consistently pro-free trade MEP is. There are unlimited angles. Just call the committee press people to ask them what the biggest, most crucial issues were.

Votewatch analyzed, for example, the voting history for the MEPs who ran for the job of president of the European Parliament in 2012. The organization chose ten votes that were much discussed and that showed clear ideological differences, including the Maternity Leave Directive, the trade agreement ACTA (Anti-Counterfeiting Trade Agreement), proposals for reducing the agricultural budget, the EU free trade agreement with India and the proposed European tax on financial transactions.

By examining the votes, you can compare what MEPs promised ahead of the election to how they actually voted. You can analyze to what extent MEPs follow the party group line and to what extent they vote 'nationally'.

One interesting analysis is to look at which issues your country's MEPs vote on 'nationally', to determine what your country specifically brings to the European table, and how the EU would look without it. Votewatch did this with the British MEPs, showing where the typical British influence in the European Parliament lies, using this as a way of measuring how EU politics in substance would change in the case of Brexit.[9]

Once again, you need to be careful not to use statistics without explaining the context. For example, you might see that an MEP has rejected a proposal to limit a dangerous chemical. You cannot draw the conclusion from this alone that he or she is an environmental villain. Perhaps the MEP actually voted for another amendment that went even further. To find this out, you must call the MEP or the assistants and ask. The best way is to call two MEPs who voted differently and ask them their reasoning and motivations. Only then can you understand the motives and judge the vote.

Pressing the wrong button?

Sometimes MEPs accidentally press the wrong button during the vote. Or, perhaps, they say that they have done that when they no longer want to justify how they have voted.

An MEP who has pressed the wrong button can, within two weeks, ask to enter into the minutes of the meeting how he or she actually intended to vote. This does not change the result of the vote; that still holds. For your own good night's sleep, check the minutes before you publish a revelation about how an individual MEP has voted, and always let the MEP respond to your claim, if for no other reason than to ensure that your disclosure will not be questioned later.

An investigation by online newspaper Europaportalen shows that, in a period of little over a year, each MEP corrected, on average, seven erroneous votes. This may sound like a lot, but bear in mind that the MEPs can vote on hundreds of amendments during one plenary session, that the voting goes very fast and that the simultaneous interpretation can lag a little bit. But a few MEPs stand out: almost all MEPs from the French Front National corrected more than 40 times during the same period.[10] It is unlikely that this happened by mistake. There is probably a hidden story behind those numbers that French reporters will hopefully look into.

What the European Parliament does

The European Parliament's main task is, as said, to amend and pass legislation, in parallel with the Council of Ministers. But it has other roles too.

Controlling the commission

National parliaments serve as a check on their governments. The European Parliament acts as a check on the other EU institutions, especially the European Commission.

The parliament:

- Asks the commission questions.
- Questions and approves the commission president and the other nominated commissioners.
- Dismisses the commission by a vote of no confidence.
- Checks if the European Commission has spent the EU budget correctly and grants discharge for the financial year; checks and discharges the other EU institutions' budgets.
- Listens to complaints from ordinary people in the parliament's petitions committee.
- Sets up special investigative committees to examine scandals and determine whether EU member states and/or EU institutions have acted in accordance with EU laws.
- Takes EU institutions to the EU court.

Questions to the European Commission

The European Parliament can be the journalist's best friend, because the MEPs often want answers to the same things as journalists. When it comes to some of the more obscure or closed EU institutions, the parliament can be the only place where you see their representatives being put up for scrutiny. You can, for example, drop in when the president of the European Central Bank presents the bank's annual report in plenary or is questioned in the Economic and Monetary Affairs Committee.

MEPs can also ask written questions to the European Commission, the ECB, the foreign affairs chief and the Council of Ministers. The commission is obliged to respond within three or six weeks, depending on the priority of the questions. You can find all the questions and answers on the parliament's website.

It can be worthwhile scrolling through the list of questions. There might be a nice story somewhere in the pile and it is easy to get ideas for articles. You can also use the parliament's questions to get an idea of what issues a specific MEP is working on in parliament. And the questions can be a shortcut for understanding the EU rules on a specific topic. Search the topic that interests you, e.g. GMOs (genetically modified organisms). By reading the questions and answers you quickly get an overview of the current state of EU laws on GMOs and what the crucial issues and political conflicts are.

MEPs ask around a thousand questions every month. During the 2009–2014 term, they tabled in total 58,840 written questions. So, it is very commonplace and not a big deal. The commission is only required to answer, not to act in any other way. Remember this when considering the news value of MEPs' questions.

In 2010, there was a short article on a Swedish news site with the headline 'EU law against Facebook'.[11] The whole story was based on a written question from Irish Labour MEP Nessa Childers, which had as subject line 'internet addiction'. Childers wrote that the use of social media such as Facebook had exploded and that, for some people, this could become an addiction.

'With the passing into force of the Lisbon Treaty, the EU now has increased powers to legislate when there is a threat to public health in Europe. Will the Commission submit proposals to Parliament to address this growing threat to the mental health of European citizens?' she asked the commission.

Putting 'EU law' as headline when the article is based on a parliamentary question leads the reader to the conclusion that a parliamentary question is the first step towards binding legislation. Nothing could be more wrong.

Many of the questions are not genuinely looking for an answer. They are often a statement – a way to show voters back home that the MEP is using all possible channels to influence the commission, for example on a local or national issue. There are also reports of MEPs who have their assistants write dozens or even hundreds of questions in order to rise up the activity rankings, as mentioned earlier.

Some MEPs make it their mission to be the link between citizens and the more difficult-to-reach EU institutions, such as the commission. They might send off questions they have received in emails from ordinary people or from lobbyists. You cannot be sure that it is the MEP him- or herself who is behind the poorly-worded question or if they believe in the values it expresses. To know that, you need to call the MEP or their assistants and ask.

Vote of no confidence

When a new commission is appointed, the European Parliament accepts or rejects the whole college of commissioners, after having questioned the nominees in the appropriate parliament committees (see chapter 4).

The European Parliament can also make the whole commission resign, by a vote of no confidence. Again, it can only sack the whole college, not single out specific commissioners. A tenth of all MEPs are needed to call for a vote of no confidence. And for the vote to succeed, it needs a double majority: two-thirds of the votes cast and a majority of all 751 MEPs.

The European Parliament has voted ten times, but never yet forced the commission to resign. In 1999 however, the commission led by Luxembourger Jacques Santer resigned over corruption allegations, after it became clear that it would otherwise be voted down in the European Parliament.

More recently, the commission president Jean-Claude Juncker survived a no-confidence motion just a month after he took office in 2014. The motion was backed by anti-EU parties such as Britain's UKIP, France's National Front and Italy's Five Star Movement, and demanded Juncker be sacked because of the 'Lux leaks' revelations: that while Juncker was prime minister, Luxembourg had agreed to possibly illegal corporate tax avoidance schemes.

Budget discharge

It is the European Commission that is responsible for implementing the EU budget. The commission hands out money from various funds to farmers, fishermen, businesses and public projects. Almost all money is paid as a lump sum to the member states, which then pay it to different people and projects. But it is still the commission that makes sure the money has been used properly, and the parliament in turn checks if the commission has done a good job at that.

Once a year, the European Parliament decides whether or not to discharge the commission accounts. In April, when the parliament votes, it either grants a discharge or postpones the decision. If it postpones the decision, the parliament takes a new look in October and then decides whether to grant or refuse a discharge. In the meantime, the commission should provide additional information and follow the recommendations of the parliament's Budgetary Control Committee.

The committee members examine the accounts and the annual reports from the commission, taking into account the recommendations from the Ecofin council (the EU countries' finance ministers) and the report from the Court of Auditors.

The report from the Court of Auditors, which typically comes around mid-October, usually contains heavy criticism of the commission, as the share of errors – whether a missing signature or actual fraud – is always too high. An error rate of two per cent is generally considered to be the acceptable level. In 2014 the error rate was 4.4 per cent. When the report from the Court of Auditors comes out, it usually leads to many articles about poor control of EU spending.

Remember that if the audit has found errors in four per cent of all payments, this does not mean that four per cent of all EU money has been lost or subject to fraud. An error can mean a wrongly completed form.

Only twice has the parliament refused to discharge the commission – in 1986 for the budget year 1984 and in 1998 for the year 1996. The latter was also a way to pressure the commission led by Jacques Santer to resign.

The European Parliament grants discharge to all the EU institutions and EU agencies, not only the European Commission. But it is only for the commission that a non-discharge has any legal consequences. For the other EU institutions and agencies that are being scrutinized, it is mostly an embarrassment and an unpleasant political signal.

For every institution and agency, the European Parliament first votes on whether to give a discharge or not, and then votes on a resolution for the institution. For example, the European Environment Agency, EEA, in Copenhagen was refused discharge in 2012. Among other things, the MEPs questioned a plant wall with a price tag of 300,000 euros that had been purchased to adorn the agency's façade, without a proper public procurement process.

These types of stories of wastefulness can be found in the 40-plus reports from the budget control committee. Check them out. Also, make sure not to miss the committee's many hearings with senior officials who have to explain their strange investments. Check the committee's website to see what is on its agenda for upcoming meetings and watch the meetings online, either on the committee's website or on EP TV.

Interview: Petri Sarvamaa, coordinator for the EPP group in the European Parliament's Committee on Budgetary Control

Explain your role as the EPP coordinator
Simply put, you're responsible for the coordination of your party group. The coordinator has a lot of practical powers in the day-to-day business. In the coordinators' meetings in the committee, we discuss the allocation of reports. And as the EPP coordinator, I allocate the reports within the EPP.

There is one rapporteur for every discharge report, i.e. every EU institution. What do the rapporteurs base their reports on?
The most important part of the information comes from the Court of Auditors' annual report. As a rapporteur you also have all the means to go and visit, say, the agencies. You always strive for a more complete picture; there is no end to that. But first you study the basics.

Do you see any problems with the discharge procedure as it is today?
The European Parliament has gained so much more power with the Lisbon Treaty 2009, but one of the things where it is still falling short is

the non-binding nature of these [discharge] resolutions. As it is today, we have an important task, but our recommendations are not binding.

The commission pays a lot of attention to the discharge. But the council has not been given a discharge from this parliament for many years and that doesn't change anything. The council building for example [the Europa building, next to Justus Lipsius, that is under construction and will be operational by the end of 2016] – nobody knows how much it has cost, because the council didn't abide by the parliament's will to disclose the figures and the contracts.

Another example is the information about the cohesion and agriculture spending. The national institutions are responsible for collecting the data and to give it to the commission. In this chain, we all know that the quality of the data from the member states is very different. It is not comparable.

What do you think journalists should cover more when it comes to the EU budget?
The free tip that I would give any journalist is to just call and ask. You can call me. There are always interesting findings, stories about taxpayers' money that wasn't spent wisely, that people don't know.

Many people who work in the EU institutions seem scared to reveal mismanagement because they think it would harm the image of the EU and play into the hands of Eurosceptics. Not you?
Well, I used to be a journalist for 25 years, that is my background. That is why I tell journalists to come over here to see what is going on. I've never personally dug up a scandal, but I give hints to journalists.

Whether or not we should be more critical of the EU is a key question. I don't have an answer, but I tend to point out the problems, I believe that it's better. It's like in a relationship, you know. If you keep problems to yourself, they keep growing, until you put it on the table, maybe you have a fight and you clear the air.

European Parliament Petitions Committee

The European Parliament's Committee on Petitions is the oddest of the standing committees. The committee does not legislate; it listens to ordinary people's complaints about the EU institutions and about how EU law is applied in their country, and mediates. The complaints must be about things that fall within the EU's power and affect the plaintiff directly.

When you, as a journalist, have overdosed on the technical negotiations on the EU's long-term budget or other stories that go on forever, it can sometimes be refreshing to check the agenda for the next meeting in the petitions committee. The complaints that are treated are wonderfully practical and you are served the case – the person affected by the matter – on a plate. Further, you get a deeper understanding of how EU law and its national implementation are connected.

The Committee on Petitions listens to about a thousand complaints every year. Typically, the complaints are about local or national authorities that have not implemented EU laws correctly, often environmental law. Other common complaints are from individuals who have not been able to move freely within the EU or have not been able to take their social benefits, like pensions or health care, to another EU country.

Most complaints come from Spain, Germany and Italy. Even if the discussions are about countries other than your own, it can give you a hint of problematic areas in EU legislation that might also be the same in your country, and can give you ideas for things to investigate. For example, airport noise has been up for discussion in the committee, with affected people from Belgium, France and Italy. The petitioners are people living close to airports that do not follow the rules and standards set by the EU. What about your country? Are the rules followed there? It might be worthwhile to check.

Members of the committee sometimes go on fact-finding missions to investigate if there is any basis for the complaint. Often, the complaining citizen comes to the committee to express his or her view. A representative of the institution deemed to have done wrong – it tends to be the commission – is also there, to explain its actions.

A typical case can be a man from Naples who thinks that the Italian government is not following EU rules by allowing waste to pile up in his city, and that the European Commission is not doing its job by allowing this to continue. A delegation from the Committee on Petitions travels to Naples and meets the mayor. At the next committee meeting the responsible MEP, the rapporteur, explains what has been said and done at the meeting. A lawyer from the commission participates in the petitions committee meeting, to explain if or why the commission has not launched an infringement proceeding against Italy.

The petitions committee has no power to promise the affected citizens any real action. But it puts pressure on the commission.

Check the committee's website to find out when the next meeting is held, and what issues are on the agenda. Follow the meeting directly on the committee's website.

Investigative committees

The European Parliament sometimes sets up temporary committees in order to investigate particular issues. Recent investigative committees include the 'Luxleaks Committee', formally the Special Committee on Tax Rulings (TAXE). It was set up in February 2015 and was tasked with investigating the revelations about some EU countries' favourable, and perhaps illegal, tax deals with multinational companies.

Another committee, set up in early 2016, is the 'Dieselgate Committee', formally the Committee of Inquiry into Emission Measurements in the

Automotive Sector (EMIS). It investigates what the EU countries and EU institutions knew about Volkswagen's cheating on emissions tests.

The committees hold hearings with involved parties. They cannot force people to come and answer their questions. But most EU politicians and representatives of major countries and companies do so anyway. It would just be too embarrassing otherwise. European Commission president Jean-Claude Juncker, who has been in the Luxembourg political centre for the last 30 years and whom few believe could have been unaware of the contested tax agreements, is one politician who has been present at hearings of the Luxleaks Committee, for example.

The European Parliament's informal power

To resume, the European Parliament has extensive power to legislate and to scrutinize the commission. But much of the parliament's daily activities are outside of what could be called its core business. As a journalist, it is important to know when the parliament has real powers and when it does not, because this of course affects how we determine the news value.

That said, the European Parliament's informal powers are not insignificant. The parliament is good at maximizing its impact by combining formal and informal powers – by adopting legislative reports, own-initiative reports, asking questions and holding hearings and seminars on the same topic, pushing it up on the EU's agenda.

Debates, seminars and speeches

Every day (except on Fridays, when many MEPs sit on the plane home), the parliament buildings are bustling with activity; there are debates, seminars, hearings and exhibitions. In one corridor, you can taste food from an Italian region; in a meeting room, there is a seminar going on about active ageing, organized by a Christian organization. There is a mix of high and low. It might seem like no topic is too obscure for the parliament, but *European Voice* reported that some Hungarian MEPs were actually turned down when they wanted to organize an exhibition with Hungarian breeds of dogs outside the parliament building.[12]

All issues that are of current interest in several EU countries will find their way to the European Parliament, including issues over which the EU does not have any formal power: extraction of shale gas, surrogate motherhood or the future of the Arctic, for example.

Occasionally checking the scheduled hearings and seminars can give you good ideas for articles. Even on issues over which the EU does not have any decision-making powers there is often an EU angle. And the European context is always a good backdrop to an article about a current political debate in your country. You get a good overview of EU countries' attitudes and legislation on the issue – an overview that often is too time-consuming and complicated to do yourself.

You also get an idea of who the informal experts are and who has an opinion about the issue at stake – who your sources and interviewees will be, both the MEPs who have organized the seminar and the invited experts.

There is no one-stop-shop for these seminars. Depending on who the organizer is, you can find them on the committees' websites or the political groups' websites.

When strolling through the parliament corridors, one sometimes gets the feeling that the MEPs do nothing but go to seminars all day long. And yes, there is a whole lot of stuff going on that has no direct link to the parliament's main job – to legislate for the whole of the EU. But bear in mind that the European Parliament is perhaps the only physical place where there is an ongoing EU debate and where people are confronted with all EU countries' culture and traditions. The parliament has made it its mission to be a forum for EU and European debate, and it takes this very seriously.

Because it is the only physical place where people from all over the EU talk about the EU, world leaders often choose the European Parliament as their venue when they want to talk directly to 'Europe'. The plenary week in Strasbourg often includes a visit and speech from an international top politician, followed by a press conference. In 2014, Pope Francis visited the parliament; in 2015, King Abdullah II of Jordan did.

It is therefore interesting for European journalists outside Brussels to time a Brussels or Strasbourg visit according to when an international top politician visits, as they would otherwise be almost impossible to see up close, let alone to ask questions of them. Important guests in committees or plenary can be found in the general agenda.

Own-initiative reports

It is only the European Commission that can propose new EU laws. The European Parliament cannot propose legislation, unlike most national parliaments. But this does not prevent the parliament from saying what it thinks anyway, for example by formally asking the commission to propose some EU law, or by adopting so-called own-initiative reports.

The European Parliament examines the commission's annual work programme (see chapter 7) to see what bills the commission will propose in the near future. The parliament anticipates the commission proposal by adopting own-initiative reports, showing what it thinks about the question. This is a clear indication of what the parliament will accept if and when a proposal is on the table.

Own-initiative reports are often formulated as a call to the commission to submit a specific legislative proposal. But it is altogether up to the commission to act. You need to bear this in mind when you evaluate the news. Many headlines about 'EU proposals' actually refer to own-initiative reports from the European Parliament, sometimes on issues that the commission is not working on (see chapter 17 about typical mistakes in EU reporting). The report says something about where the European Parliament stands on an issue, but does not necessarily say anything about future EU legislation that will have an effect on EU citizens, your readers. You need to be crystal clear about that in the article.

An own-initiative report follows the same path as a legislative report in the parliament: there is a designated committee and a designated MEP, a rapporteur, and possibly also shadow rapporteurs from other political groups. The report is debated, amended and adopted in the committee and then in plenary. But compared to legislative reports, own-initiative reports usually mean less discussion and less interest from MEPs and political groups. There are fewer proposed amendments, shorter debates in plenary and fewer MEPs present for the vote.

The European Parliament and foreign policy

There are many own-initiative reports on foreign policy, over which the European Parliament hardly has any power. A typical example is the parliament adopting a report that condemns violations of human rights in Azerbaijan.

This is only the opinion of the European Parliament. It has no effect whatsoever on the EU's policies on Azerbaijan, unlike if the EU countries' foreign ministers had adopted the text. Then it would have been linked to concrete action, such as political or economic sanctions.

If you write about an own-initiative report in foreign policy, be careful never to write that 'the EU wants' or 'the EU thinks'. Write instead that 'the European Parliament wants' and add that this is outside the parliament's power. Also bear in mind that it is easier to take a principled stance on matters over which one has little power and where one does not have to bear the consequences.

On the other hand: just because the parliament does not have any power over the EU's foreign affairs, this does not mean that its opinions and views fall on deaf ears. The European Parliament is, after all, the EU's only directly elected assembly, a parliament representing 500 million people.

The reports that the parliament adopts will be received with interest by the people directly involved. Human rights activists in Azerbaijan, for example, will in all likelihood use the report. And when the parliament is united on a foreign affairs matter, and puts its weight behind it, the really powerful actors in EU foreign policy – the EU member states – take note.

A good example of how the media misinterpret the European Parliament's positions on foreign policy matters was a resolution on the Philippines that the parliament adopted in September 2016. In the resolution, the European Parliament 'urges the Government of the Philippines to put an end to the current wave of extrajudicial executions and killings'.[13] This resolution would never have made any headlines had it not been for the Philippines' eccentric president Rodrigo Duterte, who in a speech a few days later said, 'I have read the condemnation of the European Union. I'm telling them – fuck you', and gave the EU his middle finger.

Duterte's statement of course became world news. In many articles, the position of the European Parliament was mistaken for the position of the EU.

Al Jazeera, for example, writes that 'Member countries of the European Union last week called for strict monitoring of human rights abuses in the Philippines',[14] which is not correct. The EU countries have not done so. And it is the EU countries' governments that decide the EUs foreign policy, not the 751 MEPs.

Each year, the European Parliament hands out the Sakharov Prize for Freedom of Thought to someone who has 'worked against intolerance, fanaticism and oppression'. The prize is named after Soviet physicist Andrei Dmitrievich Sakharov who was involved in developing the Soviet Union's nuclear weapons, but then worked against the arms race and was given the Nobel Peace Prize in 1975.

The Sakharov Prize is awarded in connection with the anniversary of the signing of the UN human rights declaration, on 10 December 1948. By awarding this prize to dissidents, the parliament also shows where it stands on various foreign affairs issues.

Links

European Parliament website
www.europarl.europa.eu

Integritywatch
www.integritywatch.eu

European Parliament press officers, by language and by committee/policy area
www.europarl.europa.eu/news/en/pressroom/press-service

European Parliament's information offices in the different EU countries
www.europarl.europa.eu/atyourservice/en/information_offices.html

EP TV – the European Parliament's TV channel
www.europarltv.europa.eu

European Parliament's delegations
www.europarl.europa.eu/delegations/en/home.html

European Parliament's intergroups
www.europarl.europa.eu/aboutparliament/en/00c9d93c87/Intergroups.html

Website for the plenary session
www.europarl.europa.eu/plenary/en/home.html

European Parliament's yearly calendar
www.europarl.europa.eu/plenary/en/meetings-search.html

European Parliament's weekly calendar
www.europarl.europa.eu/news/en/news-room/agenda

Votewatch
www.votewatch.eu

MEPranking
www.mepranking.eu

Written questions from MEPs to the European Commission
www.europarl.europa.eu/plenary/en/parliamentary-questions.html?tabType=wq#sidesFor

Notes

1. Votewatch, *Voting in the 2009–2014 European Parliament: How do MEPs vote after Lisbon?* third report, January 2011
2. Frantescu, Doru, Values topple nationality in the European Parliament, *European View* 14 (18 June 2015): 101–110
3. Chryssogelos, Angelos, How Brexit will affect the balance of power in the European Parliament [blog post], London School of Economics and Political Science, 29 June 2016
4. *Politico*, European Parliament scolds Poland, 13 April 2016
5. *Politico*, Brussels Playbook [newsletter], 13 April 2016
6. *Irish Independent*, EU caps bank bonuses but critics warn move will drive out talent, 1 March 2013
7. van Hulten, Michiel, *A tale of two cities: The political, financial, environmental and social impact of the European Parliament's 'two-seat' arrangement*, report for the Brussels–Strasbourg seat study group in the European Parliament, 2011
8. European Parliament, *European Parliament resolution of 20 November 2013 on the location of the seats of the European Union's Institutions*, 2013
9. Hix, Simon, Hagemann, Sara and Frantescu, Doru, *Would Brexit matter? The UK's voting record in the Council and European Parliament*, Votewatch, special report, April 2016
10. *Europaportalen*, Svenskt röstvelande sticker ut, 10 February 2016
11. *Nyheter 24*, EU-lag mot Facebook, 24 June 2010
12. *European Voice*, MEPs kept on a tight leash, 24 January 2013
13. European Parliament, *European Parliament resolution of 15 September 2016 on the Philippines*, 2016
14. *Al Jazeera*, Philippines' Duterte unleashes more profanity at the EU, 21 September 2016

6 The Council of Ministers and the European Council

What does the Council of Ministers do? Who represents my country? How do I find the officials and diplomats in the different working groups? What is the role of the rotating presidency? What are EU summits?

The Council of Ministers is the EU institution that ensures that the interests of the member states are taken into account in the EU decision-making process. The Council of Ministers is the collective name for the different configurations of member states' government representatives, who have the power to make decisions for their governments. That is typically the ministers in the national government, but it can sometimes be the state secretaries or EU ambassadors.

The official name of the institution is the Council of the European Union (Council of the EU, for short). But in order not to confuse it with the European Council (EU summits) or the Council of Europe (a European human rights organization that is not part of the EU), it is almost always called the Council of Ministers, or just 'the council'.

The Council of Ministers makes laws for the EU – either alone or together with the European Parliament. All EU legislation has passed through the Council of Ministers. This is important to keep in mind; there is no mysterious 'EU' that makes decisions behind the backs of member states, as is sometimes hinted behind headlines like 'the EU is making us' do this or that. Every single tiny rule has been discussed by the EU countries' representatives and adopted by a majority (or unanimously) of the EU countries' governments.

Unlike the European Parliament, the member states are in the loop throughout the legislative process, from start to finish. The EU countries' governments are consulted when the European Commission is preparing a proposal. Once the proposal is tabled by the commission, the council amends and adopts it. And finally, it is the member states that implement the EU rules back home; the member states transpose EU legislation into national laws and dole out money from the EU's various funds: for road constructions in poor regions, or income support to farmers, boat-scrapping premiums for fishermen and efforts to improve innovation.

The Council of Ministers is characterized by a diplomatic culture. It is all about negotiations between sovereign states. National ministers come to Brussels for a day or two to debate and make decisions, but their real political life is at home. In that, they differ from the other legislative body, the European Parliament, and from the European Commission. But many of the diplomats and civil servants who make up the lower levels of the council live and work in Brussels. That entails a risk that they will lose their national perspective. Like other diplomats, they are sometimes replaced, to avoid 'going native'.

The diplomatic – intergovernmental – nature of the council is becoming more and more relaxed the larger the EU grows. With 28 member states, it is trickier to have simultaneous interpretation into all languages, which previously was the rule. Bad English is now the most common meeting language. With every treaty change, the proportion of policy areas in which EU laws are adopted by qualified majority, instead of unanimously, increases, and with every treaty change, the European Parliament gets more of a say.

If not all countries are on board on a certain initiative, a cluster of countries (at least nine) can choose to go it alone. This is called 'enhanced cooperation' in EU jargon or, more casually, multi-speed Europe. The EU laws that the countries agree on apply only to themselves, but other EU countries can at any time choose to join the cooperation. For example, in 2016, 18 EU countries adopted new rules on how to decide which country's laws should apply and which country's courts should settle property disputes between international couples – the commission estimates there are 16 million such couples in Europe.[1]

The Council of Ministers' main tasks are to:

- Adopt laws, usually together with the European Parliament
- Adopt the annual budget together with the European Parliament
- Coordinate member states' policies, for example on economic issues
- Design the Common Foreign and Security Policy
- Conclude international agreements on behalf of the EU

The council formations

Every year, about 80 council meetings are held, with each running over one or two days. Some council configurations are more important than others. Foreign ministers, EU ministers, agriculture ministers and finance ministers are among those who most often come to Brussels to negotiate on behalf of their countries. Ministers of education, social affairs and culture meet more rarely, because there is not as much EU policy in their areas.

There are ten different council formations. Many of them are 'mixed councils'; one council can cover questions that are divided over several government ministries in the EU countries.

The General Affairs Council (GAC)

The General Affairs Council meets once a month. It consists of the countries' EU ministers – if a country has one. If not, it sends a foreign minister or a state secretary who is in charge of European affairs. The General Affairs Council meets every month.

The General Affairs Council coordinates EU policy. For example, it prepares and follows up the EU summits. It also sees to the 'horizontal issues', that is matters that have to do with many different policy areas, such as the EU's seven-year budget. Often, the General Affairs Council eats into the business of other councils. For example, it is this council formation and not the Foreign Affairs Council that takes decisions on the negotiations with countries wanting to join the EU.

The Foreign Affairs Council (FAC)

The Foreign Affairs Council also meets monthly. It is composed of the EU countries' foreign ministers. Depending on what issues are on the agenda, trade ministers, development aid ministers or defence ministers might also attend.

The Foreign Affairs Council deals with everything that concerns the EU's external relations: the common foreign and security policy, defence policy, EU trade relations and aid to countries outside the EU.

Economic and Financial Affairs Council (Ecofin) and the Eurogroup

Ecofin is made up of the countries' finance or economy ministers and it meets every month. It takes decisions relating to economic policy coordination, taxes, financial markets and the EU's annual budget.

The evening before an Ecofin meeting, the finance ministers from the countries that have the euro hold a pre-meeting, where they discuss matters relating to the common currency. The European Central Bank and the European Commission also participate in the Eurogroup meeting.

The Eurogroup is not a formal council formation and has no legal decision-making power. But during the euro crisis, the focus increasingly shifted from the Ecofin to the Eurogroup. This has made countries outside the euro nervous that the Eurogroup eventually will start discussing issues that concern the whole EU and pre-cook deals in their pre-meeting.

Agriculture and Fisheries Council (AGRIFISH)

In the Agriculture and Fisheries Council, the member countries are represented by their agriculture or rural affairs ministers, as well as their fisheries ministers, for those countries that have one. The council meets every month.

The Agriculture and Fisheries Council is a very important council, as almost all agriculture and fishery policies are decided by the EU institutions, not the national parliaments. Those EU decisions are taken in this forum.

Justice and Home Affairs Council (JHA)

The Justice and Home Affairs Council meets two or three times per semester. This council is divided into two parts: justice affairs and home affairs. The countries are normally represented by their justice ministers and interior ministers or migration ministers.

Justice affairs at EU level include criminal justice cooperation. That is based on EU countries recognizing each other's sentences. There are also EU laws relating to criminal penalties, for example to curb cross-border crimes such as trafficking.

'EU Home Affairs' may sound like an oxymoron. This applies to police cooperation, anti-terrorism cooperation and asylum and migration.

Agenda issues that deal with border control and the Schengen cooperation are discussed in a special committee within the Justice and Home Affairs Council. Norway, Iceland, Liechtenstein and Switzerland, which are Schengen members but not EU members, also participate in this committee.

The Competitiveness Council (COMPET)

The Competitiveness Council consists of countries' industry ministers or research ministers, depending on what is on the agenda. They meet two or three times every six months.

This council deals with issues relating to the internal market, EU industry and research policy, and space issues. An important EU decision that the member states in the Competitiveness Council and the European Parliament took, in December 2012, after thirty years of negotiations, was to create a uniform EU patent.

The Environment Council (ENV)

The Environment Council is made up of the countries' environment ministers and meets twice every six months. It addresses issues of water and other natural resources, pollution, climate change and sustainable development. The council coordinates the EU's implementation of the UN environmental programme.

The most important decision that has been taken in the Environment Council in recent years was when the EU climate and energy package was decided, in 2009. This means, among other things, binding laws for all EU countries to reduce the EU's carbon dioxide emissions by 20 per cent relative to 1990 levels by 2020.

The Transport, Telecommunications and Energy Council (TTE)

The TTE council is made up of the member countries' transport, telecommunications and energy ministers. They typically meet twice every six months.

Transport policy is an important area within the EU: there is much common EU law and major investments in a common transport network. Energy is also an area in which the EU is acting more and more in unison, especially since the eight countries in eastern and central Europe joined the EU, for example to make Europe independent of Russian gas imports.

The Employment, Social Policy, Health and Consumer Affairs Council (Epsco)

The Epsco Council is made up of employment, social and health ministers from all the EU countries. They meet four times a year.

The Epsco council deals with everything related to employment, labour law, the work environment and gender equality. These are politically important issues in the member countries, but there is not a great deal of EU legislation concerning them.

Instead, EU policy in this field is often about comparing countries' national policies and benchmarking, for example discussions on whether or not youth unemployment is best solved by the German model of apprenticeships. The council also deals with health and consumer issues, where there is more EU legislation, such as the Tobacco Products Directive and rules for patient mobility within the EU.

The Education, Youth, Culture and Sport Council (EYCS)

Depending on the agenda, it is the EU countries' education, youth, culture or sports ministers who participate in this council formation. It only meets once or twice every six months.

The structure of the Council of Ministers

When the EU countries' agriculture ministers meet in Brussels to adopt a reform of the Common Agricultural Policy, it marks just the final phase of negotiations that have been going on for years in the lower levels of the institution, between national officials in the working groups and between the EU countries' ambassadors in Coreper.

The more difficult a question is to agree on, the higher up the decision-making ladder it ascends. If a compromise can be reached far down in the hierarchy, the ministers only need to formally wave the decision through, without further discussion. The issues that the ministers cannot solve are forwarded to the heads

---

Fact box: The different levels of member state negotiations

- European Council – The 28 heads of state and government
- The Council of Ministers – The 28 ministers (it is this level that takes legally binding decisions for member countries. The levels above and below both hand over ready-made deals that the ministers then formally adopt.)
- Coreper – the 28 countries' EU ambassadors
- Working groups – the EU countries' officials

of state and government, who meet at EU summits. They have more opportunities to strike big bargains than the ministers, because they have the overall responsibility for government. A prime minister can compromise on an agricultural issue in exchange for some extra money for a fund that is important for his or her country, for example.

The permanent representations: the national governments in Brussels

Every EU country has **a permanent representation** to the EU – 'perm rep' for short – in Brussels. It is the government's extended arm. You can think of it as an embassy to the EU or as a miniature of a government cabinet, with every government ministry represented. For example, there might be one or two officials from the ministry of culture working at the perm rep, and thirty or forty officials from the foreign ministry.

These officials negotiate on behalf of their countries' governments in the different working groups of the Council of Ministers, and they report back to their capitals. Quite often, there are also civil servants from government ministries and agencies in the national capitals who come to Brussels to negotiate in the working groups. For journalists, it is good to know that for every issue addressed in the council, there are always at least one or two people at the Brussels perm rep and one or two people in the national capital who closely follow all the dealings.

Officials at the perm reps are excellent sources. They can explain the national governments' positions, say how far negotiations have come, what the major hurdles are and what the countries' alliances in the council are. Most Brussels-based correspondents have their own country's perm reps as their main sources to keep track of the Council of Ministers, to get the national angle on a story and to find out the national government's position. Journalists based in the member states typically speak directly to the government and various departments in their capitals.

The principle of the perm reps is that officials provide background information and only the ambassador and head of press speak on the record. 'Background' means that you get the information to better understand the subject but should not attribute it.

National officials in the perm reps will most likely start the conversation by saying 'this is background' and 'you can't quote me'. Some officials will however allow quotes when it is a non-political issue. Remember that they have pretty much everything to lose from answering your questions – their careers may be at stake – and nothing to gain. So, if you start the conversation by saying, 'I understand that this conversation is only on background and I won't quote you, but I would like to understand this issue better and I think you are best to explain it', you will get further than if you just start with your questions.

Do a background interview with the official in Brussels, who of course is often the person sitting in the room when the working group negotiates. Once you understand the question better, ask for the name of his or her counterpart in your capital. Depending on your national media culture, they might or might not be OK with being quoted. Or – of course – call the responsible minister or his or her press secretary straight away to get a comment.

Some of the perm reps have lists of officials and their policy areas, together with contact details, on their websites. Then, you can just call the officials directly without passing through the press service. With other perm reps, you always need to first call the press officer.

Other countries' EU representations

All EU countries have an EU representation in Brussels. Make sure you do not confuse it with their embassies to Belgium, if they have one.

Sometimes you may need to map all key countries' positions on a particular issue. Then you call the perm reps to find out.

In all the perm reps you find civil servants and press officers who, aside from their own language, speak at least English and often both English and French. They are also used to getting calls from foreign journalists with all levels of English, so do not let language worries stop you from making contact.

The EU countries' perm reps have more or less the same information about the council negotiations and the positions of the different EU countries, and they all spin this information to the advantage of their capitals. But they differ widely in how much information they will share with journalists. Various countries' openness to journalists shifts all the time, depending on what the issue is. Therefore, don't give up just because your country does not want to give you the information you want. Try a different country instead.

It is a little bit like the Eurovision Song Contest: the neighbours tend to stick together. So a Finn will first try to get the information from the Danes and Swedes. Or try to call the perm rep of the country that has the most interest in the information being public.

The best way to build a network of EU contacts is of course by speaking several languages and having cultural flair. In European policy-making – and EU journalism – those who understand the most national perspectives have the upper hand. This is of course easiest if you are a specialist journalist, and mainly cover just one field. Then you can invest time in getting to know the key national officials dealing with your question, or at least those from countries that tend to be important on those issues. For generalists, calling for the first time, it might be harder to get the necessary information.

Background briefings

Before all council meetings and EU summits, the press people at the perm reps will hold background briefings. The ambassador and/or officials explain what issues are important to their country, which other countries are allies and what they hope to achieve during the meeting.

All the EU perm reps organize these briefings for 'their' journalists, as well as press conferences with the minister or prime minister, once the council meeting is finished. Most other countries' background briefings are open to any journalist, as long as you can speak their language.

Contact the perm reps' press people and ask them to put you on their mailing/text message list so you get invited to these briefings. You might have to explain in detail why you are interested in that country, in order to convince their press people. A few perm reps bar other countries' reporters from attending their background briefings, but those are exceptions. Brussels etiquette dictates that all EU government representatives – civil servants, diplomats, ambassadors, ministers or prime ministers – first answer the national journalists in their mother tongue. When all these questions have been asked, foreign reporters ask their questions in English. There are exceptions to this rule too: The Hungarian perm rep, for example, often holds its background briefings in English.

The helpfulness of these background briefings varies a great deal, especially to what extent the officials and ambassadors talk about other countries' positions in the negotiations.

The information from the perm reps is filtered through the national position. If an issue would be a bit embarrassing for a country, it might not be mentioned at the background briefing unless a journalist specifically asks about it, even if it is the most important issue at the upcoming meeting. In order not to be left at the mercy of your government's version of events, you need to compare the information with that from other sources.

The more countries' representatives you talk to and the more background briefings you go to, the more angles you can find for the same story. Most of the press from your country will only go to the national briefing, and will only get that information and that angle.

The rotating presidency of the council

Every six months, on January 1 and July 1, the presidency of the Council of Ministers changes. Newspapers sometimes write that 'Austria is the EU president', but that is a bit misleading. Austria is only the president of the Council of Ministers; the other two main EU institutions are not directly affected.

The importance of the presidency has declined since the Lisbon Treaty came into force. And that is a good thing for journalists. Previously, hundreds or thousands of people would fly to the country holding the presidency every time there was an EU summit and every time some important decision was to be taken, as this would put the country's name on the decision. The Treaty of Nice, the Copenhagen Criteria and the Barcelona Process are named after the places where a few pieces of paper were signed.

The Lisbon Treaty created the EU foreign chief (see chapter 11) and the president of the European Council. The foreign chief leads the meetings of the Foreign Affairs Council (FAC), which used to be the prerogative of the foreign minister of the country holding the council presidency. And the president of the

European Council, at the moment Donald Tusk from Poland, convenes the EU summit meetings, a job that used to be done by the president or prime minister of the country holding the council presidency. The Eurogroup, although not a formal institution, is also chaired by a permanent president, at the moment Dutch finance minister Jeroen Dijsselbloem.

These exceptions apart, the rule is that all meetings in the Council of Ministers are chaired by the presidency country. During the Slovakian presidency in the second half of 2016, it is the Slovak finance minister Peter Kažimír who greets his colleagues in the Ecofin Council. It is the Slovak EU ambassador Peter Javorčík (see interview later in this chapter) who chairs the Coreper meetings and Slovak officials from the Slovak permanent representation who chair the various working group meetings.

The country that holds the presidency mediates between EU countries' representatives in the various negotiations, works out compromises and sells them to council colleagues. It is also the presidency that negotiates with the European Parliament on the Council of Ministers' behalf, in the direct negotiations on EU legislation, the trialogues (see chapter 8).

The first time the council discusses a legislative proposal from the commission, there is no deadline. The issue is discussed at the lower levels of the council hierarchy by the officials and the ambassadors. The country that holds the presidency decides if and when the question is ready to be put on the ministers' agenda, for debates and decision.

For the country holding the rotating presidency, this means a great deal of extra work. For example, the Slovak permanent representation to the EU normally employs 80 people, but had to increase the number of staff to 200 during the six months. The presidency is also backed by the council secretariat, which assists it with administration and procedural knowledge. The council secretariat comprises about 300 staff, working on policy issues, press and legal advice. They ensure that the shift between the presidencies goes as smoothly as possible. The presidency itself decides to what extent it uses the council secretariat's expertise.

During each six months, it is the presidency that decides on the council's agenda. But the agenda-setting power is limited. Many ongoing negotiations are inherited from previous presidencies. Moreover, the agenda depends on the commission presenting proposals. A key issue for a presidency cannot be dealt with unless there is a concrete proposal on the table. If the commission drags on a particular issue, it might pass the country by.

So the space to influence actual policy in a particular direction is therefore quite small. But a skilful presidency can use the limited power to its country's advantage by, in the margin, putting important national issues on the agenda. It does this through thematic conferences, for example.

In January and July, the European Parliament's different committees usually organize debates and hearings with the responsible minister from the country that takes over the rotating presidency in the council. For example, the MEPs in the agriculture committee ask the agriculture minister about his or her priorities for the upcoming six months. These meetings are public and can be viewed online.

The agenda for the Council of Ministers is planned 18 months ahead. There are always three presiding countries that jointly decide on what to do during that period. Within the long-term plan, each of the three countries plans its detailed six-month agenda.

When a new country takes over the chair, it checks how far the former presidency has come in the ongoing negotiations, and fine-tunes the agenda one month before the presidency begins. This fine-tuned agenda can be found on the presidency website. You can find a link to the presidency website in the margin on the Council of Ministers website, or according to this formula: www.eu+year.country domain. For example, the Slovak presidency website address is www.eu2016.sk.

The presidency agenda is an important journalistic tool, for covering both the Council of Ministers and the European Parliament. Because the two institutions normally have to agree in order to legislate, the activities of the parliament for the next half year depend to a large extent on the planning of the upcoming council presidency.

There are good and bad presidencies. If the presidency is well prepared and plays its cards right, it can contribute to major steps taken in the legislative process. More compromises are reached with the European Parliament and the work in the working groups and Coreper progresses nicely. Bad presidencies get stuck. But EU diplomatic etiquette still requires that the leaders of the other EU institutions commend the country for an especially brilliant presidency after the six months have passed. European Commission president José Manuel Barroso did so for Cyprus in 2012, despite the fact that everyone in Brussels knew that it had been a disaster. An EU-journalistic genre is to summarize and review an outgoing presidency. In these cases, journalists should never report the official statements from the different EU institutions, as they mean little.

As a journalist, you will also be influenced by which country holds the council presidency. If the country has a tradition of open administrations, this tends to rub off on the Council of Ministers, making it easier for all

---

Fact box: Upcoming Council of Ministers presidencies

January–June 2017	Malta
July–December 2017	Estonia
January–June 2018	Bulgaria
July–December 2018	Austria
January–June 2019	Romania
July–December 2019	Finland
January–June 2020	Croatia
July–December 2020	Germany

journalists to get information. Badly organized presidencies also tend to have bad press information.

Council of Ministers press office and website

The Council of Ministers has its own secretariat with **its own press people**. They are there no matter which country holds the rotating presidency. The press people are specialized in different policy areas/councils, such as environment, fisheries or justice and home affairs. Contact them to find out what is going on in the area that you cover, if the issue will be decided by qualified majority or unanimously, and how you can find a particular document.

The council press people tend to have more background information than the presidency press service and press officers from the other permanent representations. They have often been involved for several years and know how an issue has evolved. The press officers are also inside the actual meeting room during every council meeting, so they are real experts on the issue.

However, they are EU officials, and as such, they do not allow you to quote or name them, or even attribute any information to their institution. They are only there to provide background information. They are called 'an EU source' or 'an EU official', not 'the council press service'.

The people working for the council secretariat are expected to forget their nationality, just like the commission officials. A French press officer in the council press service does not primarily serve French journalists. Therefore, you will not find any reference to nationality in the list of the council secretariat press people, unlike in the European Parliament, where you can always find someone from your country/language. Sometimes you can guess the nationality by the name – a Pablo is probably Spanish, but of course not always. The fact remains that it is usually easier for everyone involved to talk with a compatriot, at least the first time. A person from your country knows about the media that you work for and will therefore feel more comfortable to talk freely.

Press conferences before and after council meetings

The day before a council meeting, or earlier the same day, the council press office gives a briefing in the Council of Ministers' Justus Lipsius building. Even though it is a press conference in format, the information is only given 'on background', which seems weird to many newcomers in Brussels. These briefings cannot be followed online.

After the council meeting, the 28 ministers each hold a press conference. They take place in small briefing rooms in the Justus Lipsius building, and typically only a handful of national journalists attend. These press conferences are not filmed. The minister from the presidency country holds a general press conference in a bigger briefing room, which is broadcast live on EbS and on the council's own website.

Before a council meeting or a Coreper meeting, you can check the agenda on the council's website. Go to the homepage, then 'Documents and publications', then 'Agendas of meetings' and then choose the meeting you are interested in. When the council meeting is over, the final conclusions are always on the council homepage.

Meeting calendar

Do you want to know when the agriculture ministers are meeting this year? Then go to **the general EU calendar**, tick 'Agriculture, Fisheries and Food' in the subject box, 'Council of the EU' in the box for organizer and 'this year' for the period. Then you will see all the meetings.

All the council meetings are in the presidency's calendar. Check it out on the presidency website. They are planned for six months in advance.

The council's own calendar is not good for scheduling coverage of council meetings, because it is based on the date and not the theme. Tick one day and you get a list of all meetings (European Council, the council, Coreper and the working groups) that are going on that specific day.

Where are the meetings?

Most council meetings are held in Brussels, in the dirty pink Justus Lipsius building that takes its name from a sixteenth-century Belgian philologist and humanist. It is located opposite the European Commission's Berlaymont headquarters, on the Schuman roundabout, in the centre of the EU quarter.

Most people probably know that the European Parliament has seats in both Brussels and Strasbourg. Less well known is that the Council of Ministers also convenes in a few different places. All ministerial meetings in April, June and October are held in Luxembourg; the other months in Brussels. So make sure to take a look at the calendar before you book your flight to Brussels.

At some times during the six months, the various council formations also meet up for informal meetings in the country of the rotating presidency. When the foreign ministers have informal meetings, they are called 'Gymnich', after the first such meeting held at the German castle Gymnich, in 1974.

At informal council meetings, there are no official decisions or conclusions. The point of the meetings is rather to revive debates on particular issues or to have open discussions about long-term policy. If an important decision is taken at such an informal meeting, it will be formally adopted in the next ordinary council meeting.

Follow the council meetings online

For a normal council meeting, there are about a hundred people in the room: the 28 ministers and their delegations of experts and advisors, as well as a delegation from the European Commission consisting of the responsible commissioner, the director general and some civil servants.

Council formations that meet often, for example the foreign ministers or the finance ministers, have over time developed a pretty relaxed tone. Other councils are more formal and stiff.

All votes related to legislation for which the ordinary procedure applies (see chapter 8) are public. They are **broadcast live on the council website**. The meeting minutes and all documents that form the basis for discussion are also public and available on the same website.

You can retrieve and watch videos, to check what a specific minister actually said in the meeting and how the discussion went. In the archive, you can find council meetings since 2011.

Discussions that are not related to legislation are not public. The foreign affairs meetings, for example, are held almost entirely behind closed doors. Annoyingly enough, they still film all the formalities at the beginning of the meeting, then the screen goes black for a few hours, and then it starts transmitting again when the foreign ministers pick up their stacks of paper and get up.

It may be worth having a look at a council meeting just to get a feeling for how they work and to see and hear the people behind the titles. Here you can see how the ministers joke with each other, sit and sulk, check their smart-phones or give vibrant speeches. You can also see which ones seem to like each other, who kisses whom on the cheek and who gives whom a cold handshake.

But don't expect to see anything of substance. The filmed final deliberations and votes, which the council is so proud of, is a perfect example of fake transparency. All the actual deliberations and debates take place behind closed doors and are not filmed.

So, who should I call?

When I want to know what is going on in the council, should I call my country's perm rep? Should I call the presidency's perm rep? Or the council press officers? Every journalist has his or her preference. Your country's minister and his or her press people are of course a good source. In general, most Brussels-based correspondents tend to establish good contacts with 'their' perm reps. It is then natural to go to them with questions about issues that are treated in the council.

Many EU reporters have their perm rep as first source, and then double-check the information with the council press officer. They represent the council as an institution and are not coloured by how an individual country thinks and do not spin the information to the advantage of a specific country.

The council press people are not really willing to name names, but they will confirm or contradict information that you get elsewhere. For example: 'Is it true that the Germans blocked the decision?'

When it comes to summits, the spokesperson for the European Council president is always a good source. He or she will talk on the record. The head of the council press office also speaks on the record, but then only about the practical matters relating to the institution itself. All the other press people only provide background information.

Fact box: Sources in the council

- Your government's ministers and their press people
- Civil servants at your country's permanent representation in Brussels and in your capital
- Other countries' ministers and permanent representations
- The press officers in the council's secretariat
- The country holding the rotating presidency

There is certain information that only the presidency has. That is everything that concerns the informal contacts and negotiations: the corridor talks, the bilateral meetings and the telephone negotiations. Contact the presidency's perm rep with questions about this.

The decision-making process in the Council of Ministers

- The commission presents its legislative proposal and sends it simultaneously to the European Parliament and the Council of Ministers.
- The council secretariat decides which working group should work on the proposal.
- The working group discusses the proposal and negotiates. When the national experts find an agreement or realize that they will not be able to get any further, they send the proposal up to the next level, the group of EU countries' ambassadors, called Coreper.
- Coreper continues to negotiate. When the ambassadors see fit, they send the proposal up a level, to the ministers. Or they send it back to the working group, asking the civil servants to negotiate further.
- It is the ministers that take the formal, legal decision. The ministers can also send the proposal back to Coreper and ask it to continue to negotiate.

Coreper

The level under the ministers consists of the 28 countries' ambassadors to the EU. They are the heads of the EU countries' permanent representations. The constellation is called Coreper, an acronym of the French *Comité des représentants permanents*, the Permanent Representatives Committee.

In the 1960s, Coreper split into two, in order to deal with a growing workload. Illogically, Coreper II is made up of the countries' EU ambassadors and Coreper I of the deputy ambassadors.

The EU ambassadors are called 'permanent representatives' because the EU embassies are called the 'permanent representations'. But just like the 'permanent' president of the European Council, the ambassadors are replaced every so often, so in a journalistic text it is better to call him or her 'ambassador' or 'country representative'.

Coreper II deals with foreign policy, economic policy, justice and home affairs, and prepares all EU summits. It deals with prestigious issues of a diplomatic nature. Coreper I deals with all other policy areas: employment and labour law, health, internal market, industry, transport, environment and culture. These are more technical issues, often related to the single market, where the EU has great power. Agricultural policy is an exception. It is not treated by Coreper I, but instead by the Special Committee on Agriculture (SCA), which is represented by the responsible official from the perm reps.

Coreper II, Coreper I and the Special Committee on Agriculture prepare their respective ministerial meetings, for example the meetings of foreign ministers, environmental ministers and agriculture ministers. Around three weeks before a council meeting, Coreper/SCA adopts a provisional agenda for the council meeting. No question is put on the agenda of a ministerial meeting that has not first passed Coreper/SCA.

One can say that Coreper deals with issues that are too political for the working groups, but also too technical for the ministers. Around 70 per cent of all decisions that are taken by the Council of Ministers have already been agreed to in the working groups, and an additional 15 to 20 per cent are solved by Coreper. So most things are already resolved when they reach the ministers.

Coreper II and Coreper I meet once or twice a week, in the Justus Lipsius building. The Special Committee on Agriculture meets three times a month. Because they meet so often, the member states' representatives on this level know each other and the topics really well.

The meetings can be a bit chaotic. Every Coreper meeting deals with a large number of issues that sprawl in all directions. As the different points are ticked off the agenda, national experts and commission representatives go into the room, make their contributions and leave again. The ambassador and deputy ambassador from the presidency country lead the Coreper meetings. He or she puts forward compromise proposals and holds bilateral talks with colleagues from the other EU countries.

The ambassadors in Coreper are not typical ambassadors. They deal with extremely technical stuff and need to know everything about procedure, EU legislation and 27 other countries' positions. At the same time, the ambassadors are changed on a regular basis, just like diplomats around the world, to prevent them from becoming too much a part of the system and from forgetting the country that they represent.

Working groups

Below Coreper, there are a couple of hundred different working groups. They consist of national officials – either from the member countries' permanent representations in Brussels, or flown in from government ministries and agencies in their home countries' capitals. Who represents the member states varies between different working groups.

Every day, there are a handful of meetings in the various working groups in the Justus Lipsius building in Brussels. It is here, in the working groups, that the largest part of all negotiations between member states takes place.

Some working groups convene every week for a few months in order to deal with one particular legislative proposal, and are then dissolved or lie dormant for years until their services are required again. Other working groups are fixed bodies and meet regularly. When it comes to fisheries policy, for example, there is only one working group that deals with everything related to fishing.

At every working group meeting there are also always a few representatives from the European Commission. The commission is represented by a director or head of unit from the directorate-general that is in charge of the policy area.

In the working groups, draft legislation from the European Commission is treated thoroughly, article by article. The working groups never vote and its members do not have to agree on everything. When they can't get any further, they send the matter up to Coreper.

Before an issue is sent up to Coreper, the working group should have solved most of the technical issues. Then Coreper probably solves the last tricky technical issues, leaving the highly political stuff to the ministers. The compromises that the working group has worked out are adopted by the ministers without further discussion, as so-called 'A items'. Every council meeting begins with the ministers formally adopting the A items. They then move on to debates about the tricky questions, the 'B items'.

A items are typically put on the next council meeting agenda, whichever council it is. Therefore, it could be the ministers of education who formally adopt a decision about banks.

Often journalists focus on the issues that cause debate ahead of a council meeting, the 'outstanding issues' as they are called in Brussels jargon, and sometimes miss the stuff that slips through as A items. Check the list of A items ahead of a ministerial meeting, to ensure that no titbit hiding there escapes your notice.

A working group meeting is usually structured like this: a representative from the European Commission gets the chance to describe the commission's proposal. Then all the officials around the table express their countries' positions and objections. As in Coreper and at council meetings, it is the official from the presidency country that chairs the meeting.

The commission often knows the member states' positions and their objections in advance, because the countries have been consulted during the drafting of the proposal. The commission representative who participates in the meeting often has to clarify some elements of the proposal and give the commission's view on the various amendments that the presidency and national delegations put forward.

What the national officials say in the working groups and in Coreper is always based on a mandate that they have received from their superiors, ultimately the minister in charge. Therefore, depending on your country's tradition on access to documents, after every working group/Coreper meeting, there should be at least two documents that you could request from your government: *the mandate* and *the report*.

Interview: Peter Javorčík, Slovakia's EU ambassador and current president of Coreper

Peter Javorčík on ...
...what Coreper is and does

Coreper is a special body. It's hard to compare it to anything at the national level. It's the key element between the political level and the expert level. It translates what the experts agree on and prepares the ministerial meetings for the final decisions. That is one role, a vertical one.

The horizontal role is that Coreper is the only body, except the prime ministerial level [EU summits], that can make cross-cutting deals, since it deals with issues ranging from agriculture to trade, economic affairs or foreign policy.

...being the link between the national government and the EU

In Coreper, you meet your colleagues every week; during certain periods, every day. People get to know each other. That helps build trust among the member states and makes it easier to reach compromises. Some of the ministers meet only once per presidency. Some meet every month, but nevertheless, it is not possible to achieve this kind of mutual understanding only from the capitals.

You measure the temperature among the 28 in many sensitive issues, and you are probably in the best place to explain why we need certain compromises in the EU.

...being the president in Coreper

It's a special position. You need to change your mindset, forget about the national interest and focus on the others. Otherwise you get into a schizophrenic situation that doesn't help to find a common solution.

In concrete terms, before we have discussions in the Coreper meeting itself, you get in touch with and talk to your colleagues, and understand the positions and the reasoning of those member states. And on that basis, you handle the discussion in the meeting.

You need to have a good assessment of the situation from your experts who are presiding over the working groups. It's very important to come to the meeting knowing the position of every member state and what their arguments are. And you try to pre-cook a deal and just confirm it in the meeting. If that is not possible, you try to find a solution in the meeting itself.

...how the country holding the rotating presidency can influence the course of the Council of Ministers

You try to influence the work of the council on the strategic level, not in the small, nitty-gritty files. It would be a problem, at least for myself, to think about what our national position is for every file and try to reflect that in the final compromise. And the others are not naïve. They would immediately see that you are trying to push your national interest and then you are not that trustworthy and it will be much more difficult to reach a deal.

It's rather on the strategic level that you identify your priorities, into which files you want to put the emphasis, the energy, the resources, the political weight. For example, for us, energy security is a priority, so we will probably invest more energy and political momentum into certain [energy] files than some other presidencies would.

...the system with a rotating council presidency

There are pros and cons, but still it's a good system. On the downside is that every half year, someone new comes. There is maybe not that much consistency in the deliberations in the council. But that is remedied by the support of the council secretariat, which more or less follows the files for years and has a lot of institutional memory. This is of course something that every presidency is missing. Our next presidency will be in 2030; I don't know who from this presidency will still be around then.

Even if it has some administrative downsides, the political advantages of a rotating presidency are huge. You really get in to the centre of the decision-making. Maybe for the bigger countries, Germany or France, it's not a big difference, but for small or medium-sized countries it gives you much more influence, which is good because it gives you a feeling of ownership of the European processes.

The ministers vote

The ministers, or whoever is present in the council meeting, have the power to take binding decisions on behalf of their governments. When they adopt the commission's legislative proposals, they vote.

As said before, the bulk of the negotiations between the EU countries are done at a lower level of the hierarchy. The government ministers only vote when they are ready to vote, which is when the presidency is sure that a majority supports the proposal. If a vote is likely to go the wrong way, the presidency typically puts it to the side, so that someone else can deal with it later.

The Council of Ministers has three ways to take decisions: unanimously, by qualified majority or by simple majority. Qualified majority applies to all legislative decisions that are adopted by the ordinary legislative procedure, for which the council and the parliament are co-legislators (see chapter 8). This is the way almost all decisions are taken.

A qualified majority in the council requires a so-called double majority, equivalent to:

- 55 per cent of the EU countries
- 65 per cent of the EU population
- A blocking minority must include at least four member states

In a few cases, unanimity is required to take decisions. This is the case, for example, in foreign and defence policy, when the council adopts the seven-year expenditure ceiling, when it decides if a new country should join the EU, and on all tax matters. This is also the case for some, but not all, matters of social policy. For example, an EU law on anti-discrimination is adopted by unanimity, while the Working Time Directive is adopted by qualified majority vote. Call the council press service and ask what rules apply to the vote that you are interested in.

In some cases – mainly administrative issues that concern the institution itself – only a simple majority is required. That means 15 out of 28 member states.

It is important to know that although most decisions in the Council of Ministers only formally require a qualified majority, they are often in fact taken unanimously. In the council, the EU governments strive for consensus. They tend to talk and talk and talk until everyone accepts the compromise deal. The most typical outcome of council votes is that everyone votes in favour.

The consensus culture in the council makes practical sense: if a country does not want a specific law and is out-voted, it will still have to implement the policy back home. The country will do this as reluctantly as possible. Better then to find a compromise from the beginning, that all governments feel they can live with.

The connection between the national government in the Council of Ministers and the national parliament back home

It is the national government that represents its country in the Council of Ministers. To a varying degree, it anchors its actions in the national parliament. Some national parliaments have European Affairs Committees; others deal with EU affairs in their Foreign Affairs Committee. How much oversight and power the national parliament has over its government's actions differs significantly in various EU countries.

The Finnish parliament, for example, has a strong position when it comes to getting information about the council dealings. The Finnish government is obliged to submit to the parliament all documents that relate to council deliberations, if the Grand Committee (the European Affairs Committee) so wishes. The German Bundestag and the Italian Camera dei Deputi also have extensive rights of access to information from their governments about negotiations in the Council of Ministers.[2]

The extent to which a national parliament can instruct the government on how to act in the Council of Ministers also varies from country to country. The European Affairs Committee in the Austrian Nationalrat can issue legally binding mandates for its government, as can the Estonian parliament. In Germany, Sweden and Finland, the opinions of the parliament committee are not legally binding, but 'politically binding'.[3]

Whether or not the deliberations in the European affairs committees in the national parliament are public also differs. In Denmark for example, the EU committee holds meetings with the ministers ahead of every council meeting, and with the prime minister ahead of every EU summit. These deliberations are public and can be viewed online. Journalists watch the committee meeting to get an idea of what line their ministers and prime minister will pursue in Brussels.

Winners and losers?

As mentioned earlier, EU countries strive for consensus in the Council of Ministers. In most votes, *all* governments vote for the final compromise deal. In a minority of the cases, one or a few countries oppose the deal (i.e. vote no or abstain from voting).

The UK is the EU country that most often belongs to the losing minority when the council votes, according to a report by political scientists Sara Hagemann and Simon Hix. Even so, nine times out of ten, it supports the compromise. The UK has become less consensual over time. Between 2004 and 2009, the UK voted for the majority position 97 per cent of the time; during the 2009–2015 period, this share dropped to 87 per cent.[4]

From this you should not conclude that the UK gets its way less often than other countries, or has become unhappier with the final compromises over time. Another report by Hagemann and Hix shows that it is quite the opposite. Using a dataset compiled by political scientist Robert Thomson, which is based on interviews with 350 decision-makers from the EU governments, the European Commission and the European Parliament, Hix and Hagemann compare the national governments' positions on 125 pieces of legislation, between 1996 and 2008, and how important the matter is to the government – they compare this to the actual outcome of the vote. This way they map the 'average distance' between a government's position and the outcome in the council.

Out of all the participants (27 national governments, the commission and the parliament), the UK actually came forth in terms of the rate at which it gets the results it wants. France was fifth from the bottom. Still, the UK is the country that votes against the compromise deal the most, and France almost never does.[5]

Whether a country manifests its opposition publicly is actually more a matter of different political and diplomatic traditions. The UK is probably different from the other EU countries in the sense that its government has had more interest than other national governments in publicly demonstrating that it opposes a council decision, even if it knows that the vote in itself does not change anything.

The bigger and richer EU countries are, the more resources they have to influence EU cooperation. But above-mentioned political scientist Robert Thomson has shown that all EU countries get their way about as often as each other. He reaches this conclusion by comparing the outcomes of Council of Ministers' votes with the EU countries' policy positions (as said before, based on interviews with officials).

This might come as a surprise. It depends on most votes being on very concrete, technical issues, and the countries' interests vary with every issue. A European country that has a state railway monopoly but deregulated postal services will vote against the proposal for privatization of railways and for the proposal for privatization of postal services. EU countries with large olive oil production will vote for increased EU subsidies for the olive sector, and so on. It is the national economic and political interests that determine the positions of the countries in the Council of Ministers – not high-minded principles.

As the countries' interests vary, the alliances also vary. Often, EU governments end up in two or three blocs of countries, which have different stances on a particular subject. The big countries are rarely all in the same bloc.

Admittedly, some countries usually end up in the same corner more often than others – for example on the basis of the degree of economic liberalism, geographically neighbouring countries, or countries whose governments have the same political colour or vision of what the EU should and should not do. But these factors explain the government's position to a much lesser extent than the pure national interest, Thomson shows.[6]

As a journalist, you need to be careful not to become the mouthpiece for your country's government, allowing it to characterize its own positions as principled stances and those of other countries as selfish economic interests. This is all too often the case in national EU reporting, especially when we report on the budget.

Count the votes in advance: the council voting calculator

Say the Council of Ministers will vote on a matter for which a qualified majority applies. You have called the EU countries' perm reps, the council secretariat and can now pinpoint the various national positions. On the council's website, there is a **vote calculator** you can use to simulate the various majority and minority coalitions, to see how many and which countries are required to support a decision for it to pass.

Check the votes: Votewatch

All decisions in the council that are taken within the ordinary decision-making procedure must be approved by a formal vote (although, as explained earlier, the most typical outcome is a 100 per cent yes-result, like the election result for a crazy dictator). You can find the statistics from these votes on the Votewatch website, or on the council's website.

Votewatch is much more useful as a tool to cover the European Parliament than the Council of Ministers. In the council, it is only the final vote that is public. There are no records of the deliberations that have taken place behind closed doors.

You can however use Votewatch's statistics to analyze a specific country's position in the Council of Ministers, just like the Hix and Hagemann analysis on the UK, mentioned above. You can use the voting data to see on which issues your country most often disagrees with the others and which other countries have a similar voting pattern to your country, to see which countries are your main allies in the council.

The European Council

The European Council is made up by the 28 countries' prime ministers and presidents, the European Council president and the European Commission president. When this group meets, it is called an EU summit.

The EU summits/the European Council have two important functions. The first is to set the direction for the entire EU. In its conclusions, the European Council often asks the commission to put forward concrete proposals, and the commission does as it is told. This shows that the principle of the commission's right to initiative is true but not the whole story.

It is the European Council that barters about the long-term budget, decides on treaty reforms and on new countries joining the EU, and nominates persons for diverse EU top jobs, such as commission president or head of the European Central Bank.

The other important function of EU summits is to resolve remaining difficulties after the Council of Ministers has negotiated on legislation. The European Council is no legislative body like the Council of Ministers, but the EU leaders can negotiate big deals and then instruct their ministers to vote in a certain way, to make progress with an issue that has become stuck.

Before the Lisbon Treaty, summits were the highlight of the rotating presidency – an opportunity to showcase the country as if it were the Olympics. Today, all regular EU summits take place in the council building in Brussels.

According to the treaties, the European Council shall meet at least four times a year, usually in October, December, April and June – often on Midsummer's Eve, to Nordic chagrin. Typically, however, there have been many more than four summits a year, especially during the years of the euro crisis and in 2015, during the refugee crisis.

EU summits typically take place over two days, starting on Thursday afternoon/evening and ending on Friday at lunchtime. It is not unusual for the Thursday session to go on well past midnight.

Even if you do not follow EU politics on a daily basis, it can be worthwhile to come to Brussels at least once to attend an EU summit, if for nothing else than to experience the special atmosphere and have the opportunity to ask questions directly of any of the member states' presidents and prime ministers.

For accreditation for the summits, see chapter 19.

Preparation for EU summits

The Lisbon Treaty created the post of permanent president of the European Council. Since 2014, Poland's Donald Tusk has had the job. The president prepares the summits and chairs the meetings, but does not vote. (Neither does the president of the European Commission, who also attends the EU summits.) The European Council president also sometimes represents the EU outside the EU, a further complication in the context of the old question of whom one should call if one wants to talk to Europe.

About a month before the actual EU summit, the council secretariat prepares a first draft of what will be discussed at the summit. This is approved by the European Council president's office. The agenda is discussed by the EU ambassadors in Coreper, and then by the EU ministers in the General Affairs Council.

Two weeks before the summit, the council secretariat drafts a proposal for summit conclusions, which again is discussed in Coreper and in the general council.

During this preparatory phase, the member states' governments are consulted continuously. The president of the European Council will call up and discuss directly with prime ministers and presidents from key countries, and those who might have some particular objection. The European Council president visits each member country at least once a year and there, to some extent, also prepares for forthcoming summits.

In connection to the summits

On the eve of the summit or on the morning of the same day, the leaders from the European Parliament's two major groups often meet 'their' EU leaders. So the prime ministers and presidents from centre-right parties meet up with the EPP, and the EU leaders from centre-left parties meet with the European socialist family, to try to hammer out common positions on some issues, to see if they can act together.

Ahead of the EU summit, it is also common for EU leaders to meet up in different configurations based on geography, culture or a shared opinion on a specific issue. These are called 'like-minded' groups and there are quite a few of them. Sweden, Finland, Denmark, Estonia, Latvia and Lithuania hold a Nordic–Baltic pre-meeting. The so-called Visegrad Group, comprising Poland, the Czech Republic, Slovakia and Hungary, also meet up ahead of summits. During the refugee crisis, this group consolidated itself and acted together to try to stop a scheme for redistribution of refugees among EU countries. The most established and powerful alliance is of course the Franco-German duo, which often meet before the summits to talk together.

In 2016, media reported that Greek prime minister Alexis Tsipras was planning to form an alliance of Southern European countries that oppose the austerity-driven policies of the northern EU countries. This group might include France, Italy, Spain, Portugal, Cyprus and Malta.[7]

These pre-summit meeting configurations have started to rub off on the normal council meetings. It is increasingly common that the government ministers also meet up with their 'like-minded' colleagues before important decisions.

During the spring EU summit, which is supposed to be about the economy and employment, there is also a 'labour summit' before the normal EU summit kicks off – a meeting between 'the social partners'. The participants are, apart from the European Council, the bosses of the European Trade Union Confederation (ETUC) and the employment organization BusinessEurope. This session ends with a press conference, broadcast on EbS and on the council website.

The European Parliament has no direct insight during the EU summits, unlike the commission that actually has a representative in the room. But the European Parliament president will deliver a speech at the beginning of every regular EU summit, which sometimes is followed by a brief discussion. After that, he leaves the summit to hold a press conference, while the heads of state and government get on with the meeting. This press conference is also transmitted online.

It is not unusual for there to be demonstrations in connection to EU summits, with both Belgian and visiting protesters. During the euro crisis, the summits were dogged by protests and strikes. Since the neighbourhood around the council building is cordoned off during EU summits, the demonstrations take place a few streets away.

Press on the summits

About two thousand journalists cover every EU summit – most Brussels-based correspondents and as many reporters flying in. The large atrium in the Justus Lipsius building, normally empty, is filled with benches and chairs.

One by one, the cars of the heads of state and government roll in and meet the agency photographers who are squeezed together on a podium. Typically, the EU countries' perm reps send text messages to the journalists on their lists when their prime minister or president is heading for the entrance. Most EU leaders, but not all, stop for a 'doorstep', meaning that they stop between their car and the entrance, to answer some questions from waiting journalists. Many 'doorsteps' are also filmed by the council's own TV crew and broadcast on the council website and on EbS.

In the doorstep interview you get a couple of quotes about what the prime minister hopes to get out of the meeting and what line he or she is pursuing. These can be useful for the first article that you file that evening, before the actual meeting is over and you have something substantial to report.

Sometimes EU leaders also have doorstep interviews on their way to and from the different pre-meetings mentioned earlier.

During the summit itself, make sure to follow the European Council president and the council press office on Twitter for the quickest update. The press people and expert officials from the council and from the national delegations come over to the press area to brief journalists about what is going on in the meeting.

Once the summit is over, there is a general press conference in the official briefing room. The prime minister/president from the country holding the rotating council presidency, the president of the European Council and the president of the European Commission participate in this press conference, which is filmed and broadcast online.

At the same time, the other 27 EU leaders hold their own press conferences in their national briefing rooms. Only the three largest countries' press conferences – Germany, France and UK – are always transmitted online and simultaneously translated into English.

Since all the press conferences take place simultaneously, journalists have to choose which to cover. News agencies and major media with many correspondents can spread out and go to as many of the press conferences as possible to get quotes and compare versions.

Correspondents from different countries often exchange quotes, sound bites and versions of what has happened. Different countries' media hardly compete, so they are usually helpful and collegial.

In the national press conferences, the prime ministers and presidents tell their national journalists, and perhaps a few foreign ones, how he or she negotiated, and what issues were most important for the country. Often the outcome was a success for the country, according to his or her statement. The general press conference is plainer than the national ones, but it can give you a more neutral picture of what has actually been discussed and what decisions were taken at the meeting.

What happens at EU summits that we do not see?

While the two thousand journalists hammer their laptops and chase rumours in the corridors, the heads of state and government are somewhere else in the building. Sitting around a large elliptical table are the 28 heads of state and government, the European Council president, the European Commission president and sometimes the foreign chief – some thirty people in total. In an EU context, this counts as an intimate gathering, but it is still quite far from the original idea: that ten to fifteen people could have an informal exchange of ideas around a table, look each other in the eye and speak freely.

Summit meetings take place behind closed doors. Not even close aides participate. At each seat there is a button that the leaders can press to call in a co-worker. This person is called an 'antici' in EU jargon, after Paolo Massimo Antici who created the Antici group in the 1970s. The antici is the advisor to the EU ambassador; you will find him or her high up in the staff list on the different perm reps' websites. During EU summits, anticis function as the link between the EU leaders and their national delegations, which sit in other rooms.

Two or three people take minutes during the summit meeting, but the notes are not public. On a regular basis, one of the minute takers leaves the room to go and brief the 28 anticis, who sit together in an adjacent room. They will, in turn, pass the information to their national delegations. Every now and then, press officers and other civil servants leave the national delegations and go down to the reporters on the ground floor and pass on some of the information. It is kind of a game of Chinese whispers at times, which explains how there can be completely different versions of what is happening at the same time.

When the presidents and prime ministers have lunch or dinner, the discussion is somewhat freer. No one is taking minutes and the anticis do not enter the room.

Some negotiations take place outside the summit hall. The European Council president will take some leaders from key countries – the biggest ones and those with a strong opinion on the matter – to the side and hold bilateral talks with them to see if they can untangle some knots.

The actual text that is on the table in front of the heads of state and government is the draft conclusions, which have been prepared weeks in advance. These draft conclusions circulate among journalists ahead of the meetings; you can often get them through your sources at the perm reps. If not, the online newspaper *Euractiv* usually publishes draft conclusions on its website the day before the summit.

Who has the power in the European Council?

'All animals are equal, but some animals are more equal than others', wrote George Orwell in *Animal Farm*. The European Council adopts decisions by unanimity, meaning that every country, from tiny Malta to giant Germany, has a veto. But some countries' vetoes are more of a veto than others.

Through interviews with former and current participants in the European Council, political scientist Jonas Tallberg examined what determines the extent of the influence of the member countries. Tallberg notes that the most important factor is a country's 'structural aggregate power', mainly meaning how big and rich a country is. Other structural power factors are political stability, diplomatic relations and administrative capacity. Germany, France and the UK are, of course, the EU countries with the greatest aggregate structural power.[8]

How does this structural power translate into action? The European Council takes decisions unanimously, so formally the countries have equal power. The bigger countries, however, have far more resources to use in the negotiations leading up to the actual meeting – more staff, more information and more options to play with. They are perceived to have a legitimate interest in many more issues than the smaller countries, and so their colleagues give them more space in the negotiations and seek them out and try to reach compromises. The major countries' positions are often the starting point, the foundation on which the negotiations are built.

Using the veto, or threatening to do so, is quite unusual, according to the report. But when a country does, it tends to be effective. Threats of vetoes are most common when it comes to treaty changes or money, for example the EU long-term budget. A small country that threatens to use a veto too often is not considered to be legitimate. An unnamed prime minister says in an interview in Tallberg's report that 'Luxembourg can use the veto once every ten years, the UK every week'.

But a country's influence is also affected by other factors, such as the personality of its leaders. Italy under Silvio Berlusconi is an example of a country with huge structural power that failed to transform it into real influence in the European Council. The reverse was the case for Luxembourg under Jean-Claude Juncker, who was prime minister between 1995 and 2014, the longest serving in Europe. Although he led a country of only half a million, his skills and experience led to Luxembourg being treated as a medium-sized country, according to those interviewed in the Tallberg report.

The heads of state and governments' personal contacts, seniority, personality, expertise on the topics, knowledge of EU procedures and of the other countries' positions, and their ability to propose 'European solutions' and not only national ones – all this matters in terms of who brings the most weight to EU summits.

The conclusion text

The summit adopts conclusions: a stack of paper, written in legal language. But the conclusions are important to check, because this is where everything of substance is recorded.

Read the conclusions and compare what was said at the press conference and what has really been decided. An hour after the summit meeting is over, the conclusions are out in all official EU languages, both on paper in the council building and online.

Compare the draft conclusions from earlier to the final conclusions, to understand what has been decided at the specific meeting and what is new.

When is the next summit?

Go to the EU institutions general calendar, tick the box 'European Council' and 'this year' to see all EU summits for the year.

Interview: Fredrik Reinfeldt, prime minister of Sweden 2006–2014

As concretely as possible, how do the summits work?
The first thing that happens is that you welcome any new heads of government. Then there are some agenda issues. It is Van Rompuy who speaks. [At the time of the interview, 2013, Herman Van Rompuy was president of the European Council.] Then we listen to the president of the European Parliament. There is usually a question on that topic. After that, we break and take the so called family photo.

Usually we gather again in the same room and the first working session begins. We are either in the main building or we have a lunch or dinner seating.

The floor is open, but a list of speakers quickly emerges. Everyone is very well trained for these meetings, so you tend to keep it short.

Either we go through the text [the draft conclusions]: can we change this to that? Or we have a thematic discussion. Then we usually go around the table, that is almost everyone speaks. Such rounds take one and a half to two hours.

Is there any real political discussion at these meetings, or are you reading statements?
I have been in other international fora in which there are more people and then you do read statements. But this [EU] cooperation is so rooted, we meet so often, that we have moved away from that. You might have a few talking points but I don't have the feeling that anyone is reading, you can speak quite freely.

Then there are differences between the countries: between those who have heads of government of different political colour, between north and south, between small and large countries. There are several intersections. Often, it comes down to a small group of two or three that discusses a certain sentence [in the draft conclusions].

What is most important to gain support for your position?
You always gain from being very well informed. It is hard to get to people who are well informed. That's maybe the most important. Then it's well known that large countries have a big influence, perhaps particularly Germany and France. It is also good to have the European Commission on your side. The commission president sits in and is often a driving force in the discussions, because the commission is often given the task of completing what has been decided, or the commission wants to take various kinds of initiatives.

Do you, as a representative of a small country, ever threaten to veto?
We are there to find an agreement. We are reluctant to express ourselves in terms of vetoes. This is something that I often have to defend at home. You can't threaten with a veto. Then the cooperation would quickly stop working.

However, there have been occasions over the years where I've defended the Swedish position for a very long time, and I have had colleagues who have done that too [with their positions]. Sometimes we get stuck on difficult issues and we are all experienced negotiators, then you sit there for a long time.

How do you notice the big countries' influence?
They have a tendency to get the changes they want in the text. They often have a strong team on the other side of the door. Everyone recognizes

Germany's importance and therefore many seek out Germany to try to find compromises.

You have been coming to EU summits since 2006, longer than most other prime ministers and presidents. Do you notice that when it comes to your influence?
Yes, I think so. With years of experience, I feel that the others listen more. I know the procedures, the background, and I can refer to past decisions and processes that I took part in myself. That makes a difference. And I know my colleagues better than those who come to their first meeting.

Speaking of personal contacts, how much of the alliances are based on that?
There's that, too. But one shouldn't think that there are always the same constellations. In the budget negotiations [winter 2012–2013], we had a tight group. It was us, Germany, Holland, UK and Denmark. Today we instead saw a Franco-British alliance. So that changes, it is not always the same. It should also not be underestimated that we stand closer to each other if we come from the same political family.

How much is actually decided in the meeting room and how much has been decided in advance?
If the preliminary work has been done properly, it means that we, in principle, only have to agree and correct things in the margin. Then, I think the system works. Then we've been able to anchor [the Swedish position] in the parliament's EU affairs committee and we have been able to go through what the consequences will be for Sweden.

But there are those who want to have more summits, more crisis management. That we have gone through a financial crisis since 2008 has also contributed to this. For several years now, we have had summit meetings under market pressure. This has meant that we have made more decisions there and then. But I don't advocate this. I favour the well prepared, elaborated and well analyzed.

You sometimes have all-night negotiations. Is it possible to be statesmanlike at four o'clock in the morning?
I try to be well prepared, physically fit and to eat well. It is important to stay focused, because when we sit until late into the night, it is not for fun. Every time that it takes a long time, it is because it has been really, really hard. We sat all through the night for the [long-term] budget in February. And we sat through a whole night, Midsummer night, when we were going to adopt the Lisbon Treaty. Then we are down to the fundamental things and there is a reason that it takes so many hours. You get inspired by the fact that the task is great.

But in the night, there is a greater risk that someone suddenly makes a contribution that makes the discussion go off in the wrong direction and

> you devote one and a half hours to that. We should be better disciplined and say that this is the wrong discussion here and now. Of course, it's easier to get annoyed. You feel that it's hard enough as it is, don't mix that in now at half past two in the morning.

Links

The Council of Ministers' homepage
www.consilium.europa.eu/en/home

The EU countries' permanent representations to the EU
europa.eu/whoiswho/public/index.cfm?fuseaction=idea.hierarchy&nodeid=3780
(Or google 'permanent representation' and 'EU countries')

Council of Ministers' press people, by council formation/policy area
www.consilium.europa.eu/en/press/contacts

Calendar for all EU institutions
europa.eu/newsroom/events/week_en

Council of Ministers' calendar
www.consilium.europa.eu/en/press/calendar

Video from Council of Ministers meetings
video.consilium.europa.eu/en/webcasts

Council of Ministers' voting calculator
www.consilium.europa.eu/en/templates/voting-calculator.aspx?id=244
(Or go to the homepage, then 'Council of the EU', then 'Voting system' and then 'Voting calculator')

Notes

1 Council of Ministers, *Council regulation 2016/1103 of 24 June 2016 implementing enhanced cooperation in the area of jurisdiction, applicable law and the recognition and enforcement of decisions in matters of matrimonial property regimes*, 2016
2 Mastenbroek, Ellen, Zwaan, Pieter, Groen, Afke, van Meurs, Wim, Reiding, Hilde, Dörrenbächer, Nora and Neuhold, Christine, *Engaging with Europe: Evaluating national parliamentary control of EU decision-making after the Lisbon Treaty*, Institute for Management Research, Radboud University Nijmegen, December 2014
3 Mastenbroek et al., *Engaging with Europe*
4 Hix, Simon and Hagemann, Sara, Does the UK win or lose in the Council of Ministers? [blog post], *EUROPP*, London School of Economics and Political Science, 2 November 2015
5 Hix and Hagemann, *Is the UK marginalised in the EU?* [blog post], EUROPP, London School of Economics and Political Science, 20 October 2015
6 Thomson, Robert, *Resolving Controversy in the European Union: Legislative Decision-Making before and after Enlargement*, Cambridge University Press, 2015
7 *Politico*, Greece eyes alliance of southern EU states, 5 August 2016
8 Tallberg, Jonas, *Bargaining Power in the European Council*, Sieps, 2007

Part III
Decision-making in the EU

7 The legislative process part I
The European Commission proposes a new law

The European Commission submits legislative proposals

The European Commission has the exclusive right to propose new laws for the entire EU. This is known as the commission's right of initiative. The power to formulate the first version of a bill cannot be overestimated. The EU system is based on compromise and consensus – 90 per cent of all commission proposals will make it to the other side and eventually become EU laws, albeit with many changes from the European Parliament and the Council of Ministers.

But the commission's right of initiative is not absolute. When the 28 EU countries' heads of state and government meet at EU summits, the conclusions often contain requests to the commission to put forward specific legislative proposals. And the commission usually heeds these requests.

The European Parliament also tells the commission what it wants it to do, for example by adopting own-initiative reports. Since the Lisbon Treaty, the parliament has a formal right to ask the commission to propose a certain legislative initiative. The commission is obliged to react, but does not have to actually propose what the parliament wants.

When the commission is preparing a bill it always takes into account the wishes of the council and the parliament – otherwise the proposal would of course not stand a chance later on.

From fluffy speeches to concrete legislative proposals: how to find out what is in the commission pipeline

The period between the European Commission starting work on a legislative initiative and the finished proposal will in most cases last from one to two years. If you know what the commission is working on, you can find stories along the way and prepare yourself so you are not surprised when the press release arrives.

Every year in September, the commission president gives a 'State of the European Union' speech in the European Parliament. The commission president paints a picture of the state of the EU and gives some details of what the commission will propose in the next year.

128 *The legislative process part I*

> ### Fact box: Treaties, directives, regulations and decisions
>
> At the top of the judicial hierarchy are the treaties – the union's primary law. The treaties set out exactly what the EU can and cannot do, which EU institutions decide what, and the procedures. Below the treaties is the secondary legislation, the legislative acts. These are directives, regulations and decisions.
>
> - Directives are framework laws that leave it up to the member states to adopt the necessary national laws in order to meet the requirements of the directive. The directive comes into force only once it has been transposed into national legislation. In the directive there is always a deadline for this. Once the directive is transposed, the member states must notify the commission. There can be several years between the moment when a directive is adopted in Brussels and Strasbourg and its entry into force.
> - Regulations are legislative acts that are effective immediately and are identical in all the EU countries. The member states' parliaments do not vote on any new laws to implement them.
> - A decision is addressed to a particular recipient, for example an EU country or a company. It is binding and directly applicable. An example of a decision would be when the commission fines a company for abusing its market position.

These speeches are usually extensively reported and analyzed by EU media and big national media. One can consider the State of the European Union speech as the commission's political ideas programme.

The ideas are put into practice in the commission's **annual work programme**, which is presented in October. In an appendix to the work programme, there is a list of all initiatives for the next year, legislative and non-legislative. This is perhaps the best tool for journalists who want to stay ahead of commission legislative proposals. Print it and put it on your desk. It is only a few pages long.

If you are a specialist journalist, make sure to have a look when the work programme is published to see if there are any upcoming initiatives that have to do with the topics you cover. The work programme is available in all official EU languages.

You can find more details of the specific legislative initiatives in the so-called **road maps** from the commission's directorates-general. In the road maps you can see what kinds of consultations and impact assessments the DGs are doing. The road maps are only in English on the commission's website.

In April each year, the commission presents its proposal for the annual EU budget. The EU's expenses are determined according to a seven-year expenditure ceiling, called the Multiannual Financial Framework (MFF). But on an annual basis, there is still room for manoeuvre, and therefore there are always tough negotiations between the two legislatures in November, before the budget is finally adopted in December.

The commission drafts a proposal

The legislative proposals are drafted by the most appropriate unit of the most appropriate DG. The officials in the unit prepare the proposal, conduct impact assessments and consult other DGs and national governments, local authorities, industry, trade unions and civil society.

Once the draft is finished, the responsible commissioner puts this forward to the college of commissioners. The college takes the decision to formally adopt the proposal.

Impact assessment

All important new initiatives are preceded by an impact assessment. In the impact assessment, the commission looks at the economic, social and environmental impact of the proposal. The assessment should also answer the question: should the EU act on this issue at all? The impact assessment is published at the same time as the college adopts and publishes the draft bill.

The impact assessment (usually a couple of hundred pages) is the starting point in the commission's own internal discussions, between the DGs and within the college. It is the fact basis on which the college bases its decision. Later on, when the proposal has left the commission and is being treated in the council and parliament, the impact assessment is extensively used in the debate.

The impact assessment is important for journalists too. Here you find the relevant facts and statistics to beef up your article, especially comparisons between all the EU countries on the particular topic. Here you also find the commission's reasoning behind why and how it has chosen to act. It is a good idea to consult this document if you write about an EU law that many years later is criticized, to see what the original idea was.

Consultations with stakeholders

There is today no arena for a genuine European debate. There are no newspapers that Maltese, Lithuanians and French people read. There is no place where the commission can put up a finger to see which way the wind is blowing. To determine the European public interest, the commission basically sums up the different national interests. Therefore, it is essential for the commission to consult member states early on.

But the commission also tries to determine common European interests in sectors that cut through member states, such as European farmers, European women, European consumers or European employers. It does this mainly by consulting European umbrella organizations, both corporate and NGOs. When there is a clearly defined group that is not represented by a European umbrella organization, the commission finances it itself, and then consults it.

These consultations are a way for the commission to legitimize the legislative process. The consulted parties tend to be sympathetic to the proposal when it is ready. But most importantly, the commission does not have enough expertise in-house to write good laws by itself.

Today there is EU policy in more or less all policy areas, and much legislation is highly technical. When the commission proposes to harmonize the rules of how adverse drug reactions should be reported to national health authorities, for example, it must know exactly what these rules are today in 28 different countries. There are not enough people working in the health DG to have this expertise. Contrary to the popular idea of the commission being a bureaucratic monster, the administration is quite slim, if you take into account how many policy areas it operates in. The commission borrows expertise from member states' authorities and Brussels-based lobbyists.

Consultations are done in many ways: public consultations, expert groups, meetings with 'strategic partners', stakeholder conferences, online polls and of course a great deal of informal contacts. Read more about how to use lobbyists as sources in chapter 13 and about investigative journalism and lobbying in chapter 18.

Public consultations

The commission's most visible consultation tool is the open public consultation. The commission is only obliged to have public consultations on legislative proposals, but it tends to carry them out more often. All information about ongoing and closed consultations is on the website **Your Voice in Europe**.

On the website, there is a summary of each proposed action and questions that the commission wants input on. When the consultation is closed, the answers from the consultation are also reported here. Use the public consultation to map the different interests and arguments for or against a specific EU proposal.

If you want to find out who is lobbying the commission on a particular issue, it is a good idea to check the responses to the commission's public consultations on the website. Although big corporate interests have many, often informal, ways to influence the commission, they also tend to go through the public routes. All contact with the commission is a matter of give and take. Skilled EU lobbyists know that they must participate in the formal consultations and contribute with constructive proposals to gain support for their views, and to open channels for informal contacts.

If the initiative is about something that directly concerns your readers, it could also be worth adding a link to the ongoing public consultation, to give your readers an opportunity to have their say. Anyone can respond to public consultations, but because the language is quite technical, it is often only Brussels-based lobbyists who give input.

Green Papers and White Papers

Before the commission proposes new legislation, it often starts with a green paper and a white paper. They can be likened to preparatory work on national laws.

Early on in the legislative process, the commission presents a green paper, in which it outlines some general ideas and proposals; it shows what possible action it is considering. This is a basis for debate. The point is to consult interested parties before the actual legislative proposal. The document is a maximum of thirty pages and is translated into all official languages.

Sometimes green papers become news. For example, many media wrote about the green paper on reducing plastic waste, which the commission published in March 2013. The green paper examined the measures along two different tracks: recycling and taxes.

The consultation is rather formalized. All responses from stakeholders are published on the responsible DG's website. Here, you get a good outline of what the different positions are on the issue.

The green paper is usually followed by a white paper, which is more concrete. Here, the commission has decided which track it wants to follow and explores it in more detail.

The white paper cannot be longer than 15 pages and is also translated into all EU languages. The white paper is sent to the European Parliament and the Council of Ministers, and they give feedback.

Remember not to describe a green or white paper as a finished law or even a legislative proposal. Some of them are however the first step towards a bill.

Expert groups

When the responsible unit in the commission DG lacks the expertise on a subject, it often creates a so-called expert group, which is commissioned to come up with concrete proposals. It is the DG that decides who to invite to participate in the expert group.

There are nearly nine hundred of these groups, with around thirty thousand members. Here are some: 'EU Alcohol and Health Forum', 'Commission Expert Group on Forest Information', 'Member States' Gender Experts' and 'Fertilizers Working Group'. You can find all expert groups in the commission **expert group registry**.

It is not always easy to know just by the name if it is a commission expert group. Sometimes they are called 'expert group', but they can just as well be called 'advisory committee', 'working group', 'project group', 'consultative group', 'high-level group', 'expert committee' or something along those lines.

Most expert groups are responsible to the directorates-general for industry, environment, agriculture, research and energy – those in charge of the EU's core business and where a great deal of technical expertise is needed. Some expert groups are permanent and work with overarching and long-term issues. Others have been created with clear start and end dates to work on one specific issue. Some meet monthly, others once or twice a year.

It is the commission that calls the meetings of the expert groups, writes the agendas and chairs the meetings. The expert group analyzes the issue and writes reports with recommendations to the commission. The recommendations are in no way binding on the commission.

There has not been much research on the influence expert groups actually have over commission policy. For example, no one really knows how much of the content from expert group recommendations remains in the proposals that the commission actually presents, or remains in the adopted EU law. But political scientists agree that expert groups have great potential to influence laws. Often the philosophy of the recommendations of the expert group shines through in the final bill – how the problem is framed and the ambition of the EU initiative.

Expert groups are EU lobbyists' wet dreams. It is extremely important for organized interests to have a seat at the table where the idea that sets the legislative process in motion is originally formulated. It is far superior to later lobbying efforts, which basically are about trying to change an already written text. Therefore, it is important for journalists to examine which interests are represented in the commission expert groups.

For specialist journalists, it is a good idea to keep track of the recommendations from expert groups that work on your topic, if there are any. These recommendations will give you a good indication of what the commission will propose half a year later, and what might become binding law across the EU in another year or two or three.

An important thing to remember when you write about expert groups is that they only have power in matters in which the commission has power, i.e. where the EU has power.

In the commission's register of expert groups, you can read the mandate that the expert group has received from the commission. If the mandate is to propose legislation, it is very important to examine the expert group's recommendations and who participates in the group. If the mandate is vaguer and if its recommendations will not lead to any legislation, it is less important.

Do not call recommendations from an expert group an 'EU report'. Everything with the prefix 'EU' gives the reader the idea that it is an EU institution with the power to decide on the matter that is behind the report. Instead, write that it is a consultative body and that the recommendations are non-binding. Write who the actual experts are and interview them, at least the ones from your own country.

The European Commission's legislative proposals are adopted by the college and published

When officials in the DGs' units have finished a fully formulated legislative proposal – after consultation with EU countries and organized interests, and after having done an impact assessment – the proposal is blessed by the 28 commissioners. This happens in weekly meetings of the college, usually on Wednesday mornings.

When the European Parliament, one week every month, has its plenary session in the French city of Strasbourg, the commission's weekly meeting also takes place in Strasbourg.

In principle, all decisions in the college are taken unanimously, although the formal rules state that a simple majority is enough. Once the proposal is adopted, it becomes the commission's common position. All commissioners are obliged to stand behind it and keep a united front. It is rare for information on which commissioners objected to a proposal and which supported it to leak out into the media.

When the college has adopted a proposal, the responsible commissioner usually presents it to the press at the commission's lunchtime press conference, the midday briefing. This press conference can always be watched online via the EU's TV channel EbS. When there are technical issues in the proposal – there usually are – the press conference is followed by a technical briefing, at which civil servants from the DG go through all the details. This briefing is not transmitted on EbS.

The college meetings are not public, but **the minutes** are. You can find them online, together with **agendas** for forthcoming college meetings. They are only available in English and French.

When writing about a legislative proposal from the commission

Legislative proposals from the European Commission are almost always newsworthy. In the long and sometimes complicated EU decision-making process, it is nice to have an obvious moment to write a story.

Articles about commission legislative proposals usually have the headline 'EU wants/thinks/is going to' something: 'EU wants women to have 40 per cent share on company boards' or 'EU wants to ban hunting rifles' to take two examples.

In this situation it is not wrong to say that 'the EU wants' something, since the commission *is* 'the EU' when it comes to initiating legislation. At a later stage however – when the draft law is broken down into smaller parts in the European Parliament and the Council of Ministers and various versions and amendments are voted on – you must be wary of writing that 'the EU' wants or does this or that.

Even if the commission is the EU at this stage, for the sake of precision, it is still better to actually call the commission the commission – especially if you write about a proposal that you already know is contested by some major EU player, for example a big EU country or a big party group in the European Parliament. Calling the commission 'the EU' gives the reader the impression that everyone agrees with its proposal.

The commission might resemble a national government, but unlike many governments, the commission cannot expect its proposals to automatically pass in the council and the parliament. When the commission adopts a proposal, it is the *starting point* for long negotiations, not a final decision. Its proposals are not rubber-stamped by the legislatures.

134 *The legislative process part I*

When you write about a legislative proposal, include a paragraph describing what now happens to the bill, so the reader is not left without this information. It can look like this example from an article from *Le Quotidien* on the European Commission's proposals for gender quotas on corporate boards: 'The European Parliament has already voted in favour of this project and the Council of Ministers will discuss it before the end of the year'.[1]

You should find out and could tell your readers the following:

- Who decides? Is it only the Council of Ministers, or is it both the council and the parliament? (See chapter 8.)
- Has either one of the legislatures already adopted their position on the issue? Are there others (individual EU countries, parliament political groups) that have a position?
- When are the legislatures going to start working on the proposal?
- When will they vote?

This information is available from the respective institutions. Call their press people and ask.

Yellow Card and Orange Card: when national parliaments protest against proposals from the European Commission

As seen in chapter 3, there are many policy areas where both the EU institutions and the individual countries have decision-making power, for example environmental policy. In these matters, the principle of subsidiarity means that decisions should be taken as close to the citizens as 'effectively possible' – the European, national, regional or local level.

It is of course very difficult to determine what the lowest effectively possible level is. Therefore, there is something called a subsidiarity check, or 'early warning system'. Every time the European Commission proposes new legislation, the Estonian Riigikogu, the German Bundestag and all the other national parliaments have a chance to examine whether or not the proposal violates the subsidiarity principle. The national parliaments write 'reasoned opinions' to the commission, setting out the reasons why they think the draft law does not comply with the subsidiarity principle.

If one-third of the EU countries' parliaments object, the European Commission has to reconsider the proposal. This is called a yellow card. The commission is not obliged to scrap the idea, but it has to justify its decision to move on with the proposal. For example, 11 parliaments objected to a commission proposal from 2013 to create a European public prosecutor with exclusive rights to investigate fraud that targets the EU budget. The commission reviewed its proposal but then decided to continue with it.

If instead a majority of the EU countries' parliaments raise objections, this is called an orange card. In that case, the commission has to explain why it chooses to keep the proposal, and either the parliament or the council can reject the proposal on grounds of subsidiarity. The orange card thus triggers an early vote on the draft law.

The subsidiarity test is a fairly new invention, and it is unclear what – if any – practical impact it will have. The main benefit from this new procedure seems to be that it makes the national parliaments more invested in the EU process.

The extent to which EU countries use this instrument varies. The Swedish parliament invokes the principle of subsidiarity the most. That is because the Swedish parliament examines all commission proposals on grounds of subsidiarity, which is unusual. The parliament in Luxembourg, the Dutch Tweede Kamer, the UK House of Commons and the Polish Sejm also send many reasoned opinions to the European Commission. The least active parliaments are those in Slovenia, Hungary, the Czech Republic, Greece and Estonia.[2]

Political dialogue: input from national parliaments

While some national parliaments are active in checking the commission's drafts after they have been published – the subsidiarity test – others prefer to engage with the commission at an earlier stage, through the 'political dialogue'. For example, Portugal and Italy are not very active when it comes to the subsidiarity checks, but they use the political dialogue a lot.[3]

The political dialogue was the brain child of ex-commission president José Manuel Barroso. In 2006, the commission promised to send all new proposals and consultation papers directly to national parliaments so that it could take their reactions into account. There are around 600 of these opinions from national parliaments every year. The commission says it replies within three months.

All **reasoned opinions** (subsidiarity checks) and opinions within the framework of '**the political dialogue**' are published on the commission's website.

The EU national debate: a taste of what will come in the European Parliament and the Council of Ministers

Whatever method your national parliament uses to monitor the European Commission and the legislatures, and to provide input into EU law-making, it is important to understand that national parliaments *do* have tools to check what is going on in Brussels. So, as a journalist, never accept the idea that things are decided in Brussels and then imposed on your unknowing country.

All national parliaments have one or a few liaison officers – typically a civil servant, not a politician – in Brussels, with an office in the European Parliament. These people form a group of forty to fifty people who exchange information between themselves at their weekly Monday meetings, and inform their national parliaments back home about activities in the European Parliament. Often they co-ordinate their actions in order for their subsidiarity checks of commission proposals to reach the threshold for a yellow or orange card, or so that the opinions within the political dialogue have greater impact.

Except in the very few cases in which the commission gets a yellow or orange card, the debate in national parliaments has no direct impact on the legislative process in Brussels. But it can still be a good idea to follow the subsidiarity debate in your national parliament, insofar as there is one, as the national parliaments indirectly affect the Brussels legislatures. The national parliamentarians will influence their governments (which make up the Council of Ministers) and their MEPs (through the national political parties).

Links

The European Commission work programme
ec.europa.eu/atwork/key-documents/index_en.htm

The roadmaps
ec.europa.eu/governance/impact/planned_ia/planned_ia_en.htm

Subscribe to the transparency register, to get updates on new roadmaps
ec.europa.eu/transparencyregister/public/homePage.do

'Your voice in Europe' – The European Commission's public consultations
ec.europa.eu/yourvoice/consultations/index_en.htm

The European Commission expert group registry
ec.europa.eu/transparency/regexpert

Minutes from meetings of the college of the European Commission and agendas for upcoming college meetings
ec.europa.eu/transparency/regdoc/index.cfm;jsessionid=B58B9071334FA47C60 9D2CE571C67B51.cfusion14601?fuseaction=gridyear
(or go to the commission's site for public documents – ec.europa.eu/transparency/ index_en.htm – then choose 'Access to documents', 'Register of Commission documents' and 'Commission meetings')

Opinions and replies from national parliaments and the European Commission, within the framework of the 'early warning system' and 'political dialogue'
ec.europa.eu/dgs/secretariat_general/relations/relations_other/npo/index_en.htm

Notes

1 *Le Quotidien* (Luxembourg), 40% de femmes dans les conseils d'administration, 8 March 2013
2 Mastenbroek, Ellen, Zwaan, Pieter, Groen, Afke, van Meurs, Wim, Reiding, Hilde, Dörrenbächer, Nora and Neuhold, Christine, *Engaging with Europe. Evaluating national parliamentary control of EU decision making after the Lisbon Treaty*, Institute for Management Research, Radboud University Nijmegen, December 2014
3 Mastenbroek et al., *Engaging with Europe*

8 The legislative process part II

The European Parliament and the Council of Ministers amend and adopt the law

The EU legislative process is often perceived as difficult. But it is really not much more complicated than those of countries with bicameral parliaments, such as the UK, France and Germany.

Something that can make it more difficult is that there is a long time between the publication of the commission proposal and the final law being adopted by the legislatures – typically between one and two years. This also makes it difficult to know when to actually write a story.

The two EU legislatures, the European Parliament and the Council of Ministers, deal with legislative proposals from the commission in parallel, even though, on paper, the parliament begins the process. In the council, the process is easy to understand – it follows a strictly linear hierarchy – while decision-making in the parliament is more difficult to grasp. In terms of transparency, the reverse is true: in the council most negotiations take place behind closed doors until it is time for the ministers to make a final decision. In the parliament almost everything is out in the open. There, it is rather the multitude of amendments and drafts that make it difficult to get an overview and to know exactly when the important decisions are being taken.

There are a few different ways to legislate in the EU. The most common way is that both the European Parliament and the Council of Ministers propose changes to the commission draft, negotiate with each other directly and finally agree on the amended text and adopt it. This is called 'the ordinary legislative procedure'. Sometimes, you can still hear the old term 'codecision' used in casual EU-speak.

This procedure was only introduced in the Maastricht Treaty, in 1993. Since then, its scope has steadily widened. After the Lisbon Treaty, which came into force in 2009, the ordinary procedure is used for the vast majority of all policy areas. This gives you an idea of the radically increased importance of the European Parliament since the 1990s.

Between 2009 and 2014, the European Commission tabled 658 legislative proposals. Eighty-nine per cent were adopted using the ordinary legislative procedure,[1] so this really *is* the ordinary method by now. But there are still a few exceptions to the rule.

Special legislative procedures

In order to understand what the special legislative procedure really means for the issue you are covering, you need to either look directly at the treaty articles about the specific policy area, or talk to experts in the parliament and the council. But in general, the special legislative procedures typically require the council to adopt a legal act by unanimity, and either the parliament to consent to the final law or the council to consult the parliament.

Consultation

The consultation procedure means that the Council of Ministers is the sole legislature. The council, however, has to wait for the parliament's opinion before it can adopt its final decision, which gives the parliament a sort of 'filibuster' power, to delay legislation it does not want, even though it cannot do this indefinitely. The European Parliament considers the proposal, and adopts amendments in the committee and in the plenary, as it would with a proposal under the ordinary procedure. But ultimately the Council of Ministers does what it wants with this input. There is no legal obligation for the council to comply with what the parliament wants.

This procedure, with the parliament no more than a consultative body to the Council of Ministers, was the way all EU legislation was adopted in the early days of EU politics. Today it is the exception. The issues with the greatest journalistic relevance for which this procedure applies are tax issues. One example is the proposed tax on financial transactions (FTT) that some EU countries want to impose.

When it comes to nominating people for top jobs in the EU institutions, the parliament is also consulted. It is only when it comes to appointing the commission that the parliament really has any power; in other cases, the council does as it pleases. Often, but not always, EU countries will try to avoid a clash with the European Parliament by taking into account its opinion.

In autumn 2012 the European Parliament voted on the appointment of Luxembourger Yves Mersch for the European Central Bank's six-person strong Executive Board. Because the board at this time consisted of only men, the parliament had urged EU governments to nominate both a man and a woman. When the member states chose not to, a centre-left majority in the European Parliament voted against Mersch's candidacy. But it did not matter; the council appointed Mersch anyway.

In 2013, MEPs opposed the nomination of Croatian Neven Mates for the Court of Auditors, and in 2016 they opposed Polish Janusz Wojciechowski for a top job in the same institution. In both cases, the candidates for the EU watchdog had said, in hearings in the European Parliament, that they would withdraw their candidacies if they did not get the backing of the MEPs. In both cases, after their candidacies were rejected in parliament, the council went ahead and appointed them anyway and they did not keep their promises to the parliament.[2]

When you write about a vote in the European Parliament under the consultation procedure, you need to point out that the vote does not carry any legal weight, that the parliament's opinion is only an opinion. Also avoid the term 'veto'. For example, the European Parliament's in-house magazine carried the headline 'EU Parliament vetoes Polish European Court of Auditors candidate', referring to Wojciechowski.[3] This gave the false impression that the parliament can stop the appointment.

Consent

When the consent procedure applies, it is only the Council of Ministers that can amend the proposal from the commission; the parliament does not make changes to the actual text. But the parliament can say yes or no to the final text. Here, the parliament can actually veto the decision.

This procedure is of the greatest journalistic importance when it comes to the parliament accepting or rejecting finalized international deals. In 2011, the European Parliament rejected the Swift agreement, mentioned in chapter 5, which dealt with the exchange of bank transaction information with the US. In 2013, the parliament rejected the final trade deal ACTA, after many years of hard negotiations. It will eventually have a say on both the EU–Canada trade deal CETA (EU–Canada Comprehensive Economic and Trade Agreement) and the EU–US deal TTIP (Transatlantic Trade and Investment Partnership).

Consent from the European Parliament is also required when new anti-discrimination legislation or laws for strengthening the rights of European citizens are adopted by the EU. The creation of a European public prosecutor, mentioned in chapter 7, requires the consent of the parliament.

When it comes to non-legislation, the consent of the European Parliament is needed when a new country wants to join the EU, or to make arrangements when an EU country wants to leave the union. The latter has never happened and will be tested for the first time with the UK leaving the EU.

The consent procedure also applies to 'Article 7 cases', which is when an EU country violates common EU values: human rights, freedom, democracy, equality and the rule of law. The Council of Ministers can decide to give a warning to, or impose sanctions on, the country, and this must then be approved by the European Parliament. Article 7 has so far never been used against an EU country, but it has been discussed by politicians and organizations in reference to Hungary and Poland.

What procedure applies?

Knowing what decision-making procedure applies to an EU initiative is crucial to evaluate the news value of an event. If the European Parliament rejects a proposal and it thereby falls, it is news. If the parliament is merely expressing its opinion, it is of course less interesting.

The easiest way to find out is to call someone who knows and ask them, such as the press people in the relevant European Parliament committee or in the Council of Ministers. If you look up the parliament report in the institution's Legislative Observatory (read more in chapter 9), you can see the procedure type under the heading 'basic information'. Also, all reports in parliament are assigned a reference number and the last three letters indicate the procedure:

- COD = ordinary procedure
- CNS = consultation procedure
- APP = consent procedure

Deciding the EU's budget

First, when we talk about the EU budget, we talk about two different things: There is the Multiannual Financial Framework, 'the MFF', which is the EU's seven-year expenditure ceiling; and then there is the annual budget.

The seven-year budget framework is decided like this: The European Commission drafts a proposal. The EU governments in the Council of Ministers and European Council hammer out the details. Every country has to be on board – decisions are made unanimously. The European Parliament has the right to veto the final text, but cannot amend it. Here, the so-called consent procedure applies.

When it comes to adopting the annual EU budget, the council and the parliament have the same power – the legislatures together establish the overall amount and the distribution of EU expenditure and revenue.

The annual EU budget is decided like this:

- By the end of April or beginning of May every year, the European Commission presents the annual draft budget for the EU. (According to the formal rules, the deadline is 1 September.)
- By the end of July (formal rules: by 1 October), the Council of Ministers adopts its position on the draft budget and presents this to the European Parliament. The council position is typically a cut in the commission proposal.
- In the European Parliament, the different committees debate the budget and the plenary adopts its position on the draft budget. It does so by absolute majority (a majority of its 751 MEPs).
- Once both the council and the parliament have adopted their positions, a specific 'conciliation committee' convenes. It typically meets in November. The conciliation committee comprises representatives from the council, parliament (one from each member state and 28 MEPs) and commission. The committee now has 21 days to come up with a compromise between the two texts, which the legislatures – the parliament and the council – can agree on.
- Often the European Parliament wants more money for all budget posts while the Council of Ministers wants to spend less money. Negotiations are held behind closed doors. The best chance to find out what goes on in the

meeting room is to talk directly to the MEPs who represent the parliament in there. Call the press officer for the European Parliament budget committee and ask who these MEPs are.
- If the conciliation committee manages to reach an agreement, the two legislatures adopt the joint text. If the committee fails to reach an agreement, the European Commission has to submit a new draft budget. Since the Lisbon Treaty, which created the new rules for adopting the EU budget, has been in place, the committee has failed to reach an agreement three times (on the 2011, 2013 and 2015 budgets). In all these cases, the commission presented a new draft budget which was finally adopted.[4]

Just like when you report on EU legislation that both the council and the parliament have to agree upon, you need to be sure if the decision that you are reporting on is actually the final deal or simply one of the institutions' positions. For example, in 2015 many media wrote about an 'EU ban on bullfighting', when the background to the story was in fact the parliament's voting on its position on the following year's budget (see chapter 17 about typical mistakes in EU reporting).

Something else to keep in mind when you are reporting on the EU budget is the difference between 'commitments' and 'payments'. 'Commitments' refer to money that theoretically could be spent (the value of all the contracts) during the budget year and paid in future years. 'Payments' are the actual payments that are made during the budget year in question, as consequences of commitments in the same year and the years before.

Tip: if one party claims they want to cut the budget, make sure to ask where they want to make the cut (grants for Erasmus students, research grants, agriculture subsidies etc.). Sometimes, proposed cuts are just made in the 'payments', to cosmetically achieve a lower sum. In these cases, the council and parliament usually agree to either adopt 'amending budgets' during the budget year, increasing the budget when the media attention is elsewhere, or agree to pay the bills from the end of the year at the beginning of the next year.

Before the European Commission presents the draft budget, all the EU institutions submit (typically in March) their calculations about how much they think they will spend internally, on their own administration. Check them out. There is a sort of gentleman's agreement between the two legislatures not to scrutinize each other's internal spending proposal. This is the stuff of articles about wasteful spending in the EU institutions.

The ordinary legislative procedure

For the lion's share of all EU legislation, the ordinary legislative procedure applies. The European Parliament and the Council of Ministers debate and make changes to the proposal that the European Commission has proposed, in one or two rounds, known as the 'first reading' and the 'second reading'. If the legislators have not agreed after the second reading, the report goes to conciliation, but that is rare.

The first reading

The first reading begins when the European Commission presents its legislative proposals. Formally, the European Parliament adopts its position first, ahead of the Council of Ministers. In practice however, both legislatures start working on the proposal as soon as it is presented.

The commission proposal is also sent to the consultative bodies the Economic and Social Committee and the Committee of the Regions (see chapter 11). National parliaments also get the proposal and they have two months to protest if they think that it is contrary to the principle of subsidiarity (see chapter 7).

The parliament's committee chairs together decide which committee should be responsible for the report. Several committees may be involved: one responsible committee and one or more advisory committees. For example, the parliament's Gender Equality Committee (FEMM) was responsible for the directive on the European protection order, which allows women to move a restraining order with them if they move to another EU country. The justice and home affairs committee (LIBE) was the advisory committee.

The responsible committee or committees appoint the rapporteur, or the MEP who is responsible for the report. One or more shadow rapporteurs from other party groups are also appointed.

The European Parliament can accept the commission's proposal as it is, reject it outright or amend it. In practice, it always does the latter.

The rapporteur prepares a draft report which changes the commission's original proposal. This report is discussed within the various party groups, which also table amendments. The committee or committees vote on these amendments.

After the committee has voted on the draft report, its position is typically confirmed by the whole parliament in plenary. In the committee, there is the same political composition as the full parliament. A report that has the support of a broad majority in the committee will be supported by their party group colleagues in the plenary. In the first reading, the report is adopted in plenary by a simple majority, meaning a majority of all MEPs who show up for the vote.

Once the parliament has adopted its position, it is sent to the Council of Ministers. The council can choose to accept all of it. Then it becomes an EU law.

If the Council of Ministers does not like all the changes, it will instead adopt its own report. This is called the Council of Ministers' first reading. It sends its report, with detailed explanations, back to the parliament.

Trialogues

Such is the formal process. But in reality, the legislatures do not sit around in separate bubbles, making decisions and then announcing them to an unprepared counterparty. Instead, there are ongoing negotiations between the two legislative bodies. Everyone involved knows early on what the crucial issues are.

During the 2009–2014 European parliament term, 85 per cent of all legislative reports that were subject to the ordinary legislative procedure were adopted by the European Parliament at first reading.[5] Today that figure is probably even higher. This does not mean that eight or nine times out of ten the parliament was spot on and the council liked everything that the parliament did to the proposal. Instead, this means that the two parties negotiated with each other directly, early on in the process, and that the first-reading report that the European Parliament adopted in plenary was already a compromise deal between the parliament and the council. Once the parliament adopts this deal, the council will also adopt it without further ado.

These direct negotiations are called trialogues, or tripartite conferences, because it is the three main EU institutions – the parliament, the council and the commission – that participate. It is possible to reach a compromise so early in the process because there is no deadline during the first reading. The parliament and the council can negotiate with each other without any time pressure.

Within the ordinary legislative procedure, the trialogues have become the main place where the actual deal is done. Every EU law that is adopted in the first reading has been decided on in trialogues.

The trialogues often start directly after the parliament committee has adopted a position, before the report has been voted in plenary. For journalists, this means two things. First, the European Parliament rapporteur is a very important source, because it is he or she who represents the whole parliament in these negotiations. Second, in the European Parliament, the responsible committee is the main arena for decision-making, because it is here that the stance that the parliament will take in the trialogue negotiations is hammered out. The committee vote ahead of trialogues is therefore a very important news event if you follow a specific piece of legislation.

In recent years, these direct negotiations between the parliament and the council, with the commission as a facilitator, have become widespread. It makes decision-making quicker and smoother. But it also makes the European Parliament's reading less political, with less ideological debate in the chamber and with more negotiations taking place behind closed doors.

The big party groups in the European Parliament like this system, because it gives substantial power to the rapporteur, who often comes from one of these groups. The small party groups are critical of trialogues.

Who participates in the trialogues?

Trialogue meetings are quite large – there can be somewhere between five and 20 people from every institution participating. As they become more common, they also become more and more formal in nature. The meetings are normally held in the European Parliament (Brussels or Strasbourg) and rarely in the council building. It is typically the parliament's rapporteur who chairs the meeting.

The council is represented by the Coreper ambassador from the country that holds the rotating presidency in the Council of Ministers (see interview with Peter Javorčík in chapter 6) or by the responsible official. He or she has an entourage of legal experts and officials from the council secretariat and the presidency country.

The European Parliament is represented by the rapporteur. There are also the shadow rapporteurs and/or the committee chairmen – a constellation that should correspond to the political blocs. Sometimes, the committee's press secretary is also in the room.

Finally, there is also a handful of people from the European Commission. It could be the commission civil servant who is the expert on the issue, the head of unit or the director from the responsible directorate-general, occasionally the director general him- or herself, or the responsible commissioner.

The basis for the tripartite talks is a document with four columns, called the four-column document. It lists the commission proposal, the council's amendments, the parliament's amendments and a compromise proposal for every article on which the legislatures do not agree. These articles are negotiated, one by one. For a big legislative report, there might be twenty or so trialogues, each taking a couple of hours. Moreover, there are often several 'technical meetings' held, with only one or two representatives from each institution.

No transparency

How much control the different institutions have over their representatives in the trialogues varies. The Council of Ministers is typically represented by the Coreper ambassador, who meets his or her ambassador colleagues on a weekly basis and can keep them informed and quickly get a renewed negotiation mandate.

In the European Parliament, however, the other MEPs have less control and insight into what is going on in the trialogues. Some committees have as a standing agenda item 'situation in the trialogue', but not all. Further, the committees do not meet every week. Although the group of MEPs who participate in the trialogue corresponds to the political division of the whole parliament, and even though they report back to the responsible committee, it is not certain that what is agreed on in a trialogue will get the final support of the plenary.

Getting information about the trialogues

Committee meetings and plenary sessions in the European Parliament are open events. When the EU ministers vote on legislation, this is filmed and broadcast online (although the negotiations are in secret). But the trialogues, where the crucial decisions and trade-offs are made, are completely closed to the public. They are not filmed, they are not in any agendas and there are no official minutes taken.

To find out what happens, you need to speak directly with those who are involved. There are quite a few people, so it should not be too difficult to find someone who can talk. Of the three institutions, the parliament is the most open, so start there. The rapporteur is your main source. The shadow rapporteurs, the committee chairman, their assistants and the committee's press person are other possible sources.

Go for the younger, ambitious MEPs who are often more interested in good media relations, rather than the old ex-prime ministers who also populate the European Parliament. Go for the MEPs who are either very unhappy or very proud. Go for the Greens who in are in favour of more transparency and critical of the secret nature of the trialogues. Ask them in particular for the four-column document.

The permanent representation from your country will also know what is going on in the trialogues, as their ambassador receives continuous reports in Coreper.

If an agreement is reached in a trialogue, a press person will likely tweet from the meeting. If not, the commission, the Council of Ministers' presidency or the parliament rapporteur will quickly send out a press release.

The second reading

Now back to the formal decision-making process. If the two institutions do not reach an agreement in early first reading, and if the council does not accept the report that the European Parliament has adopted, the council adopts its own amendments and then sends this text back to the parliament. This is the start of the second reading.

The same players are involved as in the first reading. Sometimes it is a new country that holds the rotating presidency of the Council of Ministers, and then it is that country's EU ambassador who sits at the table. The parliament rapporteur is usually the same person as the last time.

Again, even before the Council of Ministers has voted on its final text, the two institutions negotiate in new trialogues. If they reach consensus in the trialogue, the council incorporates the parliament's position into its own and adopts it. This report is then adopted in parliament without much fuss and becomes law.

If parliament does not adopt the council's report, there are two ways forward. Either it rejects the council position, in which case the proposal is dead. For such a rejection, an absolute majority is required, i.e. a majority of all 751 MEPs.

Most commonly, however, that parliament again adopts changes, which also requires an absolute majority.

The first and second readings in the European Parliament differ. During the second reading:

- there needs to be an absolute majority in plenary in order to take a decision
- there is a strict time constraint (three, at most four, months)
- the only report that is treated is the report from the parliament's main committee, no advisory committees
- there can only be certain types of amendments to the text

On the last point: in the second reading, MEPs cannot put completely new things on the table. They only have the right to return to the position from the first reading, propose amendments to the items that the council added after the first reading, or suggest amendments that are compromises between the two institutions.

In the first reading, the amendments will go in all directions; in the second reading, everything apart from the crucial issues on which the institutions do not agree has been dealt with. Because MEPs take decisions with an absolute majority, only the amendments that have the broad support of the party groups will be presented.

The parliament's new proposal will now go to the Council of Ministers, which has three months (in exceptional cases four) to act. If the council agrees to the parliament's amendments, they are adopted and become EU law. Again: for the council to accept all the parliament's amendments, the two institutions will first have had to agree on this in a trialogue or other direct negotiation, before the parliament votes in plenary.

The third reading, or conciliation

If, after two readings, the parliament and the council still have not agreed, a conciliation committee is convened. It consists of an equal number of representatives from both legislative bodies: 28 people each. The European Commission mediates.

The Council of Ministers is represented by the entire Coreper (thus 28 people from both the council and the parliament). The delegation is led by the ambassador from the country that holds the rotating presidency. The European Parliament is represented by the parliament's rapporteur, shadow rapporteurs and committee chairman, and around twenty members from the responsible committee, so that the numbers match. The commission is represented by the responsible commissioner.

This committee has six weeks (which can be extended to eight) to find a compromise that all can accept. If the committee fails, then the law is scrapped. If the committee agrees on a compromise, this needs final approval from both legislatures. They have six weeks to adopt the final text, but this can be extended to eight.

At this stage, the vote in the Council of Ministers offers few surprises for the simple reason that the entire Coreper is in the conciliation committee, and the ambassadors are acting on behalf of their governments. In the European Parliament however, it can happen that the parliament's conciliation delegation has agreed to a compromise that the chamber then votes down.

The work of the conciliation committee is the least open stage in the legislative process. The meetings take place behind closed doors, there are no minutes and you will not find any official information about when or where the meetings are held. Again, it is through contacts with the persons who are in the delegations – either the MEPs or the perm reps – that you have the best chance of finding out what happens.

Fact box: The ordinary legislative procedure

- The European Commission adopts its proposal.
- National parliaments give their opinions.
- The European Economic and Social Committee and/or the Committee of the Regions give their opinions, when this is required.
- First reading by the European Parliament: the parliament adopts a position (adopts amendments to the commission proposal).
- After this, the European Commission can amend its proposal if it wishes.
- First reading by the Council of Ministers: either the council adopts all the parliament's amendments, which means that the law is adopted; or the council disagrees with the amendments and instead adopts its own position (amending the commission proposal).
- Second reading by the European Parliament. If the parliament approves the council's position, the law is adopted in 'early second reading'. If it doesn't approve, it again proposes amendments.
- Second reading by the Council of Ministers. Either the council approves the parliament's amendments to the council's first reading position, in which case the law is adopted; or the council disagrees with the parliament's amendments. In the latter case, a conciliation committee is convened.
- The conciliation committee agrees on a joint text.
- If both the parliament and the council agree to the joint text, it is adopted and becomes law. If the parliament and/or the council disagree with the joint text, the law is not adopted.[6]

Fact box: Where in the process are laws mostly adopted?

Between 2009 and 2014, 488 legislative proposals were adopted via the ordinary legislative procedure.

- 85 per cent were adopted at first reading,
- 8 per cent were adopted at second reading in the European Parliament (early second reading),
- 5 per cent were adopted at second reading by the Council of Ministers (second reading), while
- 2 per cent went to conciliation.[7]

When is it news?

During the 2009–2014 parliamentary term, for the legislation that was adopted at first reading, it took an average of 17 months from when the commission presented the proposal until the final decision was taken by both legislatures. But the more complex – and interesting – a legislative report is, the longer it will take.

If you follow a specific legislative proposal through the institutions, make a folder – electronic or paper – where you collect the different drafts and amendments.

The following are some good moments to write about a legislative proposal in the ordinary procedure:

- When the European Commission presents its draft law
- When the European Parliament's main committee adopts its draft report, its position
- When the Council of Ministers adopts its position
- When an agreement has been reached between the parliament and the council in a trialogue
- When the council and/or the parliament adopts the final, compromise text

When can you write that 'the EU wants' and when can't you?

Perhaps the most common error in articles about the EU is that the journalist writes that 'the EU' has decided something, or that there is an 'EU law' or 'EU decision' when, in fact, it is only a partial decision from an institution that is not alone in taking the decision. It is almost always better to actually name the institution in question. This does not make for great headlines, but it is important for clarity.

- When the commission adopts and presents its proposal, you can say that 'the European Commission' or indeed 'the EU' wants this or that, or label it an 'EU proposal'. Bear in mind that commission proposals are only the beginning of the discussion and that the final deal will probably look very different.
- When the parliament's rapporteur tables a report, you cannot write 'EU report', or even 'parliament report'. It is still only the position of a single MEP, who is maybe from a small party group.
- When the committee has voted on the report, you can say that 'the European Parliament Economic and Monetary Affairs Committee wants …' and help the reader interpret this information. It is still not 'the EU' or 'the European Parliament' though.

The rule of thumb is that if the report was adopted with a large majority, it is reasonable to believe that this will also be supported by the whole chamber.

Was it a long and complicated compromise that demanded tough negotiations between the party groups in the committee or between the parliament and the council in trialogues? In that case, it is also likely that the chamber will follow the committee, rather than pick at details and risk undermining the deal.

- Only when the whole European Parliament votes in plenary can you say that 'the European Parliament wants …'. Add information about the status of the vote: was it the vote on a compromise deal with the council, or was it the parliament's position ahead of the negotiations with the council?
- When the Council of Ministers has voted, you can write that 'the EU governments want …' or the 'EU finance ministers want …'.
- Finally, when both the council and the parliament have voted, or when a deal between them is already completed and it is only a formality for the other institution to adopt the law, it is time to trumpet that 'the EU has decided …' and 'this is what's going to happen'.

Fact box. The Passenger Name Record (PNR) Directive. An example of how a directive is adopted by the European Parliament

The PNR directive is an EU law that obliges airlines to hand over passenger data on people entering or leaving the EU – travel dates and itinerary, ticket information, contact details and information about baggage and payment – to the EU country in question. The data will be stored by the EU countries' national surveillance authorities and can be used to identify criminal and terror suspects. The national authorities do not have to share the information with other EU countries if they do not want to.

The directive was first proposed by the European Commission in 2011. At the time, the UK was the only EU country that had a PNR system, but France was in the process of setting up something similar and many others were considering it.

In the European Parliament, British Tory MEP Timothy Kirkhope was appointed rapporteur. He says that an EU PNR system made sense, rather than eventually having 28 different national PNR systems, with different requirements for airlines and different safeguards for the protection of personal data.

The parliament rapporteur drafts the report that is the position of the European Parliament. He or she uses the commission proposal as a basis for the report.

Kirkhope states: 'One of the big mistakes that people make [about the EU] is assuming that commission proposals are being agreed by the parliament. That is far from the truth. The rapporteur writes his own report, and that report may or may not be similar to the commission's. In our case, it was very different.'

According to you, how much was the PNR directive changed, from the commission proposal to the final law?
'Probably about 50 percent, and virtually all of it was changed by the parliament, a little bit by the council.'

Kirkhope drafted his report together with the special advisor from his party group, the ECR, in the civil liberties committee. He explains that their main sources of information were meetings they had with British and French authorities, who had experience of PNR systems.

What about lobbyists?
'Oh yes, whenever you get a report like this, a sexy report, they tend to converge. I saw some lobbyists but I didn't see the generality, because some were pushing a very narrow agenda and we already knew what it was. We didn't really need to have a long talk. I know of legislators here who simply incorporate amendments and clauses that were sent to them by lobbyists. I never use anybody else's material. It may contribute to my thinking, but I will not use texts that are sent to me, as a principle.'

The rapporteur negotiates with the shadow rapporteurs from the other party groups in the committee while drafting the report. At the same time, he or she also needs the backing from his or her own party group.

'[The ECR] agreed on the general principle that the PNR system was something that we ought to have, and they supported me on the basic starting points. But there wasn't a lot of interference as I went on, only concern that it took a long time', says Kirkhope.

Timothy Kirkhope presented his report to the civil liberties committee (LIBE) in April 2013, two years after the commission had adopted its proposal. In the committee, the Kirkhope report was rejected by 30 votes to 25. MEPs voting against the report, the left and the Greens, questioned the proportionality and its compliance with fundamental rights, especially protection of personal data. The conservative party groups EPP and ECR supported the report.

Two years later, in July 2015, the civil liberties committee accepted Kirkhope's second report, by 32 votes to 27. In the meantime, momentum had built up over fears that radicalized young European Muslims were travelling to Syria to fight in the civil war, and then returning home, posing a security threat. The terrorist attacks in Paris in 2015 gave urgency to the PNR plans.

'The PNR directive was not a measure designed to deal with [Paris-type terrorist attacks], it deals with criminals, traffickers and people like that as well. But the terror attacks highlighted security. Some governments, especially the French and the Belgian, put a lot of pressure on their left-wing MEPs. In the end, that helped us get a substantial majority in the committee, and then an even better majority in the plenary,' recalls Kirkhope.

The two legislatures need to get on board with the same text for it to become law. The trialogues – meetings between the parliament, the council and the commission where their negotiators go through article after article, trying to agree on the same final text – started on 24 September 2015.

All in all, it took five of these meetings and 'loads and loads of pre-meetings', explains Timothy Kirkhope.

'Trialogues are negotiations. You go through the articles and you say, "Sorry but that's not acceptable". They say, "We'll get back on that" or "We'll have a vote" or "We might agree". There isn't that much smiling and chatting. You get straight to the business', he says.

'The rapporteur is in charge. Shadow rapporteurs are entitled to attend and listen but they can't intervene. You can invite them to speak, but I decided not to. Only the three representatives speak. I took my legal representatives along, and occasionally I would ask them to clarify a matter. The commission and the council also have experts with them.'

Once the final text was agreed by the three institutions in the trialogues, the compromise text was adopted in the European Parliament plenary session and by the Council of Ministers, in April 2016. The EU countries then have two years, with a deadline in 2018, to transpose the directive into their national legislation. All in all, from when the European Commission proposed the PNR law, to when our readers can see and feel the result of the new rules, it took seven years.

Notes

1 European Parliament, *Activity Report on Codecision and Conciliation 14 July 2009–30 June 2014*.
2 *EUobserver*, EU states overrule MEPs on Polish audit nominee, 28 April 2016
3 *The Parliament Magazine*, EU Parliament vetoes Polish European Court of Auditors candidate, 14 April 2016
4 Calatozzolo, Rita, *The Budgetary Procedure: Fact Sheets on the European Union*, The European Parliament, September 2016
5 European Parliament, *Activity Report on Codecision and Conciliation 14 July 2009–30 June 2014*.
6 European Commission, *The European Union Explained: How the European Union works*, Directorate-General for Communication, 2012
7 European Parliament, *Activity report on Codecision and Conciliation 14 July–30 June 2014*, DV\1031024EN.doc

9 Tools for following the legislative process

What is the idea behind a proposed EU law? How do I find out which institution is now dealing with the draft law? Where do I find the legal texts? When does the law apply?

All EU laws have a legal basis in the treaties

Everything that the EU does has a basis in **the treaties**, the EU's rulebooks. Check the treaties to see what the EU has the right to legislate on, and what the decision-making procedure is. If a policy area is not mentioned in the treaties, the European Commission cannot propose a law in that area. To take one example: even if every single EU commissioner personally would want to legalize gay marriage across the EU, marriage rules are outside the areas where the EU has any say, and therefore what the commission can propose legislation on.

Every legislative proposal from the commission contains a reference to a treaty article. This is the proposal's legal basis. Check that treaty article when you write about a proposal. It will not take you much time. Start with the commission proposal. Search in the document for 'legal basis'. Then google the treaty in question and search in it for the article in question.

Take for example the Ship Recycling Regulation (Regulation 1257/2013). European ships that are ready for scrapping are sent to India, Bangladesh and Pakistan, where they are disassembled on the beaches by workers who often lack protective equipment. This is much cheaper for the owners of the vessels than scrapping the boats in Europe, but it is of course dangerous for the workers and damaging to the environment, because of the many hazardous materials present in old ships.

In 2009, EU countries signed an international agreement, the Hong Kong Convention, which sets minimum safety conditions for ship recycling. In 2012, the European Commission proposed a regulation by which EU countries would implement the international agreement. The parliament and the council adopted the regulation one year later. According to this new EU law, European vessels must have an inventory of all hazardous materials on board, with the most dangerous removed, before the ship goes to the scrapyard.

The legal basis for this law is Article 192, paragraph 1, of the Treaty on the Functioning of the European Union (TFEU). That paragraph reads: 'The European Parliament and the Council, acting in accordance with the ordinary legislative procedure and after consulting the Economic and Social Committee and the Committee of the Regions, shall decide what action is to be taken by the Union in order to achieve the objectives referred to in Article 191.'

Article 191 states among other things that the objectives of EU environmental policy are to protect the environment and human health.

Or take the regulation banning the sale, import and export of cat and dog fur, mentioned in chapter 3. The legal basis is Article 114 in the TFEU, which states that the ordinary legislative procedure applies for adopting measures for the internal market to function smoothly.

In some news articles, it might be worth actually referring to the legal basis. Here is an example from the online magazine *Euractiv* about the so-called two-pack, which sets out fiscal discipline rules for Eurozone countries: 'The two regulations are being adopted under Article 136 of the EU treaty, which allows eurozone countries to adopt more stringent rules for themselves. It excludes countries that do not use the single currency'.[1]

Fact box: Treaty or treaties?

Sometimes, one reads about 'the EU treaties' and sometimes 'according to the EU treaty …' or 'in the Lisbon Treaty …'. Is there one or many EU treaties?

There are two *core treaties*: The Treaty on European Union, TEU (signed in the Dutch city of Maastricht in 1992, and also called the Maastricht Treaty) and the Treaty on the Functioning of the European Union, TFEU (signed in Rome in 1958, establishing the European Economic Community, also called the Rome Treaty). These core treaties lay out the role and the principles of the EU, its powers and its decision-making procedures.

These core treaties are updated by *amending treaties*. You might have heard of the Amsterdam Treaty or the Nice Treaty. They are treaties that amend the two core treaties. The last amending treaty was the Lisbon Treaty, which entered into force in 2009. Those are the rules that apply right now.

So both 'the EU treaty' and 'the EU treaties' are right. As a journalist, it probably makes more sense to write 'EU treaties', rather than talking about the TEU and TFEU.

All the EU legislation in one place: EUR-Lex

In the **EUR-Lex database** you will find the EU legislation in its entirety. There are a staggering three million documents. Whatever you are looking for, you will find it on EUR-Lex: EU treaties, EU countries' accession treaties, EU laws, international agreements which the EU and its predecessors have signed, the court cases from the European Court of Justice – you name it, it's there.

The website is rather messy, but it is updated frequently and everything is there. You can do simple or advanced searches on EUR-Lex. Keep in mind that there are many different types of documents that you probably are not interested in. If you just want to find a specific document quickly – say an EU law – it is often easiest to just google it and choose the EUR-Lex result, rather than search on EUR-Lex. But if you want to get an overview of a policy field, it might be worth doing a keyword search on EUR-Lex.

On EUR-Lex, you will find all the procedure regarding an EU law, all the technical information that is important to get an accurate picture: what was the legislative procedure when it was adopted? On what dates were the different decisions taken in the Council of Ministers and the European Parliament? What is the legal basis?

Under the heading 'linked documents' you can see the relationship between the EU law in question and other documents in the database, for example rulings of the European Court of Justice and the infringement procedures against EU countries that refer to this law.

Under the heading NIM (national implementing measures), you will find information about the deadlines for member states to transpose specific directives into national law, and how the member states have done that. The 'national implementing measures' are changes in national laws to conform to the directive. It can be one or many national laws. On EUR-Lex you can only see them in their original languages.

Summaries of EU legislation

EUR-Lex has a great site with easy-to-read and legally correct **summaries of all EU legislation** in a particular policy area. It is a good place to start when you want to get an overview of what EU laws there are before reading the actual legal texts. There are just over two thousand summaries.

On the first page, there is a list of 32 different policy areas. If you click on one, you get a new list with more detailed policy areas. The website is one of the few EU sites where an intuitive approach actually works. For example, one of the 32 policy areas is 'food safety'. In the next list, select 'animal welfare', then 'trade in seal products', to read about EU rules in this area.

The Official Journal

An EU decision takes effect once it is published in the daily *Official Journal*, which is available in full text on EUR-Lex.

The journal is divided into an L-series for legislation and a C-Series for information and notices.

Following the ongoing legislative process: EUR-Lex and the Legislative Observatory

The EU legislative process is long, and because the media pays little attention, you will not always be reminded when it is time for a partial decision on the matter. Say that you wrote an article when the European Commission presented its proposal for the Ship Recycling Regulation. Half a year later, you want to check what has happened with that.

The easiest way to get an idea of the stage EU legislation has reached is to refer to the databases EUR-Lex and the Legislative Observatory or, as it is nicknamed, Œil (French for 'eye' and an abbreviation of *observatoire législatif*). EUR-Lex is the European Commission's database; **the Legislative Observatory** that of the European Parliament.

Both databases allow you to follow a legal act from proposal to adoption. The Legislative Observatory is mostly focused on the European Parliament, and therefore has more documents from the parliament's internal deliberations. On EUR-Lex you can search in all official EU languages, the Legislative Observatory is only in English and French. However, if you are looking for an overview of a draft law that is adopted by the ordinary legislative procedure (with both the parliament and the council), the observatory is, in my opinion, the best place to start. It is much more user-friendly than EUR-Lex.

Here you find answers to all the when-where-how questions relating to a legal act. When did the commission present its proposal? What commissioner was responsible? When did the council adopt a position on the issue? Which parliamentary committees are responsible? Who are the rapporteur and shadow rapporteurs? What legislative procedure applies for this act? Is it a directive or a regulation? What is the legal basis? What are the next steps?

If you type 'ship recycling' into the Legislative Observatory's search field, you will get a handful of results. Scroll down and look at the document reference numbers. One is marked COD (for codecision, which is the old name for ordinary legislative procedure). That is the file you are looking for.

In the right-hand column there is a tab called 'procedure type'. If you click the 'interinstitutional ordinary legislative procedures' and/or the 'interinstitutional special legislative procedures', you only get legislative reports, not the parliament's own-initiative reports. Do this to narrow down your search if you get too many hits.

On the first page of the Legislative Observatory, there is a list of all new documents. There are the reports that are up for vote during the next plenary session, the most recent reports from the parliament's committees and new documents from the commission that have not yet been dealt with in parliament.

The Legislative Observatory's search engine is excellent. If you start with a loose query – for example you might wonder what EU laws there are on genetically modified crops (GMOs) – then type 'GMO' into the search engine. You will get a lot of hits: replies from the European Commission to questions from MEPs and legislative and non-legislative parliamentary reports. Search on keywords and limit the search to procedure, parliamentary committees, the rapporteur or something else. For example, by ticking the box for the parliament's Gender Equality Committee (FEMM), and own-initiative reports (INI), you can see how many of these reports the committee had adopted in a year or during the parliamentary term.

You can, if you wish, register on the parliament's database. Then your searches will be saved. You can also get notifications whenever there is a document that relates to your interests.

The Legislative Observatory's search engine catches more than EUR-Lex's, especially if you do not know the correct legal name for an EU law, only the EU jargon. For example, one of the two regulations in the so-called 'two-pack' is actually called the 'regulation on the strengthening of economic and budgetary surveillance of Member States experiencing or threatened with serious difficulties with respect to their financial stability in the euro area'. Combine the different databases when you do research. Start with the parliament's database, where you can search for the jargon term 'two-pack' and find the actual regulation. Then move on to searches in less flexible databases.

If you write in a language other than English or French, you can start by finding the correct term using the Legislative Observatory, then search that term in English or French in EUR-Lex, and then change the language settings to your own language.

Links

The EU treaties
Google 'TFEU' or 'TEU' and choose the EUR-Lex site. There are the consolidated versions of the two core treaties in all EU languages.

EUR-Lex
eur-lex.europa.eu

Summaries of EU legislation
eur-lex.europa.eu/browse/summaries.html

The official journal of the EU
eur-lex.europa.eu/oj/direct-access.html

The European Parliament's Legislative Observatory, Œil
www.europarl.europa.eu/oeil

Note

1 *Euractiv*, Brussels wins new powers over national budgets, 20 February 2013

10 Delegated decision-making

The European Parliament and the Council of Ministers are the EU's legislatures. However, they delegate some of their power to adopt legal acts to the European Commission. Every year, several thousand EU decisions, regulations and directives are adopted and, as noted in the previous chapters, the legislative process can take quite some time. To prevent the political system from getting stuck in the mud, the commission takes many mainly technical decisions.

It is rare that a journalist who is a generalist will write about these technical decisions. The delegated decision-making gets much less media attention than the normal legislative process, because the issues dealt with are often technical and rarely cause as much political debate or as many institutional power struggles. There are probably many Brussels correspondents who are unsure of how this delegated decision-making really works.

If you feel this is too detailed for your journalistic needs, skip this chapter. It is important if you need to get to the bottom of a decision that was adopted in the delegated decision-making. You then need to have some idea of how to find your source and have the right person to answer for the decisions taken.

How it started

The EU member states started to delegate some legislative power to the commission in the 1960s when the Common Agricultural Policy was being implemented, which required many technical decisions on grain prices and the like. The national governments – at this time only the Council of Ministers legislated, not the European Parliament – felt a need to delegate these technical decisions. At the same time, they did not want to give the commission free rein, so they kept a check on the commission's decisions in special committees, consisting of representatives from all member states. This system was called 'comitology' in EU jargon.

The Lisbon Treaty changed the comitology system. Nowadays, there are two different ways for the commission to adopt legal acts and for the council and/or parliament to retain some control: through the commission adopting delegated acts or implementing acts.

158   *Delegated decision-making*

The procedure for adopting implementing acts builds on the comitology system, and the word comitology is still used for it in the EU jargon. Delegated acts, however, are a brand new Lisbon Treaty invention.

What decisions are delegated to the commission?

Often, the legislatures delegate to the commission the detailed measures for implementing a law. The commission can also update existing EU legislation to bring it into line with new scientific findings, instead of having to adopt new laws. On the plus side, this makes EU decision-making faster and smoother; on the minus side, it makes the decision-making system opaque and complicated.

Take the Ship Recycling Regulation, mentioned in chapter 9. According to the regulation, the owner of a vessel sent for scrapping is obliged to state what substances are on board, to help manage the risks of dangerous chemicals in the recycling process. Certain substances are banned from use on board. The right to update the lists of dangerous substances was delegated to the European Commission. In the regulation, article 5, paragraph 8 states that the commission can adopt delegated acts in order to update the lists of hazardous materials.[1] If, for example, new research shows that a substance used in ships can have adverse health effects, the commission can put the substance on the banned list, without the matter having to go through the entire time-consuming legislative apparatus.

The legislators decide on the procedure

Every time the European Parliament and the Council of Ministers adopt a new EU law, they also decide if they should delegate powers to the European Commission and, in that case, which procedure should apply. This is a strategic and political matter and is therefore up for discussion at an early stage in the legislative process.

Should it be an implementing act or a delegated act? If an implementing act, it is decided whether a control committee should be created for the purpose, or if an already existing committee should be given the task.

The European Parliament has more control over delegated acts than over implementing acts. Technical decisions that might be political are therefore typically delegated acts. Purely administrative decisions are typically implementing acts. In the case of the Ship Recycling Regulation, deciding what substances should be prohibited is not an administrative task; it can be politically sensitive. So the way the commission does this is by adopting delegated acts, which the parliament also has the power to scrutinize and stop.

Adopting implementing acts

The procedure for adopting implementing acts is as follows: the European Commission proposes the implementing act. A committee made up of member states' representatives either votes for or against it.

Depending on the issue, the committee's opinion carries different weights. If an advisory procedure applies, the committee's view is, as you can imagine, only advisory. Formally, the commission can ignore the committee's opinion, though this rarely happens.

If an examination procedure applies, the committee has a veto over the commission's decision. Roughly speaking, an examination procedure is often used when the commission takes decisions in politically sensitive areas, and an advisory procedure for technical decisions, concerning the internal market.

As you can imagine, the European Commission itself prefers the advisory procedure, and therefore often proposes this in the basic act (remember: it is the commission that proposes the EU law in the first place). If the issue is politically sensitive, the Council of Ministers usually pushes for an examination procedure. But quite often, the different EU governments want different things, and each country makes an assessment of what procedure will benefit them the most. If a country's position is close to that of the commission's, it will probably advocate an advisory procedure, and vice versa.

What are the committees and who is there from my country?

For want of better terminology, these committees are still called 'comitology committees' in everyday EU-speak. The comitology committees that control implementing acts consist of one representative from the European Commission, who chairs the meeting, and one or two representatives from each EU country. There are around 300 active committees that in total hold about 800 meetings every year. Sometimes a committee disappears or a new one is formed, but, on the whole, these committees are fixed units. However, who actually represents each member state may differ. Most committees deal with the internal market, transport, environment and health and food safety.[2]

Media sometimes mix up the comitology committees with the expert groups, which are also groups of member state officials that are consulted by the commission. The national officials are there in different functions – in the comitology committees they control the commission and in the expert groups they provide the commission with advice and expertise. In practice, there is probably a large overlap between the two groups, as well as the working groups in the Council of Ministers. They are civil servants from government ministries or agencies in the member countries or from the permanent representations to the EU.

To find out who from your country was in the committee, start by looking at the European Commission's **committee register** online. There you can see what government department or agency represented your country. Call them and ask who they sent to Brussels.

Officials go to Brussels with instructions about how to act in the committee and will report back to their authority. That means there are at least two documents per country for every committee meeting in the commission: the instruction/mandate and the report. Depending on your country's tradition on openness to the media, these documents can be requested from your government.

> **Fact box: Step-by-step guide to sources in the comitology committee**
>
> - Start by reading the basic act – the regulation or the directive that the European Parliament and the Council of Ministers have adopted. Find it on EUR-Lex or google it.
> - What power is delegated to the commission? What procedure applies? All this is stated in the basic act. Search for the term 'delegate'.
> - Which government department/agency from your country is responsible? Check the committee in question in the commission's comitology register.
> - Who was there from your country's government? Call the ministry/agency and ask.
> - Request the meeting minutes from the European Commission and the national documents (mandate, report) from your national authorities.
> - Even though it is the national governments that take final decisions in the committees, the committees are still under the mandate of the European Commission. So any questions about them should be directed to the commission's press people, not those of the Council of Ministers.

The commission publishes an annual report that summarizes the work of the committees during the past year. Find the report on the comitology register website.

Delegated acts

Delegated acts are adopted in a completely different way to implementing acts. The system was created in the Lisbon Treaty and responded to a trend of more and more political decisions, rather than only technical ones, being taken in the comitology system.

The developments in the past two decades have seen the European Parliament being given greater equality with the Council of Ministers when adopting almost all EU legislation. But the control over the commission's delegated powers was exclusively exercised by member states' governments, via the comitology committees. The Lisbon Treaty reform was also a response to this.

The procedure for adopting delegated acts is something between adopting implementing acts and the normal legislative process. It is done like this: the commission adopts a delegated act. If neither the Council of Ministers nor the European Parliament protest within the time-frame that is specified in the basic act, the delegated act is adopted. In January 2016, for example, MEPs vetoed a

Fact box: GMOs and delegated decision-making

In recent years, there have been a few cases of delegated decisions on 'technical issues' making the headlines. The most contentious issue is genetically modified organisms (GMOs).

The authorization, tracing and labelling of GMOs is regulated by two EU laws: regulation 1829/2003 and directive 2001/18/EC. These basic acts set out that the decisions to authorize new GMO products on the EU market should be taken by the European Commission, through the adoption of an implementing act, via the examination procedure.

If a company wants to start cultivating a GMO crop in the EU, it sends a request to the European Commission. The commission asks the European Food Safety Authority, EFSA (see chapter 11 about decentralized EU agencies) to risk assess the GMO crop in question. The commission bases its decision on whether or not to allow the crop purely on EFSA's scientific assessment.

The commission then tables a draft decision, in which it authorizes or does not authorize the crop. This decision is accepted or rejected by the national governments in the comitology committee, by qualified majority. If there is neither a qualified majority for or against the draft decision, the result from the committee is 'no opinion'.

On the issue of GMOs, the examination procedure applies, meaning that the EU countries can stop the commission's proposed action. But if the EU countries cannot agree an opinion, the commission has the right to push ahead and adopt the implementing act.

Since regulation 1829/2003 came into force, the member states have *not once* delivered a qualified majority either for or against the commission's draft decision to authorize a GMO. The EU countries are split almost 50–50 and consistently vote according to their entrenched preferences, whatever EFSA's scientific assessment says. The issue is political, not scientific.

Sometimes the European Parliament also says what it thinks. In February 2016 for example, MEPs objected to the commission implementing acts that would approve three types of genetically modified soy bean. This opinion from the parliament is however not binding.

Because GMOs are very controversial in some EU countries, it would be politically impossible for the commission to go ahead and adopt the implementing act when there is no opinion from the committee, even if the commission has the legal right to do so. On the question of GMOs, the delegation of decision-making power does not work. The commission has therefore proposed, in 2015, to 're-nationalize' the decision-making power – basically to make it possible for EU member states to restrict or prohibit a GMO crop, even if it has been authorized by the EU for the EU market.

> At the time of writing (September 2016), this proposal is being considered by the EU's legislative bodies.[3]

delegated act concerning sugar in baby food, because they feared the sugar amounts that the commission was allowing were too high.[4] The legislatures can stop the delegated act on whatever grounds and they can also take back the power that they have delegated to the commission.

The legislatures that check the delegated acts are not as hidden as the representatives in the comitology committees that control the implementing acts. In the European Parliament, it is the MEPs that vote, in committee and plenary, and there is a rapporteur who proposes a position. In the Council of Ministers, it is the Coreper ambassadors and the member state ministers who are in control.

Links

The European Commission's register for 'comitology committees'
ec.europa.eu/transparency/regcomitology/index.cfm?CLX=en
(Or google 'comitology' and 'registry')

Notes

1 Regulation (EU) No 1257/2013, Article 5, paragraph 8
2 European Commission, *Report from the Commission on the Working of Committees during 2014*, SWD (2015) 165 final, COM (2015) 418 final, 9 March 2015
3 Proposal for a regulation of the European Parliament and of the Council amending Regulation (EC) No 1829/2003 as regards the possibility for the Member States to restrict or prohibit the use of genetically modified food and feed on their territory, 22 April 2015.
4 European Parliament, *Objection to a delegated act: specific compositional and information requirements for processed cereal-based food and baby food*, 20 January 2016

Part IV
Other EU sources

11 Other EU institutions

European External Action Service, EEAS

The EU's foreign service, **the European External Action Service**, is a creation of the Lisbon Treaty. It is an institutional hybrid born out of the merger of the foreign policy arms of the Council of Ministers and of the European Commission. It can be likened to an EU foreign ministry and an EU diplomatic service. The EEAS is a separate EU institution with its own budget.

The EEAS is led by the High Representative for Foreign and Security Policy, also known as the EU foreign policy chief. The first foreign policy chief was Briton Catherine Ashton, who was followed by Italian Federica Mogherini in 2014.

The foreign policy chief is *both* the foreign affairs commissioner in the European Commission *and* the president of the Foreign Affairs Council in the Council of Ministers. She thus represents both the European Commission and the EU countries in terms of the EU's foreign policy – she is 'double-hatted'.

The foreign affairs chief acts when the national governments give her a mission

Foreign policy is at the core of a country's sovereignty. The EU countries are very different from each other and have different national interests. Among them are nuclear powers, former great powers with close relationships to ex-colonies, NATO countries, non-aligned states, permanent members of the UN Security Council and countries who were at war with their neighbours as recently as the 1990s.

When it comes to foreign policy, there is no mandatory EU legislation. On the EU level, the 28 national governments merely co-ordinate their policies. The countries use the EU as a forum for cooperation through which they can pool their resources and act together – a complement to, not a replacement for, national foreign policies.

The 28 foreign ministers and the EU foreign affairs chief meet in Brussels on a monthly basis to discuss current international issues. If the interests of the EU countries coincide and collective action could achieve better results than the countries acting alone, they adopt a common position. That could be, for example, to impose sanctions on the Syrian leadership, to prohibit the diamond trade with Zimbabwe, to denounce electoral fraud in Belarus or to put the armed wing of Hezbollah on the EU terrorist list.

All decisions in the Foreign Affairs Council are adopted unanimously. As a journalist, remember that there is no EU foreign policy that is not also government policy in your country. Critical questions are best directed at your country's foreign minister and government.

When the 28 foreign ministers decide on a common position, they give a mandate to the foreign affairs chief, who then acts on their behalf. Catherine Ashton was for example commissioned by the EU countries' foreign ministers and by the UN Security Council to lead the international nuclear negotiations with Iran.

EEAS spokespersons and press service

What is the EU doing to resolve the ongoing conflict in Syria? What is the EU's relationship with Norway? How are the EU-led negotiations between Serbia and Kosovo going? All questions about the EU and its foreign policy are best answered by the EEAS's spokespersons. They are also the only ones from EEAS who can and will speak on the record.

On the EEAS's website you can find the contact information for the **EEAS's two spokespersons** and a handful of press officers. The same information is also in the list of European Commission spokespersons. One of the EEAS's spokespersons is always present at the European Commission midday briefing press conference, along with the other commission spokespersons.

In the secretariat of the Council of Ministers there is also a press officer who follows the foreign ministers' meetings, and can answer questions about this, on background. However, if you need a quote, you need to turn to the EEAS spokespeople.

Both the council press officer and the EEAS spokesperson sit in on all the foreign ministers' meetings (Foreign Affairs Council, FAC), so they have the same information and will say the same things. However, the council press office might have a more in-depth understanding of the process – like the different views of the national governments and how the compromise was reached – and are better at explaining the procedure.

So, background questions about the procedure for imposing sanctions on Russia, for example, are best directed to the council press people. But if you want to ask about Mogherini's visit to Cuba, it is the EEAS spokespeople you should ask.

What counts as foreign affairs?

Even seasoned EU reporters think that the organization of the EU's foreign and security policy is confusing. Foreign and defence policy are within the remit of the foreign affairs chief and the EEAS. But foreign aid, EU enlargement, migration and trade policies are overseen by other commissioners and other commission directorates-general, and are dealt with by other ministers in the Council of Ministers.

If you are curious about the EU's relationship with Russia, you should probably first call the EEAS's spokespersons. If you are wondering more specifically about Russian gas, they will direct you to the commission spokesperson for energy. And if your question is about visa restrictions for Russians, they will refer you to the spokesperson for home affairs.

There is a large overlap in the administration too. Under the enlargement commissioner there is the enlargement directorate-general, which has a directorate working on negotiations with the Western Balkan countries that aspire to be EU members. Within the EEAS, there is also a unit that works on the political developments in the Western Balkans.

Delegations

The EEAS has 139 delegations and offices scattered around the world, in countries and international organizations. They are much like EU embassies. The EU has delegations in, for instance, Burma, Iraq, Guatemala and Papua New Guinea. Their main task is to implement EU policies on the ground, report back to the EEAS on local developments and, possibly, negotiate on behalf of the EU.

These delegations used to be the European Commission's delegations. But with the Lisbon Treaty, under which the EU became a legal person that can sign international agreements, they have become EU delegations. In situations in which the EU countries have agreed on a common approach, the EU delegations have the authority to speak and act for the whole EU.

You can find all the **delegations** listed on the EEAS website together with contact information. They can sometimes be a good source for journalists. They can, for example, help you find contacts or get information from the ground in places where your country does not have any diplomatic presence and you have a hard time finding sources. If you have questions on EU policy, they will probably refer you to the EEAS spokespersons in Brussels, but if you have questions about local development or EU-funded local projects, they can be helpful.

What is the EU foreign chief called?

'High Representative of the Union for Foreign Affairs and Security Policy' is of course unfit for a journalistic text, although 'the high rep' can sometimes be seen in articles. 'EU foreign affairs chief' or 'EU foreign policy chief' are the most established terms. 'EU's foreign minister' is also quite common. Personally, I think the latter is confusing. If you write for an American or Chinese audience, who see the EU as a bloc, from a distance, it might make sense to call Mogherini the 'EU's foreign minister'. But if you write for European media, it is just confusing to add a twenty-ninth foreign minister, whose job is completely different from the other 28.

When Mogherini is out in the world on an EU mission, it also makes sense to call her the 'EU chief diplomat', 'chief negotiator' or something along those lines.

Court of Justice of the European Union

On an overcast autumn day, I visited the Grand Duchy of Luxembourg. On a plateau in the capital, also called Luxembourg, two golden towers rose out of the grey mist. That was the EU Court of Justice – Europe's highest judicial body and interpreter of EU law.

An important negotiation was underway in the large courtroom. It was a complicated affair in which EU and international law were in conflict, after the European Commission had frozen the assets of a British citizen, placed on the UN terrorist list. Fifteen European judges, dressed in maroon robes, sat in a semicircle and questioned the parties. The plaintiff's representatives were eloquent British lawyers in grey wigs. The defendants were the European Commission and several other EU countries that had also frozen the assets. An Italian lawyer had some kind of golden curtain tassels hanging from his shoulders.

These images from the EU Court of Justice are rarely painted in European media. The court is the EU's perhaps least known institution. But it is very powerful.

What the court does

When an EU country fails to implement EU laws on time or in the correct way, the European Commission can take the country to court (see chapter 4). The court can order the country to implement the EU law under threat of further proceedings that could ultimately result in a fine. However, it is very rare that fines are actually levied. The size of the fine depends on the gravity and length of the country's infringement (especially if it led to negative consequences for other EU countries), how important it is that the infringement not be repeated, and the country's ability to pay. When the court imposed a fine on Sweden, in May 2013, for failure to transpose the data retention directive, it took into consideration that Sweden had previously always followed the court's rulings without fuss, and reduced the fine from the eleven million euros that the commission had proposed, to three million euros.

These cases, where the European Commission acts as a sort of prosecutor and the court rules on whether EU countries are respecting the commonly decided EU rules, are called in court language 'failure of a member state to fulfil its obligations'.

Many cases that reach the EU court are of a different type: preliminary rulings. This is when a national court asks the EU court how an EU law should be interpreted. The EU court interprets the EU law and gives its verdict. Once the EU court has ruled, the national court can rule in the particular case.

The two courts of the EU Court of Justice

The European court is in fact made up of two courts. The highest court is called the Court of Justice. It interprets EU rules and investigates violations of the EU treaties.

In the court, there is one judge from each member country. They are appointed by their respective national governments for six-year terms. But just like the 28 commissioners, the 28 EU judges work for the whole EU and never for their home country. The cases that the judges deal with are not distributed according to nationality; the Spanish judge does not automatically handle Spanish cases, for example.

In addition to the 28 judges, the highest court also comprises 11 advocates general, in line with the French legal tradition. The advocates general give opinions, which are not binding but seem to weigh heavily. Research shows that about 70 per cent of the time, the opinion of the Advocate General coincides with the ruling of the court.[1] The Advocate General's opinion is therefore a strong indication of what the final verdict will be. When the advocates general give their opinions, journalists tend to report on it, and then write again when the final judgement is handed down.

The second, lower, court is called the General Court. It consists of 44 judges as of September 2016. In 2019, after the final phase of the reform, the total number of judges will be 56 (two per EU country).

In the General Court, individuals or companies can file cases against the EU institutions, or an EU member state can file against the European Commission. Rulings by the General Court can be appealed to the Court of Justice.

Also in 2016, the third and lowest court, the Civil Service Tribunal, ceased to operate. Its jurisdiction - to resolve disputes between the EU institutions and their employees - was transferred to the General Court.

How political is the court?

The EU court only treats the cases that are referred to it. It does not pick and choose the most interesting and important cases like the US Supreme Court can do. This is something that the EU judges themselves point out whenever the court is criticized for pursuing a political line.

The court interprets the texts of EU directives and regulations, as well as the recitals that explain the purpose of each law. EU laws are often deliberately vague in order to facilitate political compromises. This allows for different interpretations, and gives the court real political power in its role as interpreter.

During certain periods, the court has actively pursued deeper European integration. In the 1960s, the judges ruled that EU law trumps national law, a matter that before this time had not been crystal clear in the treaties. This ruling marked a huge step towards supra-nationality. Several court judgements also established the protection of the internal market. In more recent years, the European Court has ruled in several labour law cases, with the effect that protection against discrimination in the EU has been strengthened.

The EU Court of Justice and the media

The EU court is extremely powerful. Given the weight that its rulings have, the court is significantly under-reported. This is both strange and problematic. Hearings in the court are generally open to journalists but they are not filmed, so you need to be in Luxembourg to attend. Contact **the press service** for accreditation.

The EU court has no spokespersons who speak on the record for the institution. But the press officers are helpful and can explain the background to judgements and help you find the necessary documents. They also send out press releases with the most important judgements and opinions of the Advocates General. The Twitter account @EUCourtPress is used to quickly get the rulings out.

The press officers are organized by country, so there is one person who keeps an eye on everything that concerns your country. Call him or her to ask what ongoing cases there are.

On the court's website, there is a pretty good calendar which lists future hearings, the opinions of the Advocates General and the rulings, and which provides links to all the background material. The calendar, however, is only for the coming month. Dates of rulings are typically only set two to three weeks before the verdict. But the date of the Advocate General's opinion may be determined further in advance. Call the secretariat and ask. You can also find all the court rulings in the EU law database EUR-Lex, but in a less user-friendly format.

The EU Court of Justice and the European Court of Human Rights

Quite often media mix up the EU Court of Justice, in Luxembourg, with the European Court of Human Rights in Strasbourg. The latter is the court of the Council of Europe – an international organization that is not part of the EU. One EU judge has told me that he actually receives emails that apparently are meant for the human rights court.

Be very careful with the terms you use when you write about either the EU court or the Council of Europe court. If you write about the latter, you should make it explicit that this is not the EU court, as many people otherwise will think it is.

Read more about the Council of Europe and the European Court of Human Rights in chapter 17, about typical mistakes in EU reporting.

The European Central Bank

The European Central Bank (ECB) is based in Frankfurt, Germany. It was created in 1998, a year before the euro was introduced.

Since the euro crisis struck, the bank has become an increasingly important political player, and consequently the journalistic interest in it has grown. As the European economies are so intertwined, even the EU countries that are not in the euro are affected by the decisions taken by the ECB.

Those in power in the ECB are the six people on the Executive Board. The main decision-making body of the ECB is the Governing Council, which is the Executive Board plus the central bank bosses of the 19 euro countries, in total 25 people. The Governing Council formulates monetary policy for all the countries that have the euro as their currency.

The Governing Council usually meets every other week. Every six weeks, it sets the key interest rate. The decision on the interest rate is announced in a press release at 13.45. At 14.30, there is a press conference that you can attend in Frankfurt or watch online via EbS or the **ECB's website**.

At the other meetings, the Governing Council takes all other decisions. They can be about payment systems, financial stability, banking supervision, etc. These decisions are announced the day after the meeting.

Check the ECB's calendar for all upcoming Governing Council meetings. On the ECB's website, there is a great deal of other useful information: official statements, financial analyses, statistics and filmed press conferences.

Court of Auditors

The European Court of Auditors reviews the EU institutions' accounting and budgets to see if EU money has been spent properly. The Court of Auditors typically gets media attention just once a year, when it presents its annual accounts. This is followed by a press conference, which can be seen on EbS. Articles written at this time tend to focus on the many errors in the EU's accounts. Most errors are in regional aid and agricultural aid. This is also where most money disappears.

But the Court of Auditors also publishes a handful of special reports every month. It is worth checking the audit's homepage now and again, or following the institution on Twitter, in order not to miss reports that may be of interest to you, such as a special report on public procurement by the EU institutions or a report about how the EU delegations around the world manage their buildings.

These reports get less media attention, but if there is a special report in an area that you cover – say an audit on animal disease monitoring programmes or EU grants for Roma inclusion – they can be easy stories to write. They can also point you in the direction of problem areas and provide ideas for investigations in your country or on the EU level.

OLAF: the EU's counter-corruption agency

The EU's anti-corruption agency OLAF (from the French *Office Européen de Lutte Antifraude*) was formed in 1999 in the wake of a corruption scandal that led to the entire European Commission resigning.

OLAF investigates corruption related to EU expenditure and EU revenue. Most expenditure corruption occurs in the EU member states. Investigations are usually led by national police in collaboration with OLAF. On the revenue side, OLAF investigates corruption related to the EU's own income, such as tariffs. For example, OLAF has a task force that investigates cigarette smuggling into the EU.

OLAF should also investigate corruption in the EU institutions, and, in doing so, should be independent of the European Commission. But this independence is questioned. The counter-corruption watchdog is often criticized by an independent monitoring committee that has the role of ensuring that OLAF acts within its powers, and by the European Parliament's Budget Control Committee.

The European Economic and Social Committee and the Committee of the Regions

The European Economic and Social Committee (EESC) represents unions, employers, farmers, environmental organizations and consumers. The Committee of the Regions (CoR) represents local and regional authorities. These two committees are consultative bodies for the three main EU institutions and are supposed to be a bridge between civil society and the EU institutions.

The European Commission, the European Parliament and the Council of Ministers are obliged to consult the committees every time they legislate on something that relates to economic and social policies, and to regional policies, which of course can be almost everything. The committees' opinions however are in no way binding.

When the European Parliament's liberal party group ALDE had their say on the EU's seven-year budget for 2014–2020, it suggested, as a way for the EU to save money, that the two consultative committees be scrapped altogether. Another suggestion, regularly proposed by different MEPs, is that the committees should move into the European Parliament building in Strasbourg, so that the building would have a new use and MEPs would not have to go back and forth every month. These suggestions will in all likelihood stay on the drawing board – remember, the seats of the European Parliament and the role of the consultative committees are set out in the EU treaties, and changing the treaties requires unanimity among EU countries – but they give you an idea of how unimportant the two consultative bodies are considered to be by many EU politicians.

The committees adopt positions, both on legislative reports for which their input has been requested, and on their own initiative. You can find these documents on their respective websites. Remember to report on their opinions as opinions, nothing else.

How did they vote?

Even if the committees have marginal influence, you might once in a while want to check to see how the committee members voted on a certain issue, because sometimes the committees vote on things that interest you and that no other EU institutions deal with. For example, Swedish magazine *Dagens Medicin* wrote that a couple of representatives for big Swedish organizations had voted for a resolution in the Economic and Social Committee that stated that electromagnetic hypersensitivity was a real and growing problem, contrary to science.[2]

If you contact the committee press people and ask them how the committee members have voted on something, they will most likely say no on reflex, which they did in the example above. All institutions get secretive when no one forces them to be open, and these consultative committees are used to nobody asking for information. If that happens, just ask again and again until they give you the vote record, which they will eventually – there are no valid arguments that their votes should be secret when the votes in the European Parliament and the Council of Ministers are not.

Plenary sessions

The Committee of the Regions holds six plenary sessions a year; the Economic and Social Committee holds nine on average. Check their websites for upcoming dates.

When the Committee of the Regions' 350 members arrive in Brussels, there will be among them mayors of big cities and other high-profile local and regional politicians. Plenary sessions in the committee can therefore be a good time to travel to Brussels and set up interviews with local politicians from across the EU. There are many topics for which it is interesting to compare how different cities or regions handle similar challenges, for example how they deal with radicalization or with an influx of poor EU citizens from Romania and Bulgaria who beg on the streets.

In autumn (typically October), the Committee of the Regions and the European Commission's DG for regional policy organize the conference open days – European week of regions and cities. Many local and regional politicians from across the EU come to Brussels to participate in the workshops and debates. For journalists, it is easy to find interesting news angles and interesting interviewees.

Decentralized EU agencies

Overall, there are some forty EU agencies, not to be confused with the European Commission's directorates-general. The agencies are not mentioned in the treaties; they have been set up for a specific purpose and they can easily be dismantled again. For example, the European Agency for Reconstruction was set up in 2000 and closed its doors eight years later. From its headquarters in Thessaloniki, Greece, it managed the EU's various aid programmes to Serbia, Kosovo, Montenegro and Macedonia, on behalf of the European Commission.

In the agencies you can find technical and scientific expertise in particular fields. For specialist journalists, the EU agencies can be very good sources. Some agencies, but not all, have press services. And some EU agencies, such as the environment agency EEA, are often in the media spotlight, while others are rarely or never heard of.

What do they do?

The agencies are supposed to reduce the commission's workload and help it implement EU legislation. For example, the European Medicines Agency handles applications for selling new drugs in the EU and the European Food Safety Authority does risk assessments when someone wants to cultivate a GMO crop in the EU, as mentioned in chapter 10.

Some agencies have coordinating functions. Eurojust deals with legal cases that concern several EU countries, bringing together judges and prosecutors to plan coordinated prosecutions and the like. For example, Eurojust coordinated a prosecution team from the countries with nationals aboard flight MH17, which examined possible criminal charges.[3]

Other agencies have been created to gather and disseminate information. For example, Eurofound disseminates information on living and working conditions in the EU. And the EU agency monitoring drug use and abuse, EMCDDA, publishes Europe-wide surveys about school students' experiences of, and perception of, alcohol, cigarettes, drugs and online gambling.[4]

These agencies often produce reports and statistics that can be of interest for national or local journalists, or specialist reporters. For example, the European Environment Agency, EEA, together with the European Commission's environment DG, every spring publish a report about the water quality in 20,000 European lakes and coastal areas, within the framework of the EU's Bathing Water Directive.

For example, the BBC writes: 'Even as recently as 2015, 31 bathing water sites in the UK were classed as 'poor' in the European Environment Agency's annual report. ... By 2015, 97 percent of England's bathing waters had passed the commission's minimum standards, compared to only 27 percent in 1990'.[5]

The Agency for Fundamental Rights (FRA) publishes an annual report in spring and many thematic reports and surveys throughout the year that are of journalistic interest. FRA shows in a special survey that doctors in some EU countries still view homosexuality as a disease and transsexuality as a mental disorder.[6] In another survey, where FRA has polled over 90,000 LGBT persons across the EU, 26 per cent state that they have been physically attacked or threatened with violence in the last five years.[7]

Other EU agencies are executive agencies, managing EU programmes. They are typically located close to the European Commission in Brussels. If you have ever applied for an EU grant to translate Romanian poetry or to set up an Italian film festival in your home town, it is to the Education, Audiovisual and Culture Executive Agency (EACEA) that you have sent your application. It deals with the culture and education programmes that are funded by the EU budget.

The EU agencies have been created for different purposes and their activities may differ widely. If you are particularly interested in one agency, have a look at the EU legal act that created it. On most agencies' websites, you can find it under the heading 'mandate', 'legal basis' or 'legal framework'. If not, you can always find it on EUR-Lex, by searching for the name of the agency.

Fact box: Decentralized EU agencies

Agency for the Cooperation of Energy Regulators (ACER)
Ljubljana, Slovenia
www.acer.europa.eu

Body of European Regulators for Electronic Communications (BEREC)
Riga, Latvia
www.berec.europa.eu

Community Plant Variety Office (CPVO)
Angers, France
www.cpvo.europa.eu

European Agency for Safety and Health at Work (EU-OSHA)
Bilbao, Spain
www.osha.europa.eu

European Agency for the Management of Operational Cooperation at the External Borders (Frontex)
Warsaw, Poland
www.frontex.europa.eu

European Agency for the Operational Management of Large-scale IT Systems in the Area of Freedom, Security and Justice (eu-LISA)
Tallinn, Estonia (seat) and Strasbourg, France (operational management)
www.eulisa.europa.eu

European Support Office on Asylum (EASO)
Valletta, Malta
www.easo.europa.eu

European Aviation Safety Agency (EASA)
Cologne, Germany
www.easa.europa.eu

European Banking Authority (EBA)
London, United Kingdom
www.eba.europa.eu

European Centre for Disease Prevention and Control (ECDC)
Stockholm, Sweden
www.ecdc.europa.eu

European Centre for the Development of Vocational Training (Cedefop)
Thessaloniki, Greece
www.cedefop.europa.eu

European Chemicals Agency (ECHA)
Helsinki, Finland
www.echa.europa.eu

European Environment Agency (EEA)
Copenhagen, Denmark
www.eea.europa.eu

European Fisheries Control Agency (EFCA)
Vigo, Spain
www.efca.europa.eu

European Food Safety Authority (EFSA)
Parma, Italy
www.efsa.europa.eu

European Foundation for the Improvement of Living and Working Conditions (Eurofound)
Dublin, Ireland
www.eurofound.europa.eu

European GNSS Agency (GSA)
(GNSS stands for Global Navigation Satellite System. GPS is an American GNSS. Galileo is the future European one.)
Brussels, Belgium
www.gsa.europa.eu

European Institute for Gender Equality (EIGE)
Vilnius, Lithuania
www.eige.europa.eu

European Insurance and Occupational Pensions Authority (EIOPA)
Frankfurt, Germany
eiopa.europa.eu

European Maritime Safety Agency (EMSA)
Lisbon, Portugal
www.emsa.europa.eu

European Medicines Agency (EMA)
London, United Kingdom
www.ema.europa.eu

European Monitoring Centre for Drugs and Drug Addiction (EMCDDA)
Lisbon, Portugal
www.emcdda.europa.eu

European Union Agency for Network and Information Security (ENISA)
Crete, Greece
www.enisa.europa.eu

European Union Agency for Law Enforcement Training (CEPOL)
Budapest, Hungary
www.cepol.europa.eu

European Police Office (Europol)
The Hague, The Netherlands
www.europol.europa.eu

European Railway Agency (ERA)
Valenciennes, France
www.era.europa.eu

European Securities and Markets Authority (ESMA)
Paris, France
www.esma.europa.eu

European Training Foundation (ETF)
Turin, Italy
www.etf.europa.eu

European Union Agency for Fundamental Rights (FRA)
Vienna, Austria
www.fra.europa.eu

European Union Intellectual Property Office (EUIPO)
Alicante, Spain
www.euipo.europa.eu

Single Resolution Board (SRB)
Brussels, Belgium
srb.europa.eu

The European Union's Judicial Cooperation Unit (Eurojust)
The Hague, The Netherlands
www.eurojust.europa.eu

Translation Centre for the Bodies of the European Union (CdT)
Luxembourg
cdt.europa.eu

Agencies under the EU common security and defence policy

European Defence Agency, EDA
Brussels, Belgium
www.eda.europa.eu

European Union Institute for Security Studies (EUISS)
Paris, France
www.iss.europa.eu

> European Union Satellite Centre (SatCen)
> Torrejón de Ardoz, Spain
> www.satcen.europa.eu
>
> *Executive agencies*
>
> Education, Audiovisual and Culture Executive Agency (EACEA)
> Brussels, Belgium
> eacea.ec.europa.eu
>
> Executive Agency for Small and Medium-sized Enterprises (EASME)
> Brussels, Belgium
> www.ec.europa.eu/easme
>
> Consumers, Health, Agriculture and Food Executive Agency (CHAFEA)
> Luxembourg
> www.ec.europa.eu/chafea
>
> Research Executive Agency (REA)
> Brussels, Belgium
> www.ec.europa.eu/rea
>
> Innovation and Networks Executive Agency (INEA)
> Brussels, Belgium
> www.ec.europa.eu/inea

There is also a regional dimension to the creation of decentralized EU agencies: the agencies set up after the EU's 2004 expansion have typically been placed in eastern and central European countries, so that all countries can host their own agency.

When writing about EU agencies

The EU agencies can be called things like 'centre', 'office', 'agency', 'fund' or 'institute'. When you write about the EU agencies, you should explain what they are, not only write the name.

A good example of how to explain such matters is provided by a *Guardian* article about the European Environment Agency (EEA) reporting a fall in average carbon dioxide emissions from new cars sold in the EU: 'The agency's research guides EU policymakers, who are reviewing proposals by the European commission to tighten laws on air quality, emission limits and new vehicle authorizations following the Volkswagen emissions scandal'.[8]

Links

EEAS
www.eeas.europa.eu

EEAS spokespeople and press officers
eeas.europa.eu/press-media/spokespersons-service/index_en.htm

Council of Ministers' press office for foreign affairs
www.consilium.europa.eu/en/press/contacts
(Scroll through the list to find the press officer for foreign affairs)

EEAS delegations
eeas.europa.eu/delegations/index_en.htm

The European Court of Justice
www.curia.europa.eu

The European Court of Justice press service
curia.europa.eu/jcms/jcms/Jo2_25870

The European Central Bank
www.ecb.eu

The European Court of Auditors
www.eca.europa.eu

OLAF – the EU's anti-corruption agency
ec.europa.eu/anti-fraud

European Economic and Social Committee
www.eesc.europa.eu

Committee of the Regions
www.cor.europa.eu

Notes

1 Arreola, Carlos and Mauricio, Ana Julia, Measuring the influence of the Advocate General on the Court of Justice of the European Union: correlation or causation? [blog post], eulawanalysis.blogspot.be, 17 January 2016
2 *Dagens Medicin*, EU-representanter för LO och HSO tror på elallergi [blog post], 2 February 2015
3 AFP, *Countries with MH17 victims agree prosecution team*, 28 July 2014
4 EMCDDA, *Results from the European School Survey Project on Alcohol and Other Drugs*, ESPAD Report 2015
5 BBC News, Could Brexit affect beach water quality?, 5 September 2016
6 European Union Agency for Fundamental Rights, FRA, *Professionally speaking: challenges to achieving equality for LGBT people*, March 2016
7 European Union Agency for Fundamental Rights, *European Union lesbian, gay, bisexual and transgender survey*, 2013
8 *The Guardian*, Emissions from new cars sold in Europe fell 3% last year, 14 April 2016

12 Statistics, opinion polls, sound, photo and video

Eurostat

Eurostat is the EU's statistics agency and has its home in Luxembourg. It is also a directorate-general of the European Commission. Eurostat collects a huge range of statistics from the EU countries – statistics that are used as the basis for decisions by the other commission DGs.

The rule of thumb is that if there is some sort of EU cooperation on an issue, there are also EU-wide statistics on it. The EU's growth strategy, Europe 2020, has the goals that school drop-out rates should be no higher than 10 per cent and that 3 per cent of the EU's GDP should be invested in research and development. Therefore, there are comparable numbers from all 28 EU countries on how many students drop out of school and how much is spent on R&D.

However, if there is no EU cooperation or EU policy, there will not be any EU statistics ready for download, even if it might be very interesting to compare the countries. On social topics such as abortion, no EU-wide statistics are collected.

Every autumn, the Eurostat yearbook is published in English, French and German. Eurostat also publishes a regional yearbook, with the same statistical indicators but for the European regions. Sometimes comparing regions instead of countries can make newsworthy stories.

Eurostat classifies EU regions in three different ways, from major to minor units, called NUTS (nomenclature of territorial units). In the current NUTS classification there are 98 NUTS 1 regions, 276 NUTS 2 regions and 1,342 NUTS 3 regions. In the UK, for example, Wales is a NUTS 1 region, Merseyside a NUTS 2 region and the metropolitan borough of Liverpool a NUTS 3 region.

For Germany, the NUTS 1 regions correspond to the German *Bundesländer*. For France, the NUTS 2 and NUTS 3 regions correspond to the French *régions* and *départements*.[1]

There is another Eurostat publication that may also be of interest: 'The EU in the world'. It deals with the EU as a bloc and compares it to the 15 G20 countries that are not EU members.

It is easy to get article ideas from EU statistics. National media usually make news out of fresh Eurostat figures when their country is at the top or the bottom of any list. For example, Romanian publication *Curentul* wrote that Romania comes last in the EU in terms of the minimum wage – only 157 euros per month, compared to Luxembourg's minimum wage of 1,874 euros per month.[2]

Bulgarian daily *Trud* also used Eurostat statistics when it wrote that 'as many as 94 percent of primary school teachers [in Bulgaria] are women, compared with 85 percent in the EU'.[3] And Greek *Naftemporiki* wrote that Greece is among the least-connected EU countries: 54 per cent of households have internet access, compared to the EU average of 76 per cent.[4]

Eurostat economic statistics for the EU or euro area are often newsworthy, such as fresh GDP figures. 'According to the latest figures from Eurostat, the EU's GDP dropped by 0.8 percent between 2007 and today, while the euro area's GDP declined by 1.3 percent', writes Poland's *Rzeczpospolita*. The article contrasts this to the figures from Poland showing 18 per cent growth over the same period.[5]

Much of the data continuously put out by Eurostat are economic indicators. On the website, there is a publication calendar for euro-area statistics, such as inflation or jobs in euro-area countries. On the **Eurostat press page**, you will also find a list of press releases and contact details for the press service.

The decentralized EU agencies (see chapter 11) also produce many interesting statistics and opinion surveys that you can build stories on, or use for European context.

Eurobarometer

Eurobarometer is the EU's own opinion research institute and is funded by the European Commission. Every year, some 150 new reports based on opinion surveys are published, and Eurobarometer has been polling for more than 40 years. The database with accumulated surveys is quite extraordinary. It is a goldmine both for journalists and political scientists. Some of the standard questions recur over long periods of time, which allows for comparisons between countries and over time.

The classic poll is called the Standard Eurobarometer. It has asked more or less the same questions since 1973: about Europeans' attitudes to society in general, to the EU, and to national and European institutions. For each edition, 1,000 people are interviewed in every EU country, except for small countries like Malta, Luxembourg and Cyprus, where 500 people are polled.

The Standard Eurobarometer comes out twice a year, in June/July and November/December. Media tend to focus on the countries that like or dislike the EU the most, or where there has been a big change in attitude towards the EU.

This is what it normally looks like, from *The New York Times*: 'Public confidence in the European Union has slumped to record lows, according to survey data compiled by Eurobarometer, the union's polling arm …'.[6]

Or like this, from *Politico*: 'The EU has a mostly positive image in 15 member countries, with the highest levels of support in Romania (62 percent) and Ireland (57 percent) …',[7] or like this op-ed in *Politico*: 'data from the Eurobarometer – the closest we have to a gauge for measuring public opinion in

Europe – suggests that Europeans want more, not less, integration. The difference is whether or not they live in the eurozone'.[8]

There are also special Eurobarometer surveys that look at Europeans' attitudes to specific issues, such as the common agricultural policy or young Europeans' attitudes to drugs. They are usually carried out by Eurobarometer on behalf of the commission's DGs.

These polls can be good for providing context for a national debate on a certain topic. If there is a political debate in your country about changing the pension age, for example, then you could have a look through the Eurobarometer archive to see if there has been a poll on future pensions systems.

A third category is Flash Eurobarometer. These are quickly produced polls done via short phone interviews. They could be about, for example, Cypriot or Maltese businesses preparations before joining the euro, or any other EU-related subject. There are a few dozen of these polls every year.

In order not to miss any interesting survey, you can subscribe to updates. Then all new publications arrive in your email, usually in English and French. Or follow Eurobarometer on Twitter.

The European Commission often refers to a Eurobarometer study when it presents a legislative proposal or some other initiative. That can sometimes give the impression that there is a real popular demand for the commission's initiative, which is sometimes misleading. Double-check how the polling question was phrased before you refer to the Eurobarometer numbers from the commission's press release.

Sometimes the Eurobarometer questions are about things that people clearly do not have an opinion on. What is, for example, the point in stating that however many Europeans 'tend to trust' or 'tend not to trust' the European Economic and Social Committee, when it is obvious that most of the polled people have never heard of the institution?

The European Commission claimed, in a press release, that an overwhelming majority of Europeans were in favour of the EU establishing its own navigation system Galileo.[9] But in the Eurobarometer survey that the commission refers to, 60 per cent of the respondents had also stated that they had never heard of Galileo. Researchers have pointed out that errors and methodological problems in the Eurobarometer studies are not random; they systematically steer responses in a pro-EU way.[10]

There are suspicions that Eurobarometer excludes questions where the answers don't match what the commission wants to communicate. In the June 2010 issue of the *Standard Eurobarometer*, the question of whether membership in the EU was a good or bad thing – a question that had been asked in every standard poll since 1973 – was suddenly missing. In spring 2010, only 49 per cent of interviewed Europeans had replied that EU membership was a good thing for their country, compared to 53 per cent in November 2009.[11]

EU opinion polls are a great tool. But use them to compare public opinion between countries or between periods of time, rather than to make statements like '60 per cent of Europeans think Frontex should receive more funding'.

And when the European Commission refers to public opinion as supporting a proposed initiative, do not copy-paste that line into the end of your article without first checking that the question was neutrally phrased, gave the respondents an equal chance to agree or disagree and did not include concepts that most people have never heard of.

European Values Study

In each country there are typically several opinion polling institutes, providing survey results to government, media or other organizations. But in surveying EU public opinion, Eurobarometer has a quasi-monopoly. For everyone else, transnational surveys are too expensive to do.

There is however one other EU-wide public opinion poll: the European Values Study, carried out by the EVS Foundation, which brings together social and political scientists.

The study asks Europeans what they think about family, work, religion, politics and society. The **EVS** carries out a survey every nine years, compared to the Eurobarometer twice-yearly standard poll.

When it started in 1981, the EVS polled all countries that were EU members at the time. The latest survey, from 2008, covered 47 European countries. In each country, 1,000 people are interviewed. The next EVS survey will come out in 2017.

Photo, audio and video from the EU institutions

All three major EU institutions have **audiovisual archives** from which you can download and publish photos and audio/video files for free. You must be a registered user to download the files, but that is done in a couple of mouse clicks. In these archives you can find the photos needed to go with your article and the sound bite for your radio story. But the EU institutions are also unlikely treasure troves for free celebrity photos. Hugh Grant, Bono and Colombian singer Juanes are just some of the celebrities who have dropped in on a Brussels visit and left behind traces in the institutions' photo archives.

The European Commission's archives contain audio and pictures from 1950 onwards, video from press conferences and high-resolution images of the commissioners shaking hands with foreign dignitaries. The European Parliament has video from all its plenary sessions, most committee meetings, and press conferences and ceremonies, as well as feature pictures of MEPs. All public meetings in the Council of Ministers are on film and on photos, downloadable in mp4, mp3 and embedded code (which allows you to embed the video on a website).

Links

Eurostat
ec.europa.eu/eurostat

Eurostat's press site
ec.europa.eu/eurostat/help/press-media-support

Eurobarometer
ec.europa.eu/public_opinion/index_en.htm

European Values Study
europeanvaluesstudy.eu

European Commission's photo, audio and video archive
ec.europa.eu/avservices

European Parliament's photo, audio and video archive
audiovisual.europarl.europa.eu

Council of Ministers' photo, audio and video archive
tvnewsroom.consilium.europa.eu

Notes

1. Eurostat, *Regions in the European Union. Nomenclature of territorial units for statistics NUTS 2013/EU-28*, Publications Office of the European Union, Luxembourg, 2015
2. *Curentul*, România, pe ultimul loc în UE la salariul minim pe economie: 157 euro/lună, 5 March 2013
3. *Trud*, Every third manager in Bulgaria is a woman, 8 March 2013
4. *Naftemporiki*, Eurostat: Greece stands low in Internet connection, 19 December 2012
5. *Rzeczpospolita*, Unia słabo sobie radzi z kryzysem, 8 March 2013
6. *The New York Times*, Europe facing more pressure to reconsider cuts as a cure, 26 April 2013
7. *Politico*, We love the EU – sort of, 3 August 2015
8. Otero-Iglesias, Miguel, A united Europe is closer than you think [op-ed], *Politico*, 19 May 2015
9. European Commission, *Eurobarometer on GALILEO: Europeans support EU setting up its own navigation system*, Press Release IP/07/764, 5 June 2007
10. Höpner, Martin and Jurczyk, Bojan, How the Eurobarometer blurs the line between research and propaganda, Max Planck-Institute für Gesellschaftsforschung, MPIfG Discussion Paper, 15 June 2015
11. Signorelli, Salvatore, The EU and public opinions: a love-hate relationship? *Notre Europe*, November 2012

13 Lobbying

This chapter is about how to find and use lobbyists as sources. In chapter 18 you can read about EU lobbying as a subject for investigative reporting.

In many languages and national contexts, lobbying – both the term and the concept – is a negative one. In the EU context, it is almost neutral; lobbying is seen as a natural part of political life. Contrary to what many believe, lobbying in Brussels is neither secretive nor embarrassing.

Imagine the following: an Italian MEP is responsible for a major legislative report about employment regulations for small businesses throughout the EU. She lives in Belgium, speaks German, French and English, has a Polish husband and a holiday home in Croatia. Even so, she could never grasp how this proposal will affect people in every corner of the EU. A Cypriot farmer? A Danish accountant with a small business?

There is no European public debate, no European media or political parties to make the link between citizens and EU political power. The void is to some extent filled by EU lobbyists. Lawmakers will consult them and use them as sounding boards. The Italian MEP might talk to European umbrella organizations for farmers and accountants. If Cypriot farmers or Danish accountants would be affected in a particular way by the proposed law, chances are she would find out by talking to these European organizations.

Most people working on EU affairs do not see lobbying as a problem in itself, but think that it is a problem that interests are unevenly represented and that there is a lack of transparency over who is influencing whom. The lobby watchdog Corporate Europe Observatory warns that the combination of money and a complex and opaque decision-making process has enabled large companies to take over the political agenda.

As a journalist you will need EU lobbyists as sources: both for their views as affected parties, or stakeholders, and for actual facts. But check their facts against other sources and always be clear about what interests the lobbyists represent.

EU people tend to label all those who try to influence EU policy as lobbyists – be they multinational companies, environmental organizations, trade associations, unions, law firms, consulting firms or civic associations. In many national contexts, the word lobbyist is exclusively used for corporate lobbyists. Keep this difference in mind when you interview an MEP who criticizes his opponent for running lobbyists' errands while at the same time complimenting himself for listening to civil society.

Unions, churches and non-profit organizations of course do not like to be called lobbyists, and there is a difference between representing a for-profit company and an organization that seeks a better environment for all. But from the perspective of a journalist, you need to take the same critical approach towards all organized interests that want to influence EU policy. I have found that the 'good' Brussels interest groups spin as much as the 'bad' ones. Even if the purpose is not profit, they still need to justify their existence to receive continued funding for their projects. That is sometimes enough of an incentive to distort reality.

And remember that the professional influencers who work for Amnesty's Brussels office are recruited from the same pool as those who work for BusinessEurope, and that many of them change jobs with each other.

Lobbying is any activity that aims to influence EU policy. It is impossible to say how many individuals there are in Brussels whose work fits that description. The most often cited figure, both by the EU institutions and interest groups, is between 15,000 and 20,000 people. But many more people than that will come to Brussels on a regular basis, to participate in a commission expert group or a parliamentary hearing, attend a conference or talk to politicians.

The media image of EU lobbyists is sometimes that they are all-powerful. But lobbyists are not a homogeneous bunch. There are often lobbyists on both sides of the argument, just as there are EU member states and members of the European Parliament that want different things.

Who are the Brussels lobbyists?

Organized interests in Brussels fall into three categories:

- Companies or for-profit organizations, such as Volvo, BusinessEurope or the chemicals industry.
- Non-profit organizations such as Oxfam, the European Women's Lobby or the EU trade union ETUC.
- Public sector or official representatives, such as Bavaria, the city of Vienna, Tibet or Western Sahara.

Corporate lobbying

Companies clearly dominate the Brussels scene. A few hundred companies have their own Brussels offices in the most prestigious locations in the EU quarter. Here you will find Deutsche Telekom and Ericsson. But most companies do not have their own Brussels representation. Instead they pay a membership fee to a trade organization and let their professional lobbyists do the work. There are about 1,500 European trade organizations in Brussels.

The rule of thumb is that if you can think of any profession or economic sector, then most probably there is a European trade association representing their interests to the EU institutions. There are for example professional organizations for potato starch producers, fur farmers and amusement parks.

Most industry associations only have one or two people in their Brussels bureau, while the largest trade association, the chemical industry federation Cefic, has more than 150 employees in Brussels.

Industries such as chemicals, food, pharmaceuticals and cars are very active in lobbying the EU. They try to influence environment, health and competition policy – basically everything that might lead to increased costs for them and/or affect their competitiveness outside the EU. Through active lobbying, they have gained great influence over decision-making.

Companies are grouped not only by industry but also by nationality. For example, the French corporate lobby Medef has its own Brussels office, representing French companies. It is also a member of BusinessEurope – the European umbrella organization for EU employers' associations.

Companies often use many channels simultaneously to influence EU legislation: they have their own lobbyists in Brussels; they are members of both national and European industry associations that advocate pro-business policy in general; and they buy consulting and PR services for specific campaigns from some of the approximately two hundred Brussels-based consultancies. These consultancies primarily sell their expertise on how EU decision-making works. They might, for example, identify all the key players in a given area and compile their contact information – a fairly easy job that can appear next to impossible for an outsider. Finally, companies also sponsor think tanks (see next chapter) and take part in debates that they organize. Think-tank research and events are perceived to have greater credibility than those coming directly from a company.

Fact box: Some large business organizations

Copa-Cogeca
www.copa-cogeca.be
Copa-Cogeca is an umbrella organization of European farmers and agricultural cooperatives. The organization has tremendous power in all matters related to agriculture.

BusinessEurope
www.businesseurope.eu
BusinessEurope represents European industry. All EU countries and many European countries have organizations that are members of BusinessEurope, for example the Turkish Confederation of Employer Associations, the Malta Chamber of Commerce, Enterprise and Industry and the Confederation of Danish Industry.

> European Association of Craft, Small and Medium-sized Enterprises, UEAPME
> www.ueapme.com
> Representing SME associations from 34 countries. According to UEAPME, these associations in turn represent 12 million companies with 55 million employees throughout Europe.
>
> Acea
> www.acea.be
> Acea represents 15 European automotive, truck and bus companies. Among the member organizations are Volkswagen, BMW and Volvo.
>
> FoodDrinkEurope
> www.fooddrinkeurope.eu
> The voice of the food and drink industry in Europe. Among its members are national food and drink federations, EU-wide umbrella organizations like the Europe Fruit Juice Association or the Confederation of EU Yeast Producers, as well as companies like Coca-Cola and Unilever.

Non-profit organizations

Non-profit organizations and trade unions are far fewer in number than corporate interests – a few hundred organizations in Brussels – and they have much less money.

Most active and established in Brussels are the major international environmental and human rights organizations, such as Greenpeace, WWF and Amnesty International. Environmental organizations established themselves early in Brussels and they lobby professionally. All environmental legislation is closely scrutinized and the organizations speak to politicians, suggest improvements and provide ready-made arguments.

Trade unions were late to understand they have to be in Brussels to influence EU policy. Their counterparts, employers' organizations, earned a head start by understanding this from the beginning.

Many non-profit organizations that lobby the EU are actually partly financed by the EU. When there is a clearly organized business interest but no counter-interest, the European Commission funds one itself, and consults it. To consult lobbyists is, as said, an integral part of the EU decision-making process, because the institutions do not have all the necessary competence.

The non-profits are often organized in much the same way as corporate organizations: there is a European umbrella organization with a small team of professional lobbyists in Brussels that advocates the issues that the national member organizations entrust them with. The same rule of thumb as for trade associations applies here: if you can identify a group of people or a community, there is probably a European umbrella organization. It could be broad categories – such as women, the young, the old, consumers, LGBT people – or it can be small and specific categories – history teachers, Quakers or girl scouts.

If you are looking to interview someone who belongs to a specific sub-group, the big umbrella organizations are a good place to start. In their membership lists you will find the smaller, more specific organizations. Take, for example, the European Women's Lobby. It represents some 2,500 organizations from across Europe, including big national women's rights organizations and smaller European umbrella organizations representing, for example, women entrepreneurs, young Christian women or Roma women.

The large umbrella organizations are also represented within the EU institutions, for example in the commission's expert groups. They therefore have detailed knowledge of specialist topics, know the key players and are keeping an eye on the process. They may also have documents that you as a journalist want. The European Women's Lobby for example participates in the advisory committee on equal opportunities for women and men.

Fact box: Some large non-profit organizations

European consumers' organization, BEUC
www.beuc.org
Umbrella organization for European consumer organizations.

European Women's Lobby
www.womenlobby.org
Organization representing 2,500 national or EU level women's organizations.

European Environmental Bureau, EEB
www.eeb.org
Europe's largest coalition of environmental organizations and the environmental movement's main lobby in Brussels.

European Trade Union Confederation, ETUC
www.etuc.org
Representing more than 80 European national trade unions.

AGE Platform Europe
www.age-platform.eu
AGE is an umbrella organization that looks after the interests of old people, especially in relation to discrimination and health.

Amnesty International Europe
www.amnesty.eu
International human rights organization.

Climate Action Network Europe, CAN-E
www.caneurope.org

Umbrella organization that advocates changes to society to reduce the impact of climate change.

European NGO Confederation for Relief and Development, Concord
www.concordeurope.org
Umbrella organization for various aid and disaster relief organizations.

International Lesbian, Gay, Bisexual, Trans and Intersex Association, Ilga
www.ilga-europe.org
The umbrella organization for organizations working with LGBT rights.

Social Platform
www.socialplatform.org
Umbrella organization for other European umbrella organizations that are involved with various social issues. Members include organizations representing women, the elderly, children, the disabled, the unemployed, the poor, LGBT persons or families, and organizations working with issues such as health, racism and homelessness.

Transparency International
www.transparencyinternational.eu
International anti-corruption organization. Best known for its corruption barometer, which measures perceived corruption around the world.

WWF European Policy Office
www.wwf.eu
WWF (World Wildlife Fund) is one of the world's largest environmental organizations. WWF works to stop the destruction of nature, preserve biological diversity and reduce pollution.

Governmental/national representatives in Brussels

In Brussels, there is a multitude of national missions to the EU (not to be mixed up with embassies to Belgium) and chambers of commerce from countries outside the EU. Even breakaway regions and political movements are present, trying to persuade the EU to advocate their causes with their respective governments. For example, the Polisario Front, the independence party in Moroccan-occupied Western Sahara, has an EU ambassador, who is often seen in European Parliament corridors.

EU regions

Municipalities and regions from EU countries are very active in lobbying the EU institutions, for their own interests and without passing through their national governments. Some of these regions, for example Bavaria in Germany, are both more populous and wealthier than some EU countries.

Budapest has a Brussels bureau. So do Umbria, the Basque Country and Wales. Google the region or city that you are interested in plus 'EU' or 'Brussels' and you will find it easily. The different bureaus that lobby for regions and cities from one country tend to be grouped together at a few Brussels addresses.

Some of the regional lobby offices are actively trying to influence the EU's legislative process; some regions focus on establishing contacts with other countries' regions, in order to apply for EU funds for joint projects, for example connecting the regions by rail. Other regional offices see themselves as a link between the residents of the region and the EU, and spend a lot of time and resources hosting visitors in Brussels. All regional offices highlight their best example so that other European regions should copy them.

Regions and cities are also often represented through national associations, such as Regions in Hungary, Local Governments in Denmark, and the UK Local Government Association (LGA). They are a good starting point when you do not know where to turn.

And lastly, there are plenty of EU-wide umbrella organizations for regions that share some characteristics or interests. These include the Covenant of Mayors, Union of Capitals of the EU (UCEU) or Polis (European Cities and Regions Networking for Innovative Transport Solutions).

How is the lobbying done?

I take a walk through the European Parliament's corridors with Frank Schwalba-Hoth. He is a former MEP for the German Green Party, a former head of Greenpeace's Brussels office and a former PR consultant. Nowadays he calls himself an 'independent political analyst and strategist' and is a real spider in the Brussels web. He knows almost everyone.

We have lunch in the parliament canteen with a group of teenage asylum seekers in Germany. They are in Brussels to hand over a petition to the European Parliament's president, calling for a more humane asylum policy. We say hi to a PR consultant who is setting up a meeting room – he is helping a former MEP with a book launch. A woman runs by with a big stack of papers in her arms. Schwalba-Hoth whispers to me that she is a Google lobbyist. We wave to a freelance journalist who slips into a committee meeting, looking a little embarrassed. He earns money on the side by taking notes from parliamentary committee meetings for a consulting firm – information that the firm then repackages and sells to companies at high prices.

Lobbying in the European Parliament is more sprawling and colourful than in the European Commission. Every day hundreds of lobbyists pass the parliament's security checks to follow a committee meeting, have a coffee with a parliamentarian or assistant or participate in a debate as an invited expert.

The most-lobbied MEPs are the rapporteurs and shadow rapporteurs for legislative proposals, but other MEPs who sit in the committees that deal with issues that are important for industry are also often contacted by lobbyists. Lobbyists of course allocate their resources to where the pay-off will be greatest, so they will assemble lists of MEPs who are friendly to their causes and provide these MEPs with the best arguments, rather than try to convince hostile MEPs. They will call and set up a meeting to talk about their company/organization, what they think about the proposal on the table and suggest changes to it.

According to Swedish former Social Democrat MEP Åsa Westlund: 'Say we're voting on a small bill, then there are perhaps ten stakeholders that contact me about that. For a larger bill, it might be between 50 and 60. If I'm the MEP in charge, I will try to meet everyone. Otherwise, I prioritize Swedish organizations and environmental organizations rather than industry'.

Someone who did the lobby maths is Swedish former Green MEP Carl Schlyter: 'On average, I get 237 emails a week from lobbyists. There are emails, trade magazines, some letters and phone calls and a lot of invitations for breakfasts and dinners'.

The main target of lobbyists is often the European Commission, from where all legislation originates. It is also where lobbying is the most institutionalized. Lobbyists usually put the most of their effort into making their voice heard here, although the European Parliament has become more and more interesting to lobbyists as its legislative power has increased.

The commission's attitude towards lobbyists is basically positive. Those who will be affected by the law are invited to have their say (see chapter 7). The commission prefers European umbrella organizations to national associations, which has led to more and more umbrella organizations being established. Overall, the commission shuns organizations that smell too much of national interests.

European umbrella organizations – for both business and non-profit interests – lobby all the EU institutions simultaneously. The European organization has seats in commission expert groups and is in contact with MEPs. It coordinates its efforts through the national member organizations, for example by writing letters that the national member organizations can send to 'their' national politicians and MEPs.

To lobby the Council of Ministers basically means lobbying the EU countries' governments. The governments already have their positions when they start negotiating in Brussels, so it is primarily in the capitals that lobbyists deploy their firepower to influence ministers before they go to Brussels.

Interview: Lobbyist Daniel Guéguen

French Daniel Guéguen has over 40 years in the EU lobbying business. He was the head of the European sugar lobby and the European farm lobby Copa-Cogega and now specializes in 'comitology' lobbying.

Daniel Guéguen on …

…the number of EU lobbyists

The figures that are used are a pure fantasy. Around 20,000 people work with public affairs in Brussels, but that doesn't mean that there are 20,000

EU lobbyists. Lobbyists are those who actually engage with the legislators and the commission, that's perhaps 2,000 people. But there are around 3,000 lobbying structures in Brussels, for the most part very small.

...EU lobbying now and then

There were fewer people involved before, so it was easier. And you had direct access to the commission. You just knocked on the door, you didn't have to set up a meeting.

In the 1970s, the lobbyists were people who took decisions. Today they don't, they want to avoid adversaries. Society has become more diplomatic and consensual. I think EU lobbyists are losing in influence, by their own fault, because they are in a consensual mode and because they don't master the new post-Lisbon decision-making procedures [referring to the new 'comitology' procedures]. Lobbying is to defend a dossier, sometimes robustly. It is not a diplomatic game.

...the commission's lobby register

I'm in it, of course, but I think it's ridiculous. First of all, because it's not mandatory. Secondly, it is not clear what you should actually declare [concerning the money spent and personnel designated to lobby the EU institutions]. In general, consultancy firms declare a lot because they want to seem big, and companies declare little because they want to seem small. There is no control.

The register needs to be mandatory, also for law firms, and there need to be sanctions. Most serious lobbyists share that view. You know, lobbying is not a dirty business, but it is sensitive. Today, civil society wants transparency, so you need to be transparent.

...lobbying various EU institutions

With the commission, the approach is individual and personal. There is one person that's the most important: the desk officer. In the parliament, lobbying is more political and collective. You talk to clusters of MEPs.

The more experience you have, the more credible you are and the more you know the right people. You get to meet the people you need to meet and get the information that you need. That is the most important.

...corporate interests and NGOs

The big issues are put on the agenda by NGOs: endocrine disruptors, GMOs, nuclear power ... The industry plays a reactive role, it's always late and it's fragmented. It doesn't have the capacity to oppose the big trends that are imposed by civil society.

How to find the lobbyists

The lobby register

The European Parliament has had a register of lobbyists since 2006, the European Commission since 2008. These two systems merged in 2011, to create a **common**

lobby register, called 'the transparency register'. In September 2016, it covered more than 9,800 companies, organizations, consultants and think tanks. In the register, lobbyists state what policy areas they are trying to influence, how many people they have working on lobbying and how much they spend on this.

The registry has enormous shortcomings. Most obvious is that it is voluntary. The report *Rescue the Register* by Alter-EU, an umbrella organization for transparency organizations, showed that, in 2013, more than a hundred major companies that actively lobby the EU institutions were missing from the registry, including Goldman Sachs, Apple and Amazon.[1] Two years later, Transparency International found that 14 of the 20 biggest law firms in the world, all with Brussels offices, were not in the register. Of these 14 law firms, 11 were registered as lobby organizations in Washington DC, where registration is mandatory.[2]

Another shortcoming is that the registry is not controlled particularly well. When Transparency International's EU bureau checked the register in 2015, they found that half of the entries contained factual errors or were outdated.[3]

The transparency organization Corporate Europe Observatory has checked the registry and found made-up organizations in the list. The online newspaper *EUobserver* reported that an Irish cheerleading team had signed up to the register and stated that they spend 50,000 euros on lobbying. They had ended up there because they thought it was an application form for EU grants.[4] According to *EUobserver*, both under- and over-reporting of how many lobbyists work and how much money is spent is usual.

Despite these shortcomings, the registry is a goldmine if you want to know who has an interest in influencing the institutions on a specific question. Use it as a shortcut to find sources. If you are writing about EU tobacco policy, search for 'tobacco' in the lobby register and you will quickly get a list of all businesses and organizations – tobacco producers and anti-smoking organizations – that say they want to influence tobacco legislation.

Stakeholder – *the Brussels bubble's* Yellow Pages

A good source of information about who's who and what they are doing is the phone catalogue *Stakeholder*, which is edited by the previously mentioned Frank Schwalba-Hoth.

It is a brick of more than a thousand pages, with the names and contact information of about 14,000 people who in various ways are active in the EU. Apart from the EU institutions, you will find companies, associations, consultants and journalists.

This huge phone book costs about 100 euros. If you write extensively about EU lobbying, it might be a good investment. But all these organizations and companies are of course easy to find online.

Start with your country's organization and then look up the European umbrella organization

When you hear about some new EU law, you could probably, off the top of your head, think of a few organizations, companies or economic sectors in your country that would have a stake or that could be positively or negatively affected if the proposal goes through. These are the ones you would want to talk to. These organizations and companies probably will not know all the details about EU procedures, but there is some likelihood that they will be members of a European umbrella organization that does.

Start by checking out the national organization. On their website, there might be a tab that says 'international work' or something like that. Find out who is representing them in Brussels.

Talk to people in this European umbrella organization to get all the necessary EU information and comments. Then you can get back to your national organization/company with questions about specific national issues.

...and vice versa

Sometimes you read that, say, a Polish or Italian organization thinks so and so about an EU proposal, but you are not really familiar with the organization and therefore it is difficult to assess the value of what they are saying. In order to get a better idea, look up the equivalent counterpart in your own country.

Start by finding out if the organization is a member of a European umbrella association. It will often be mentioned on its website. Otherwise, just google the name of the organization together with 'European federation' or 'Brussels office'.

Once you find the umbrella organization, you can see what organizations from your country are members. This way, you can better assess whether it is a serious organization or not, and can more easily understand the interests it represents.

Also remember that your readers probably do not know the European organizations that are your sources. Therefore, compare to something that they know. For example, for French readers, 'BusinessEurope, of which Medef is a member, was satisfied after the vote'.

Beware of lobbies that sound like EU institutions

Often the EU institutions, think tanks, organizations and corporate lobbyists use the same word(s) in their names. At a quick glance, it may be difficult to distinguish them. For example, the European Investment Group is a lobby group, while the European Investment Bank is an EU institution. Eurochild is an advocacy group; Eurofound an EU agency.

If you write about a lobbying organization or think tank called something that begins with 'EU', 'euro' or 'European', you should probably explain that it is a lobbying organization or a think tank. Otherwise the reader might think it is an EU institution.

The French newspaper *Le Figaro* wrote an article that Visa Europe might be sold to US Visa Inc.[5] In the article, a person from the Fédération Bancaire Européenne/European Banking Federation is quoted several times, without the reporter explaining that this is a trade organization for European banks. Many readers might think that this is the EU taking certain positions, while in fact it is a special interest, represented by a lobbying organization.

Links

The EU lobby register
www.europa.eu/transparency-register

Stakeholder
www.stakeholder.eu

Notes

1 Alter-EU, *Rescue the Register – How to make EU lobby transparency credible and reliable*, June 2013
2 Transparency International EU, *7000 and counting – Lobby meetings of the European Commission*, 1 December 2015
3 Transparency International EU, *7000 and counting*
4 *EUobserver*, Irish cheerleaders mistake lobby register for grant application, 19 February 2009
5 *Le Figaro*, Les banques européennes pourraient vendre Visa Europe, 21 March 2013

14 Think tanks and research

Think tanks are research organizations that have a specific goal or ideology – a mix of academic and advocacy work. Some European countries, especially the UK and Germany, have a strong tradition of think tanks. For other countries, like France, it is a fairly new thing.

In Brussels, there are plenty of think tanks. Since it is difficult to draw a clear line between a think tank and an interest group, there are no exact figures, but the EU institutions' lobby register has more than 700 registered entities under the heading 'think tanks, research and academic institutions'.

Think tanks are very useful for journalists. They publish reports and organize debates that will provide ideas for articles, background information on a topic and an overview of who to talk to about a particular issue.

The researchers involved in the EU think tanks tend to be extremely knowledgeable and are easy enough to interview. Often they have previously worked in EU institutions and can explain complex EU issues in an understandable way. Phone numbers and emails are on the think-tank websites. The British and American media in particular often use think-tank researchers as expert sources.

All think tanks have a more or less declared ideology, which to some extent determines what they choose to research. Some think tanks are financed by companies, others by the EU institutions themselves. When you use their research or interview their experts, you should be aware of this. Check the EU lobby register, in which think tanks declare where their funding comes from.

Ideology in the EU contexts is not only about left and right, but also 'more or less EU'. A pro-EU think tank, funded by the EU institutions, will probably, in its research, show there is a need for more 'European solutions'. A Eurosceptic think tank, funded by business, might tend to show how EU rules are a burden on member states' companies. If your topic has a clear for- or against-the-EU dimension, you should mention where the think tank stands.

Think tank or interest group?

The border between think tanks and interest groups is blurry. Lobby-critical network Alter-EU highlighted this fuzzy border by citing a debate about investment in growth and health in Africa, which was organized by the think tank

Friends of Europe. The participants included the European commissioner for development and several MEPs. The event was sponsored by the French oil company Total and two people from the company were also on the panel. A company can, by giving money to a think tank, buy access to EU decision-makers, and probably influence the questions that are raised in the debate.[1]

The Centre for European Policy Studies, CEPS, organized the European Gas Policy Forum 2012, which Exxon and Chevron sponsored with 10,000 euros. Their sponsorship bought them a seat at a pre-conference dinner attended by EU policymakers on the topic of shale gas development.[2]

There are interest groups that call themselves think tanks because that sounds more neutral and scientific. And there are some think tanks that are governed by ideology to the point that they sometimes tip over and act as an interest group. A think tank that sometimes crosses that border and becomes a campaign organization is British organization Open Europe, which advocates looser EU cooperation. Open Europe's research has a huge impact on European (mainly British, but also other EU countries') media, thanks to a daily press summary in which current EU issues are analyzed under provocative headlines, and which arrives in the mail boxes of most Brussels correspondents.

The think tank label leads journalists to report findings without asking the critical questions they would ask a campaign organization. Open Europe is often just described as a 'think tank' or 'liberal think tank', and more rarely 'Eurosceptic think tank' or 'campaign organization'.

Some of the main EU think tanks

Bruegel

www.bruegel.org
Economic think tank, highly respected for its economic expertise. Bruegel's main research areas are European macro economy, international finance, financial regulation, innovation and growth. During the euro crisis, Bruegel experts often commented on and interpreted the outcomes of Eurogroup meetings or EU summits.

The think tank is funded by contributions from countries, companies and international organizations. It has very close ties to the EU institutions. A small hint is that the current (2016) chairman of Bruegel's board is Jean-Claude Trichet, who was European Central Bank chairman between 2003 and 2011. Mario Monti, the ex-commissioner who led a technocratic government in Italy during the turmoil of the euro crisis, is a former chairman.

Carnegie Europe

www.carnegieeurope.eu
The global think tank Carnegie Endowment for International Peace has offices in Washington, Moscow, Beijing, Beirut and Brussels. The organization was

founded a century ago and fights for international cooperation and disarmament. It is not affiliated with any political party.

If you want to find experts on EU foreign policy and EU relations with its neighbours, this is the right place. Contact Carnegie to talk about the EU's response to the Arab Spring, ask about the EU membership negotiations with Turkey or explore the EU's relationship with China.

Carnegie's Brussels office analyzes EU policy from an international perspective: it compares the EU with other international giants, such as the US, China and Russia, rather than carrying out analysis of the EU's internal conflicts and the differences between EU countries.

Centre for European Policy Studies

www.ceps.eu
CEPS was founded in 1983 in Brussels and is one of the oldest and most influential EU think tanks. It is politically independent, but is generally business friendly. Industrial interests are often represented in debates and seminars.

CEPS has some thirty researchers from across the EU. Together they cover most EU policies: economy and welfare, financial markets, regulation, energy, climate change, legal and home affairs, agriculture, EU foreign policy and institutional issues.

The funding comes from the EU institutions and from EU countries' governments that buy research from the think tank, from membership fees and from an annual grant from the European Commission. Former ministers, commissioners and business people are on the board of directors.

Centre for European Reform

www.cer.org.uk
A British think tank/campaign organization that is, in its own words, 'pro-European but not uncritical', and run by Charles Grant, a former Brussels correspondent for *The Economist*.

CER wants a more efficient and international EU. CER is independent from party politics and is funded by private-sector donations. The think tank is much respected and often quoted in the British broadsheets.

European Council on Foreign Relations

www.ecfr.eu
ECFR claims to be the first pan-European think tank: it has offices in Berlin, London, Madrid, Paris, Rome, Sofia and Warsaw. ECFR doesn't have an editorial line; all the opinions in articles and blog posts are those of their respective writers.

Like Carnegie Europe, ECR focuses on foreign policy. ECFR has three major research fields: Europe, China and the Middle East. Their experts are often quoted in European and American media. An example of this is when ECFR's China expert makes an educated guess about how China will respond to EU anti-dumping duties on solar panels.

The European Centre for International Political Economy

www.ecipe.org
Ecipe is a small think tank that focuses on trade policy and international economy. Talk to their experts about the EU's free trade agreements, customs policy and foreign aid.

Open Europe

www.openeurope.org.uk
Market liberal, Eurosceptic think tank/campaign organization, with offices in Brussels and London.

European Policy Centre

www.epc.eu
Broad EU think tank that explicitly advocates more EU integration. EPC experts are very knowledgeable and frequently interviewed by European media.

Friends of Europe

www.friendsofeurope.org
EU think tank that carries out research on most aspects on the EU agenda: everything from the internal energy market to the EU–China relationship and youth unemployment in Europe.

Notre Europe

www.institutdelors.eu
Explicitly pro-European think tank, founded by former commission president Jacques Delors. It does research on most EU policies, but distinguishes itself from other think tanks by also studying sociological questions, such as ideas of European citizenship and European identity.

Fondation Robert Schuman

www.robert-schuman.eu
The other main French think tank. Notre Europe is left-leaning; Fondation Robert Schuman is right-leaning. Pro-European think tank with offices in Paris and Brussels.

German Marshall Fund of the United States

www.gmfus.org

Transatlantic think tank with dozens of experts in Brussels and many more in Washington. Knowledgeable on trade issues and foreign and security policy.

Notes

1 Alter-EU, *Bursting the Brussels Bubble*, 2010
2 Weis, Laura, *'Foot on the gas' – Lobbyists push for unregulated shale gas in Europe*, Corporate Europe Observatory, 2012

15 Media

Other media is of course a major information source for journalists. When it comes to EU politics, you need to read some of the other countries' media too. The EU stories that become news vary a great deal from country to country, and in most EU countries there is just not enough EU reporting to cover all the major stories.

EU media

Now and then there are ambitious attempts to create a European newspaper or magazine to convey news without looking through a national lens. All such projects have failed. The most famous example was the weekly magazine *l'Européen/The European*, which was launched in 1990 and died a quiet death eight years later.

The magazine aimed to show the differences between European countries without falling into stereotypical descriptions. It took a clear 'European' position and wanted be a counterweight to narrow national interests. It was perhaps a miscalculation of what the readers wanted. Very few people have the European identity that *The European* expected of its readers.

The problem with pan-European media is that although it can be objective in the sense that it does not take a stand on a particular issue or for a political party, its very existence incarnates European cooperation, which in many EU countries is a party political position. A 'European perspective' is an elusive concept. It is difficult – and perhaps even undesirable – to go beyond the national angles.

It is also very expensive to produce European news. One solution is to have editorial offices in different countries and translate the texts/features. The EU-funded satellite TV channel Euronews is such a medium. The channel, which has its headquarters in Lyon, France, broadcasts daily in 13 different languages.

In Brussels, there are a few media outlets that specifically focus on the EU and mainly cater to the Brussels bubble – politicians, officials, lobbyists and journalists. They cover the political game but almost never illustrate how these policies affect normal people in the EU countries, for obvious reasons: their journalists are based in Brussels.

There are some online magazines that deliver fast and mostly free EU news: *Politico Europe*, *EUobserver* and *Euractiv*. They dig up their own stories and sometimes carry out relatively ambitious investigations into the EU institutions.

The EU news agency Agence Europe has been around since the 1950s and has a good reputation and excellent sources inside the EU institutions. The other main EU news agency, Europolitique/Europolitics, founded in the 1970s, closed down in 2015.

There are a few highly specialized EU media outlets: MLex covers competition, regulatory and antitrust news, ENDS covers environmental news with a regulatory focus and Agra Europe covers the Common Agriculture Policy. They are of very high quality but written for specialists and are behind pay-walls.

National media that write about the EU

EU news has always struggled to find a place in the national media. In part, this is probably because of the traditional structure of newspapers: should news from Brussels be on the domestic, political, economic or foreign pages? EU decisions are taken outside the country's borders but the EU laws are just as much national laws as if they were passed in the national parliament.

This is the case in all EU countries. And it does not really seem to change over time. Even media in countries that have been part of European cooperation from the beginning in the 1950s have a hard time knowing what to do with EU stories. The EU simply does not pop up on the editorial radar. The editor is not interested because the public is not interested, and limited and shallow reporting contributes to the lack of interest.

A few English-language mass media outlets reach beyond national borders and write about the EU without a national angle: *Financial Times*, *The Economist*, *The New York Times* and the *International Herald Tribune*. But they are elite newspapers that cater to a small clique of well-educated people.

Most national newspapers and trade magazines however choose to take a national angle on EU news. Therefore, other countries' media are great sources of ideas – just do the same story for your country. The best way to find ideas is simply to read other countries' media, follow other countries' EU debates and share ideas with colleagues from other European countries.

If you do not speak languages other than English, you can access other EU countries' national media through *Voxeurop* or *Eurotopics*, which take a selection of European articles and translate them into major EU languages. Also, more and more national media now translate into English articles that they think will be of interest to an international audience.

The specificities of the UK media

The UK media is different from the other European national media when it comes to covering the EU. You need to be aware of this if you ever re-write stories from British media, which many journalists do because English is the foreign language that they know.

If you look at what is going on in EU politics from only one country's perspective, it always leads to a distorted picture. But if you look at the EU only through a British lens, it will be more skewed than if you were to try to understand the EU by solely reading Polish, French or Spanish media, because in the EU context the UK government and UK public opinion is further from the centre than government and public opinion in other EU countries.

Some UK newspapers are, in addition, committed opponents of the EU to the extent that they actually fabricate news, not very different from April Fools' articles. The European Commission's London office has set up a 'Euromyths' page on its website, to rebut some of the made-up stories. What these made-up stories have in common is that they are hardly ever written by a Brussels-based reporter. If you re-write an EU story from a British newspaper, check where the journalist is based. That is the easiest way to avoid the worst urban legends about the EU.

British Brussels correspondents tend to be more critical of the EU than their colleagues from other EU countries. They often ask the toughest questions at press conferences and their news angles often deal with wasteful EU bureaucrats and British small business being weighed down by the burden of EU regulatory zeal. But the facts are accurate. Much of the best EU investigative journalism has been done by British journalists. The British media landscape offers not only the worst EU reporting but also the best. Once the UK has left the EU, the number of British EU correspondents will probably decline in Brussels and with that a big chunk of the best EU reporting will disappear, which affects all other EU countries' media as well.

The Brussels press corps

There are around one thousand Brussels-based journalists who are accredited to the EU institutions. Between 2003 and 2013, the total number was more or less constant, somewhere between nine hundred and a little more than a thousand, according to the European Commission's accreditation bureau.[1] EU journalist Gareth Harding, who obtained up-to-date statistics from an EU source, puts the number at 955 in October 2015.[2]

The UK, Italy, France, Germany and Spain have the biggest media presence in Brussels. In 2013, there were between 30 and 50 media outlets from these countries with accredited journalists. The Baltic states have the fewest correspondents. There are only one or two media organizations with accredited EU journalists from Estonia, Latvia, Lithuania and Malta (see interview with Ina Strazdina).[3]

Many Brussels veterans say that the EU press corps is shrinking. With the press crisis, many traditional newspapers no longer have a full-time correspondent in Brussels. This impression of a shrinking press corps is not supported by the commission statistics. However, the commission's numbers are inflated by the fact that some journalists based in their capitals have an accreditation. There has also been a sharp rise in the number of freelance journalists among the accredited journalists. Ten years ago, there were only 11 freelance reporters, in 2012 there were 64 and in 2016 there were 159.[4]

To some extent the scaling back of traditional media in Brussels is compensated for by the EU institutions becoming better at posting information online, which makes it possible to cover some aspects of EU politics from home. This is also becoming an argument for editors to save the cost of sending correspondents to Brussels. EbS and EP TV transmit most major press conferences and meetings, and background information is available online.

The fact that so much information is made available online has a downside. The institutions invest more in re-packaging information into 'news', rather than making raw information accessible and making people available to answer journalists' questions. And the balance of power has shifted. Today there are probably more people who work with communication in the EU institutions than there are independent journalists who investigate the EU institutions.

Interview: Ina Strazdina, correspondent for Latvia's Public Radio

I came here in 2006 to open the Latvian Public Radio's Brussels office. At the time, we were four Latvian correspondents: myself and my colleagues from the public service TV, the largest newspaper and the second largest newspaper. We helped each other. This was how it was until 2009, when the [financial] crisis came. The Latvian government slashed the budget, including for state media. First the newspapers brought back their correspondents. Then my colleague from TV left. I was the last one.

I made an offer to my boss that I would stay here on half my salary if they would let me freelance at the same time. First and foremost, it was personal. I liked my job here so much that I didn't want to give it up. And then I thought that it would be crazy to close the office and destroy everything that we had built up. At this time, Latvia was asking the EU for emergency loans and the decisions were taken here in Brussels. How could you as a journalist leave then?

For a year I worked for television, radio and the second largest newspaper, for a total of around 1,200 euros a month. It was a crazy year. I could hardly pay the rent. I had savings that I used to pay for the office.

People started hearing about my situation here. I won a prize: European of the Year. After a while, the radio started paying me more again. But I was still the only Latvian journalist in Brussels. I kept all three clients. I earned around 2,000 euros a month and the radio paid for my apartment and telephone. An ordinary working day started at six-thirty and ended around nine. I worked at least 12 hours a day. My calendar was so booked that I didn't have any time to take French lessons.

I was so responsible that it bordered on paranoia. I thought hard before I went to a party. But we journalists have a professional intuition that helps us to not make mistakes. So far I have not made any big mistakes.

> The attitude from my country has been great. I feel they respect me. The prime minister always came out after a summit to give me a statement. Before the summits, the ambassador has a briefing. It was only me there.
>
> Now, since the Latvian [council] presidency in 2015, we are three Latvian journalists in Brussels, one for public television and two for public radio. I now work for the radio and for the daily newspaper Latvijas Avize. I cannot compare the life before and now. It is much, much better.
>
> The interest in the EU is moderate in Latvia. Specific groups, such as farmers, are very interested because there is so much legislation that affects them, that comes from here. We are still in the process of building our EU membership. There are still many questions to answer. Now we have joined the euro, I have no problem convincing my editors to take in EU news.

EU and European media

Politico Europe

www.politico.eu

English-language *Politico Europe* started in 2015 and promised to completely change how the EU is reported. It builds on the US-based *Politico*, which was founded in 2007. *Politico Europe* is a joint venture between Politico and German publisher Axel Springer, and incorporates some of the editorial staff from the newspaper *European Voice*, which it bought and closed down. It has by far the biggest press corps in Brussels, with around fifty staffers.

At least in tone, *Politico* is something different from other EU reporting. It has an American matter-of-fact tone and is less polite to and respectful of EU hierarchies and received ideas. When *Politico* listed 'the 28 people who shape European politics', controversial Hungarian PM Viktor Orbán was for example included, but not Angela Merkel, which sparked some outrage. It mixes the serious with the nerdy, gossipy and fun, such as quizzes on 'Who said it? Star Wars or the European Union?'

Politico has a free online edition and a pay version, called *Politico Pro*, which provides specialized reporting in some policy fields. There is also a weekly paper edition, which can be picked up for free in some hotels and cafés around Brussels, London, Berlin and Paris. Check the Politico Europe website for information on where to find a copy.

The *Politico* daily newsletter 'Brussels Playbook' is a must for EU connoisseurs. Journalist and former commission official Ryan Heath mixes high and low in his insider's account of the Brussels bubble. The podcast 'In the loop', which comes out in several language editions, has the same mix of gossip and facts.

Agence Europe

www.agenceurope.com

European news agency mainly known for its daily newsletter on EU and European affairs: *Europe Daily Bulletin*. The articles are written in French and translated into English, German and Italian. The journalists are also predominantly French.

The news agency sometimes lacks the necessary critical distance from the EU institutions. Nevertheless, with its group of knowledgeable reporters, it is one of the primary sources of information for many who work in the EU system.

The online version costs about 1,500 euros per year.

EUobserver

www.euobserver.com
English-language online newspaper, which often breaks stories and is read by most EU people in Brussels. It has a small group of reporters who both cover the big events and dig up their own stories. But with only a handful of articles a day, the coverage is far from comprehensive.

Most content is free but exclusive interviews and big investigations are behind a pay wall. Subscription costs 150 euros a year.

Euractiv

www.euractiv.com
News-wise, *Euractiv* is second to *EUobserver*, with coverage that is close to the EU institutions' own press material. The line between editorial material and opinion articles written by interest groups is not always clear.

But to find background information and to get an overview of a topic, *Euractiv* is fantastic. The site has a great system with links to past articles and official documents, and for every topic it lists the key positions of politicians, campaign groups, business federations and other interested parties. It is the best place to look if you are in a hurry and need to find material for a fact box to go with your article. *Euractiv* is also quick to post leaked documents to its website.

Financial Times

www.ft.com
The only European national mainstream newspaper that regularly puts EU news on its front page. All decision-makers in Brussels read the *FT* with their breakfast coffee and it is also through the *FT* that most prefer to leak stories.

In a report by consultancy firm Dober Partners, 80 EU correspondents replied to the survey question: Which are the most important media sources about the EU for you? *Financial Times* came first with 18 per cent, followed by *EUobserver*, *Euractiv*, *Politico* and Twitter.[5]

FT's daily *Brussels Briefing*, written by its Brussels correspondents, is a free newsletter and is indispensable for keeping up with the twists and turns of EU politics. Even if you do not agree with the analysis, you can usually rely on the information.

Arte

www.arte.tv/sites/en
The German–French culture TV channel was created in 1992. It is co-founded and co-financed by the EU and has its headquarters in Strasbourg. It shows the same programmes in French and German, but some programmes are also subtitled in English, Spanish and Polish. You can feel that there is EU money involved because of the lack of sharp or funny angles, and because of the slightly diplomatic and educational tone. Some of the documentaries put one in mind of the material social studies teachers use in class.

Nevertheless, most content is high quality, and their news shows and debate programmes in particular are interesting. The perspective is different from what we are used to – European, not national – even if most of the topics are the same as in national news shows.

Voxeurop

www.voxeurop.eu
With the motto 'the best of the European press', the Paris-based news site every day publishes a selection of articles from a few hundred international newspapers, translated into nine languages (English, French, Spanish, Romanian, Italian, Dutch, Portuguese, Polish and Czech).

Voxeurop is more about Europe than the EU. It is a good place to get an overview of how the big stories, the refugee crisis for example, are viewed across Europe.

Eurotopics

www.eurotopics.net
Editorials and opinion pieces from about one hundred media from across Europe. Read it online or get it as an email newsletter, in English, German and French. Like *Voxeurop*, it is a good place to get an overview of the national conversations about major EU issues.

The institution behind the project *Eurotopics* is the German government body Bundeszentrale für politische Bildung (Federal Agency for Civic Education).

Debating Europe

www.debatingeurope.eu
An online European debate platform, run by the think tank Friends of Europe. It collects readers' ideas for discussions, questions and comments, brings them to European leaders and then publishes their responses on the website. Between its launch in 2011 and 2016, some 75,000 comments were sent in and more than 1,800 politicians and experts (including more than 180 MEPs) were interviewed.

The site is one of the few places where EU politicians and normal people actually meet and talk. Browse by theme or by participating politician.

Berlaymonster

www.berlaymonster.blogspot.be
Funny and clever EU satire with fake news à la *The Onion*. Also good on Twitter.

Politikportal.eu

Daily summaries of EU news from German-speaking media.

The Economist

www.economist.com/blogs/charlemagne
The Economist's Brussels chronicle Charlemagne usually offers a new angle on the week's major EU story.

Coulisses de Bruxelles

www.bruxelles.blogs.liberation.fr
Only in French. Jean Quatremer, correspondent for the French leftist newspaper *Libération*, is one of the best EU reporters, with a critical eye and amazing sources. His blog is widely read in the Brussels bubble.

Twitter

Much of the EU debate has moved to Twitter. The top-three Brussels-based journalists on Twitter are Jean Quatremer for *Libération*, Ryan Heath from *Politico* and Bruno Waterfield from *The Times*. They have in common that they know a great deal about EU politics and engage in discussions with readers and with EU folks alike.

Most EU politicians – nearly all commissioners and MEPs – have Twitter accounts. Check out the **European Parliament's and the European Commission's public lists** of their MEPs/commissioners on Twitter. The commission also has other public lists of interest if you want to put together a good group of EU people to follow: journalists and bloggers, EU staff, commission spokespersons …

The problem with EU politicians on Twitter is that many of them do not write on their own account and do not interact. For the politicians that do, however, Twitter is a good way of getting in touch with them directly.

Links

European Parliament's public list of their MEPs on Twitter
twitter.com/Europarl_EN/lists/all-meps-on-twitter

European Commission's public list of the commissioners on Twitter
twitter.com/EU_Commission/lists/juncker-commission

Notes

1 European Commission, Journalist and media summaries, no provisional – gender and nationality, 10 May 2016
2 Harding, Gareth, Everything you wanted to know about the Brussels Press Corps but were afraid to ask [blogpost], www.cleareurope.eu, 23 May 2016
3 European Commission, Journalist and media summaries
4 Harding, Gareth, Everything you wanted to know
5 Dober Partners, *EU Media relations report – Brussels Journalists Survey & what the findings reveal for Communicators*, 2016

Part V
Practical EU Reporting

16 Bringing the EU home

How will EU proposals affect people in my country or region?
How can I find countrymen working in the EU institutions?
What is the local angle on an EU event? How did my government vote? What EU stories are there other than big politics?

Making the connection between Brussels and home

Distance is of course a major factor for newsworthiness. The principle is: the closer to the reader, the more newsworthy the event. But is the EU far away or near? The decisions are taken outside the country's borders, but often they affect us just as much as if they were taken inside the country.

Most EU policies are domestic affairs, not foreign affairs. If we were to treat EU politics as domestic affairs – which I believe we should – it would require us to examine political proposals while there is still time to influence them, and not to write about the decisions only when they 'come home'. It would also require us to link EU decisions to our readers' lives and to hold our national politicians, who take decisions at EU level, accountable.

Write about an issue when the decision is taken, not when it 'comes home'

In May 2013, the European Court of Justice ruled that Sweden should pay a three million euro fine for failing to implement the data retention directive on time. The EU law, which was conceived in the aftermath of the terrorist attacks in Madrid in 2004 and London in 2005, required telephone and internet operators to store information about their clients' internet and telephone traffic for at least six months and for a maximum of two years, and to hand it to law enforcement and counter-terrorism agencies on request. The stored information covered time, place and recipients of all phone and email communications but not the actual content of those emails and calls. The directive was controversial in many EU countries, including Sweden.

The deadline for transposing the directive into national law was 2007. The EU court ruled against Sweden for non-implementation in 2010. A year later, Sweden had still not implemented the directive and the European Commission again took Sweden to court. This time, the court ordered the three million euro fine. (Eventually, the EU court invalidated the data retention directive, in April 2014, on the grounds that it violated fundamental rights. This was in no way because of Swedish resistance; it was the Irish High Court and the Austrian Verfassungsgerichtshof that had asked the EU court to examine the validity of the directive.)[1]

The delay in Sweden was due to a fierce political debate in the Swedish parliament at the time the laws needed to implement the directive were to be adopted. Several political parties argued that the directive violated human rights and freedoms. In 2012, the directive was eventually approved by parliament, five years late. The same year, several demonstrations against the data retention directive were held in Sweden – six years after it was first adopted in Brussels. The final decision on the directive was taken in December 2005 in the European Parliament, and in February 2006 in the Council of Ministers.

Searching for 'the data retention directive' in the largest Swedish article database, Mediearkivet, you get more than three hundred hits for the years 2010, 2011 and 2012, when the heated political debate was going on in Sweden. At that point, the decision to adopt the directive had already been taken and *could not be changed* by the Swedish parliament, which only had to vote on the formal incorporation of the directive into Swedish law, not on substance. Before February 2006, when the final decision was taken, there is only one article about the data retention directive in the Swedish media archive – an opinion piece written by a PhD student.

This is just one example of the failure of media to pick up the big EU stories in time. There are many more examples. In every EU country, there are laws that cause national debate only when they come home from Brussels – laws that no one talked about when the decisions were actually on the table.

To explain early what impact EU proposals and EU decisions will have once they come home is one of the most important tasks of EU reporting. But then you need to be able to figure out the connection between a proposal presented at a press conference in Brussels and the reality at home, which is not always easy.

How will an EU law affect my country?

The most obvious choice of persons to contact when you, as a reporter, want to establish the consequences of an EU decision in a specific EU country – your own – are the many national civil servants who work on EU matters in national government ministries and agencies and in the permanent representation in Brussels. These civil servants are best placed to answer the question 'How will this EU decision affect my country or local/regional community?' Either call the appropriate government department or agency in your capital, or your country's permanent representation in Brussels.

These civil servants are involved from the very start until the very end of the legislative process. They are consulted early on when the European Commission is preparing EU legislation, and they always know what proposals are in the pipeline.

Bringing the EU home 215

They participate in the negotiations in the Council of Ministers' working groups. Once a law has been adopted at EU level and subsequently becomes national law, they are often the ones who must implement that law.

What about the local level?

Are there any important companies or economic sectors in your town or region? You can contact the trade association that represents them in Brussels (see chapter 13) and ask about the most important current issues for their member organizations.

As explained earlier, the European regions are also very active in lobbying the EU institutions. Your region is probably present in Brussels. The people who work in the regional offices spend their days making the connection between the EU level and the local or regional level. They might not know all the specifics about the ongoing legislative process, but they can often provide concrete examples of how EU laws affect the local and regional levels, or at least hint at who knows more.

The Committee of the Regions (see chapter 11) in Brussels might be a good source. As a mere consultative body in the EU legislative process, the Committee of the Regions is not very important, because its opinions have no real legal weight. But the job of the regional representatives in the committee is to look at proposed EU laws from a regional point of view. Maybe someone from your municipality or region in your national delegation can explain what the consequences of an EU draft law might be for your region.

Your countrymen in the institutions as sources

Apart from your countries' political representatives in the EU institutions, many people from your country work directly for the EU, as civil servants in the different EU institutions. All in all, there are some 47,000 people. About 30,000 (or 20,000 if you exclude interpreters and translators) are employed by the European Commission. There are for example around 2,300 Spaniards and 1,400 Poles in the commission.[2] If you are a journalist from Spain or Poland, it is a good idea to try to find some of these people.

Even if they do not represent your country, they will interpret EU actions through their national lens, just like you. They will be better sources than EU officials from other countries because they intuitively know what information you need and can give examples that your readers understand. Because they know the media that you are working for, or can get an idea of who you are by a quick google search, they will probably be more easily convinced that you will respect their anonymity (see the off-the-record rules in chapter 4) and will talk freely to you.

If you are from a small country, you might think that your countrymen in the big EU institutions are few and far between. But officials from any country tend to be over-represented in policy areas that traditionally interest that specific country. In EU foreign affairs, there will be more Finns and people from the Baltic states who are experts in the former Soviet bloc, and more Spaniards and Portuguese with an expertise in Latin America, for example.

So how would you find these people? Ask around. Everyone who works in EU affairs – politicians, civil servants, lobbyists or journalists – has an interest in finding people in the Brussels bubble according to nationality, so you can be sure that there are many such lists and compilations. An academic told me that when he started in Brussels as a PhD student, before the internet, it only took a week before he received a phone call from someone from his home region's lobby office in Brussels.

Your national government and its permanent representation in Brussels have probably compiled unofficial lists of 'their' people employed by the EU. The Swedish permanent representation for example has a 'Sweden list' with names and contact details of all Swedes that they know who work in the various EU institutions. The perm rep does not advertise this list openly, but if you know that it exists and ask for it, they reluctantly hand it over, because they are legally obliged to. Most other EU countries with a narrower definition of what constitutes a public document will probably not hand out their lists, but you can be sure that they have something similar.

Articles based on interviews with your EU countrymen

Interviewing your countrymen who work for the EU institutions is not only a shortcut to finding good information, and to help understand what impact 'the EU' will have on your country. It can also be a way to give the EU a name and a face. Therefore, most people from your country in the EU apparatus are potentially interesting interviewees.

An interview with a countryman or woman in the ranks of the EU institutions in Brussels is an easy story to do and an easy story to sell if you are a freelancer, especially to the local paper from the region or city where the person in question comes from. You can interview your country's EU ambassador, a high-ranking commission official or anyone else with a top position in the EU capital. 'The most powerful Latvian in the EU' or 'He's lobbying for Italian businesses in Brussels' are typical headlines in big newspapers and specialist magazines.

People who work in the EU institutions are often reluctant to talk about politics, and will prefer to refer you to the designated spokesperson. But they are more willing to talk about their work on a general level and the twists and turns of life that brought them to Brussels.

Ask the man on the street about EU decisions

One morning when I was working as a political reporter for a regional newspaper, my editor handed over a press release and told me to 'do something' with it. The then minister for gender equality had proposed a government inquiry into whether a scrapped income ceiling on parental insurance would make more men take paternity leave.

A photographer and I went to a café where I had often seen men on paternity leave hang out with their babies. The text I wrote was rather dry, about how the different parties in a centre-right government coalition disagreed over parental leave. But next to the piece there was a local survey and photos of five smiling dads, which drew the reader's attention to the newspaper page and ultimately to the drier, political text.

This is an example of simple interplay between a political decision taken in the capital and the local people who will be affected by that decision. We do this all the time when we write about local, regional and national decisions. But we tend to stop at the border.

When the European Commission presents a green paper or white paper, or an actual legislative proposal, we almost never go out onto the street to ask people what they think about it. Most of the time, Brussels correspondents write about the proposal but would not go out onto the streets of Brussels – why would their home readers care what Belgians think anyway? Probably this is also because Brussels correspondents are more interested in, and focused on, the political games played inside the Brussels apparatus, and less on the impact of EU laws on society. EU news is rarely illustrated using real people, something which enhances the feeling of the EU being a bureaucracy far from ordinary people.

But for a local or regional reporter, who is not in the capital and cannot interview the political players there in person, it should not matter if political decisions are taken in Brussels or in their own country's capital. It is just as easy to go out into Perpignan, for example, and ask people what they think about a proposal from Brussels as it is to ask them what they think of a proposal from Paris.

In a perfect world, EU political reporters would cooperate more with their colleagues at home by teaming up and reporting together: one on the political game in Brussels, while the other finds relevant material back home. But the direction the media business is taking means that fewer journalists must do more on their own. Instead, local, regional, national and specialist journalists could learn to follow the EU more, and Brussels-based journalists could make phone calls to affected people, organizations and companies back home, in order to make a bigger effort to bring EU news home.

Holding your politicians accountable

EU institutions and national political institutions are intertwined; they are not separate, not two different things. The idea that there exists an 'EU' outside the control and influence of our national governments is false. This false idea is strengthened by headlines like 'the EU has decided to …' and every time we let national politicians get away with talking about 'the EU' instead of 'us' or 'we'.

How did they vote?

As you have seen in chapter 8, there are some EU laws that are adopted without the European Parliament having a say on the matter. But there is *no* new EU legislation in which the Council of Ministers is not involved. No EU law is adopted without your and my governments having a seat at the table. They might not have loved every single detail in every decision, but they have had all the information every step of the way and have on almost all occasions endorsed the compromise agreement that came out of those long negotiations.

Our national officials and ministers in the council represent our governments, which have been elected and can be replaced at the next election if people are not happy. It is important that we investigate and expose how our government acts at the EU level. The same thing goes for our national MEPs; they can be replaced at the next EU election.

Whenever you write about an unpopular EU decision, check who from your country was there when the decision was taken. How did your government vote? How did your country's MEPs vote?

There is no mystery here: call the press people in the Council of Ministers and the European Parliament who cover the topic. Ask them when the final decision was taken and ask them to help you find the vote record, or check it yourself via Votewatch or the respective institution's website (see chapters 5 and 6). Then call your countrymen who took the decision and let them explain why they voted the way they did.

Do not become a spokesperson for your government

We would never publish a statement from our government as objective fact without checking. We would probably talk to opposition parties and report both the government's and the opposition's arguments. But when our national government talks about decisions taken in Brussels, often we seem to automatically file it as diplomacy and not politics. Our government becomes synonymous with our country, and we become less critical towards it and allow it to explain events as if it were a neutral party.

Since all Council of Ministers meetings take place behind closed doors, there is no way you as a reporter can check for yourself what was really said between the ministers. The only way to get close to the truth is to compare many versions, and for that you need to have sources in other EU countries. Talk to the other EU governments or permanent representations directly, and compare your stories with those by journalists from other countries. The absolute minimum is to check your government's version of events with the council press office.

The EU vs your country

Also, try to make it a bit harder for your national politicians when they declare that 'the EU' should not get involved in this or that national affair, which is essentially saying that the commonly decided rules should apply to everyone but us. Swedish politicians, for example, can at the same time hold the opinions that 'the EU' should not tell us to stop hunting wolves, while it is outrageous that Malta does not follow EU rules when allowing hunters to shoot migratory birds passing the island on their way north.[3]

Whenever a national politician says that the EU should stay out of our business, pressure them to take some ownership of the EU law in question. Refuse the false dichotomy of the EU/your country. Start by checking who it was from your country who participated in making that law in the first place. Was the current government involved? If not, was the current government – then in opposition – also critical when the law was formulated? Who from your country is to blame if EU rules that go against the national interest have been put in place? Who did not do their job at the time?

Secondly, ask politicians some follow-up questions: is the EU law bad in itself? In that case, how is the government trying to change it? Is the government lobbying the European Commission and is it building alliances with the other EU countries to change the law? Or, if the law is good in principle, why does the politician think that it should only apply to everyone else?

The EU budget and your country

The EU budget mainly comes from direct payments from the member countries; this accounts for 70 per cent. The rest comes from customs duties on goods from outside the union and a small EU share (0.3 per cent) of the VAT that every EU country collects.

All EU countries pay into the EU budget according to the size of their economies. In 2014, the EU fee was 0.7 per cent of the countries' Gross Net Income, GNI. That means: the richer the country, the bigger the EU fee. Relatively rich EU countries are net contributors – they pay more money into the EU budget than they get back from different EU funds – and relatively poor EU countries are net recipients.

Some EU countries have negotiated (quite complicated) rebates, arguing that their net contribution is too high. The biggest rebate is the British one, from 1984, which is permanent. Since then, the UK gets 66 per cent of its net contribution back. The cost of the British rebate is carried by the other EU countries, although Germany, the Netherlands, Austria and Sweden have a 'rebate on the rebate', which is also permanent. On top of that, there are other, temporary rebates, which need to be renegotiated in the next budget period.

When it comes to writing about the EU budget, national media tend to be uncritical of their national governments and often calculate the country's contribution to the EU budget in a way that proves that it pays too much, by looking at a country's contributions to or benefits from a specific part of the EU budget instead of the whole budget.

For example, *Le Monde* makes a point in showing that France is the country that pays the biggest share of the British rebate. That is really a pointless statement; only the total net contribution is important, which, to be fair, is also mentioned in the article.[4] British media, on the other hand, often point out that France is the biggest recipient of EU agriculture subsidies (because it is the EU's biggest agriculture producer).

Media in big EU countries, such as the UK and France, prefer to talk about *total* rather than *relative* net contribution to the EU budget. But if you are making an argument about whether a country's contribution is fair or not, compared to the other EU countries, you of course need to take into account the size of the countries' economies, i.e. how much the country pays to the EU minus how much it gets back from the EU (adjusted for the rebates) and divided by the country's GNI. Find that information on the **European Commission's budget website**.

Approach stories from alternative angles

When journalists cover EU summits, the given angle is a national angle. EU negotiations are seen as a zero-sum game, in which some countries win and others lose. A typical newspaper headline is that this or that country 'won'. The country-versus-country aspect is always present in EU politics, but it is not the only angle and not always the most interesting.

We should not forget other divisions, of political ideology for example, or of different interests: what do unions think, employers, environmentalists, or young people in Europe?

For example, the long-term budget negotiations always lead to intergovernmental bickering, and media tend to be uncritical of their national government's position. Every country makes a calculation of how much it will earn or lose from the different options on the table. To take the most typical example: countries with large farm sectors, such as Ireland and France, want to keep the union's farm support as it is, while EU countries with fewer farmers want to reduce it.

But even within the countries that want to reduce EU farm subsidies, such as the UK, there are of course many people who would like to keep farm subsidies at a high level: most farmers, foresters and landowners. And relatively poor UK regions want the regional support maintained at a high level, even if London wants to cut it.

It is often more interesting to show divisions within a country than to only focus on the different countries. It will also make the reporting fairer. If a British journalist writes an article about the EU budget, in which he describes opposition between the British government and British taxpayers on one hand and French farmers on the other, the journalist will most likely fall into a stereotypical description of the latter. If he instead notes the differing interests of the British government and British farmers, who are reading his newspaper, he would probably interview them, give them a voice, and try to understand their motives, rather than only report the British government's position as fact.

To get an idea of these interests, you can start by contacting big European umbrella organizations, for example for farmers, banks, coastal regions or something else, as described in chapter 13. If you write about a subject that is discussed at EU level or that is in any way related to EU law and labour law, start by talking to the European Trade Union Confederation (ETUC) and the business organization BusinessEurope.

Specialist journalist? Integrate the EU into your reporting

As explained in chapter 3, somewhere between ten per cent and fifty per cent of all new laws in your country were actually decided at EU level. And when it comes to the local and regional levels, EU rules widely affect the scope of action. But this is an average. In some policy areas, the EU has sole discretion, while the EU has almost no influence in other areas.

If you are a reporter specialized in a field over which the EU has major powers, you need to cover the policies pursued in Brussels – there is no getting around that. That goes for environmental politics, agriculture and fish, consumer affairs and economics. The Brussels correspondents have neither the knowledge nor the time to cover everything. It is easier to learn rudimentary EU procedure than to build up the expertise of an experienced environmental or consumer journalist. As a specialist journalist, you have everything to gain by integrating the EU more into your coverage.

First and foremost, you have to change your mindset and start to see the EU level as part of the national political process. The first step towards a national law is often taken in Brussels, so you cannot wait for it to be debated in your national parliament or for stakeholders in your country to start discussing it.

Also remember that you can never evaluate the newsworthiness of EU events based on what your colleagues in your country are writing about. The total volume of EU articles in any EU country is too small for this to be a reliable method – many really big questions will never be reported on. The best thing is to read many EU and European media in your field. There are some specialized EU magazines focusing, for example, on environmental policy and agriculture policy.

Check out trade magazines from other EU countries. Their angles can often be copied straight off and applied to your country. If a Spanish medicine magazine writes that the EU's new overtime rules will affect Spanish doctors, it is a good bet that those rules will also affect German doctors.

Sign up to the newsletters of the main EU organizations in your field, to the commission DG that works on your issues and to the relevant council groups and parliament committees. And get in touch with the press people who deal with your topic, so they know that you exist and you get the necessary invitations and information.

Consumer journalism

The EU is not only big politics. There are thousands of rules – big and small – and more are decided all the time. Often we focus on overzealous EU rules or EU rules that have weird consequences for companies or for special interests.

But many of the technical rules would be interesting in themselves for plenty of people if someone would simply explain what they mean and provide some helpful graphics. The body of EU law is a goldmine for consumer journalists, travel journalists and journalists at magazines that target students or anyone who might move abroad.

Take, for example, the 2004 EU regulation that gives passengers the right to compensation if they are denied boarding, or if their flight is delayed or cancelled. The regulation was tried in the EU court in 2009, and the EU court ruled that passengers were entitled to financial compensation if the flight was three hours late. Only extreme circumstances beyond the airline's control (like an ash cloud from an Icelandic volcano) are excluded. And in 2013, the EU court ruled that the three-hour delay meant delay in reaching the final destination. Even if the first flight is just one hour late, but that delay means missing a connecting flight, which in turn makes the delay in the arrival to the final destination exceed three hours, the consumer is entitled to compensation. These EU rules and case law apply to all EU countries, even if the airlines do not advertise the information.

Since many EU rules aim to increase mobility within the EU, they will also often affect tourists travelling inside the EU. During spring and summer, there are always a number of given travel and consumer articles to write. There is for example the European health insurance card that allows you to get the necessary medical care in all EU countries under the same conditions as the citizens of those countries. Before the summer holidays, why not write an article about how to get the card, with a graphic showing what some typical vacation illnesses will cost with and without the card, for some popular European holiday destinations?

Or take the European pet passport. There are common EU rules for travelling with cats, dogs and ferrets, and a special EU pet passport that you can get from your vet. For other animals, there are no harmonized EU rules. Instead, national rules apply. An explanatory article about what rules apply to what animals and in what countries could be interesting for pet owners.

How do you find all these rules? The European Commission has a website called **Youreurope**, which provides EU citizens with practical information, such as EU rules on driving licences or retirement in another EU country. Many EU countries also have this kind of practical EU information put into a national context, often on a government site.

Another place to look is **Solvit**. This is a help centre set up by the European Commission in 2002 that people or companies can turn to when authorities in an EU country do not respect the EU rules on free movement and the internal market. It is a means to solve problems quickly at a low level, instead of forcing the European Commission to open an infringement procedure against an EU country, or having the case dragged to the European Court of Justice.

There is a national Solvit centre in every EU country, and in Norway, Iceland and Liechtenstein. The centres work together through an online database. If a person leaves a complaint at one Solvit centre, that particular centre gets in touch with the Solvit centre in the country where the problem has occurred, and together they look for a solution. Typical complaints are problems of recognition of professional qualifications and driving licences. Check the annual report on Solvit cases or talk to your national Solvit centre to get an idea of what the problem areas are for your nationals. There might be an interesting article there.

Men and women – who are your sources?

The Global Media Monitoring Project's 'Who makes the news?' showed, in its 2015 report, that women make up 25 per cent of media sources in Europe, which is just above the global average of 24 per cent. These percentages have hardly changed in recent years.

The report calculated that of the 12,000 sources quoted in print, on radio and TV from around 30 European countries and regions, only a quarter were women. But when it comes to the sections 'politics and government' and 'economy', women only make up 19 per cent and 21 per cent of the sources. When reporters use an expert/commentator, only 18 per cent of them are women.[5]

In the paper version of a randomly chosen edition of *Politico*, I counted a total of 61 sources named and quoted in the articles. Out of these 61 sources, only 9 were women (15 per cent).[6]

EU political reporting is often focused on the political game in Brussels. We tend to talk to politicians and their spokespersons and we let experts from think tanks and organizations comment. If we do not actively think about it, we all – both men and women – tend to choose men as sources more than women, and reporting will suffer because some perspectives will be lost to our readers.

There are two explanations for the relative lack of women: it reflects reality and it reflects the reporters' and editors' prejudices.

When it comes to the first explanation, it is true that the top EU political jobs tend to be taken by men. In September 2016, the president of the European Council, the president of the European Commission and the president of the European Parliament were all men. In the European Parliament, the leaders of the four largest political groups – EPP, S&D, ECR and ALDE – are men. So, if you just talk to whoever is in power, this person tends to be a man. This is of course something you would want to keep in mind when looking for sources.

The filling of the top EU jobs tends to involve two main aspects: nationality and party politics. It would be unthinkable that all major posts would go to centre-left politicians. It would also be unthinkable that they would all go to politicians from southern EU countries, new EU countries or big EU countries. These considerations are labelled 'respecting a balance' and never need defending. Whenever gender is mentioned, however, it is called 'imposing a quota', which is generally frowned upon. Gender is very slowly becoming a part of the discussion, but the idea of a 50–50 representation, or even 40–60, is still considered a rather extreme position in the EU context.

What about the second explanation, that gender imbalance in journalism is not only a reflection of reality, but also a reflection of the reporters' and editors' choices and prejudices?

Around half of the *Politico* sources (31) were politicians, civil servants or spokespeople. They were 25 men and 6 women (19 per cent). Twenty-one sources were experts of some sort: scientists, analysts and representatives of organizations or companies who were commenting on someone else's actions. They were 20 men and only one woman (5 per cent).

While you might not always get to choose the 'political sources' for your story – the competition commissioner holding a press conference *is* Margrethe Vestager and no one else – the 'expert sources' in my little study could almost all be changed for someone else. The fact is that the *Politico* reporters talked to *fewer* women, not more, when they themselves were free to choose their sources, when the choice of sources was not merely a reflection of reality.

Links

European Commission's interactive charts for EU expenditure and revenue
ec.europa.eu/budget/figures/interactive/index_en.cfm

Youreurope, the European Commission's website with practical information for EU citizens
europa.eu/youreurope/citizens/index_en.htm

National Solvit centres in the different EU countries
ec.europa.eu/solvit/contact/index_en.htm

Notes

1 Court of Justice of the European Union, *The Court of Justice declares the Data Retention Directive to be invalid*, Press Release No 54/14, Luxembourg, 8 April 2014
2 European Commission, Officials, *Temporary staff and contract staff by nationality and grade*, Statistical Bulletin on 01/02/2016, ec.europa.eu/civil_service/docs/europa_sp2_bs_nat_x_grade_en.pdf
3 Nilsson, Ylva, Allt eller det allra mesta du trodde att du visste om EU är antagligen helt fel, Paradigmmäklarna Media, 2014
4 *Le Monde*, 'Brexit': que pèse le Royaume-Uni dans le budget européen?, 16 February 2016
5 Global Media Monitoring Project, *Who makes the news?* Regional report, Europe, 2015
6 *Politico*, vol. 2 No. 20, May 19–25, 2016. In this edition was the article 'The 40 MEPs who actually matter', which listed 14 women and 26 men. Anticipating criticism, the reporters wrote that 'Power, like life, is rarely fair. As such there are no quotas for gender, age or nationality for this ranking'. The ranking did not use a method that allows for replication; it was a list of MEPs that the reporters themselves considered important, which of course also reflects the reporters' own prejudices. It was this article that convinced me to count the sources in the whole newspaper.

17 Common mistakes in EU reporting and how to avoid them

'The EU wants to ban low-cut tops': when someone wants to make a boring EU directive sexy and takes it too far

It is not always easy to sell the technical and complex EU legislative process to readers. It does not make it any easier that many EU meetings are held behind closed doors and that the key players are largely unknown to them. There is no conflict or drama to report. Therefore, the media often tries to spice up the technical laws with something funny or sexy. And often this goes very wrong.

In 2007, several European media reported that the EU was going to make it illegal for waitresses to wear low-cut tops, so that their skin would not get damaged by sunlight. The German press worried about the future of the Bavarian barmaids and their traditional 'dirndl' dress. British tabloid *The Sun* launched the campaign 'Save Our Jugs'.[1]

There was of course no mention of low-cut tops in the Directive on Optical Radiation.[2] The law would however require managers to assess health risks for employees who work outside in the sun all day, which would more likely cover farm and road workers than waitresses. How the health risks should be assessed and the measures that should be taken, if indeed there seemed to be a health risk, would be up to each EU country to decide for itself.[3] This is what an EU directive in labour law typically looks like. It sets a basic standard, so that EU countries do not compete with each other through social dumping. EU countries can decide on their own if they want stricter rules than the bare minimum.

If there truly is an EU ban in the making, there is always a proposal from the European Commission. This can be found for example in legislative databases EUR-Lex, the Legislative Observatory or on the commission's website. Check for yourself to see if the headlines are right. Or call someone who knows: the health spokesperson in the European Commission, the health committee press officer in the European Parliament or the press officer who covers health questions in the Council of Ministers. Did they really want to ban low décolletages on waitresses?

Read the actual proposal. There might be a story there that is worth reporting on – probably less spectacular, but a story nevertheless. Some EU myths have a grain of truth in them, and that small grain can in itself be very interesting.

226 Common mistakes in EU reporting

The Directive on Optical Radiation will affect other professionals and it might be interesting to write about it for their industry press.

Pure fabrications and EU myths

Some EU news is completely off the wall and lacks even that small grain of truth. They are not mistakes but fabrications. UK tabloids are the main arena for made-up EU news.

When illegal phone tapping by Britain's *News of the World* was revealed in 2011, it led it to the setting up of a committee of inquiry, the Leveson Inquiry. The subsequent Leveson Report stated, under the heading 'Inaccurate reporting of political issues to fit the world view of a title', that 'articles relating to the European Union, and Britain's role within it, accounted for a further category of story where parts of the press appeared to prioritize the title's agenda over factual accuracy'.[4]

UK tabloids have falsely claimed that the EU wants to ban the Scottish kilt, curry and bulldogs, that the EU flag should replace the Union Jack outside 10 Downing Street and that British soldiers will in future have to take orders in French.

Journalists from other countries who re-write British news sometimes spread these EU myths. To avoid passing on fake EU news, never re-write news about the EU from British tabloids and always call someone who actually knows the issue and ask them.

A Brussels colleague of mine sometimes holds lectures for journalism students on EU reporting. She usually starts by reading the following headline from the tabloid *Daily Express* aloud: 'EU wants to merge UK with France';[5] pauses to let the full meaning of those words sink in; then asks, in a very, very tired voice: 'Really?' If you read anything about the EU that sounds too weird to be true, it probably is. Read the headline aloud to yourself and hear how it sounds. Really? Is Queen Elizabeth really going to come out on her balcony and announce to the people that the kingdom has ceased to exist, simply because some bureaucrat in Brussels has said so?

The idea of the EU wanting to merge UK with France seems to be a twisted interpretation of the European Commission providing the British and French channel regions with EU money for things like harmonizing signal systems for boats crossing the channel, or language learning trips across the water for children on both sides. It brings to mind the articles in Swedish local newspapers and even in the respected daily newspaper *Dagens Nyheter*, according to which 'the EU' had decided that Öland – the second largest island in Sweden – in fact was not an island at all.[6] The news is a (deliberate?) misinterpretation of European Commission criteria for funding for particularly vulnerable regions. Only islands without a bridge to the mainland could apply to this specific fund. Öland is of course an island regardless of whether it has a bridge or not.

But you cannot dismiss all articles about wacky EU rules as EU myths. Sometimes reality goes beyond fiction and the European Commission suggests really strange stuff. An authentic commission proposal in 2013 was that restaurants should be prohibited from serving olive oil in their own jugs and bowls, and should instead use non-refillable bottles that would then be discarded, for hygiene reasons and to ensure that the oil was not diluted. After much heckling the commission made a U-turn and withdrew the proposal.

'The EU wants to ban porn': exaggerating the impact of European Parliament own-initiative reports

One of the most common mistakes in EU reporting is to give too much weight to the European Parliament's agenda-setting power. A textbook example of this was when a number of European, and even American, media outlets reported in 2013 that pornography soon would be banned in the EU. Behind this story was an own-initiative report on the elimination of gender stereotypes adopted by the European Parliament's Gender Equality Committee (FEMM). The report was due to be voted on in the plenary session, thus becoming the position of the entire parliament. In the report, the parliament urged the EU and its member states to act according to a resolution from 1997 'which called for a ban on all forms of pornography in the media and on the advertising of sex tourism'.[7]

In plenary, the report was adopted but the porn paragraph was scrapped. Even if the paragraph had passed, though, this would *not have led* to a ban on porn in the EU. The European Parliament's own-initiative reports do not have any legal weight; they are only opinions. In the pornography ban case, the parliament had already adopted in 1997 the report that the new report in 2013 referred to. An advisor in the Gender Equality Committee joked about the ostentatious headlines: 'What are they talking about "the EU wants to ban porn"? We banned that already in 1997'.

Most articles about the porn ban included a paragraph at the end stating that the report did not carry any legal weight and should only be seen as the parliament's opinion, but this information was contradicted by headlines such as 'The EU wants to ban pornography' and 'The European Union votes to ban porn'. In headlines and introductory paragraphs, the phrase 'EU proposal' was used, which gives the idea greater importance than it has. There were few concrete factual errors. More problematic was the tone, choice of words and especially the evaluation of newsworthiness.

Now, you might say that it is still news that a majority of the MEPs in the Gender Equality Committee supported this paragraph, even if it does not lead to an actual ban. To examine the values of a committee that can legislate on *other* matters is of course journalistically interesting. But in order to write that article, you would need a bit more context: how many own-initiative reports does the Gender Equality Committee adopt every year? What other issues has it adopted a position on? And what other positions have other committees adopted?

Bear in mind that all the committees have more extreme views than the parliament as a whole, because MEPs with strong opinions about particular policies tend to choose those committees. This evens out when the parliament votes in plenary. It is also easier to be idealistic when you do not have to face the consequences of the politics you propose. In matters over which the parliament has actual power, the views tend to be more middle-of-the-road.

European Parliament own-initiative reports, reports from the Committee of the Regions and the Economic and Social Committee, questions from MEPs and various reports from independent EU agencies – these should all be seen as merely input into ongoing European debate. As such, they might be of interest to report on. They can show the direction EU politics is heading in, or its diversity. But they should not be reported on as if they were a step towards laws and rules that will affect the reader. Therefore, do not write 'the EU' – say what person, group of persons or institution has put forward the opinion.

To find out if the report you are set to cover is an own-initiative report, find the report in the parliament's Legislative Observatory. Own-initiative reports have a reference number that contains the letter combination 'INI'. For example, 'Elimination of gender stereotypes in the EU (2012/2116 (INI))'. If you see 'INI' you know that the document carries no legal weight.

'EU ban on bullfighting': forgetting that there are two, not one, legislatures in the EU

If you write about a decision or a vote in the European Parliament or in the Council of Ministers, on a matter that is subject to the ordinary legislative procedure, you should also explain to the reader what the other legislature thinks of the question. Otherwise it will be difficult for the reader to interpret the information you are serving up. If you don't, you might make the same mistake as many journalists did when they, in 2015, reported on a ban on EU money being spent on bullfighting.

The articles were about an amendment to the annual budget for 2016, which was adopted by the European Parliament in October 2015. The amendment said that EU agricultural subsidies should not go to farmers who breed bulls for bullfighting, and the amendment was indeed adopted by the parliament.[8] After the vote, newspapers in Europe and the rest of the world had headlines along the lines of 'EU cuts subsidies that support Spanish bullfighting'.[9]

The annual budget is decided on jointly by the European Parliament and the Council of Ministers. What was adopted in October 2015 was the parliament's *position* ahead of the negotiations, not the final deal. The parliament still had to agree with the council, and in the council bullfighting nations Spain and France also have a seat at the table. When the final text for the annual budget was adopted in the parliament and the council, the bullfighting amendment had disappeared. But there were no follow-up articles about the 'bullfighting ban' that hadn't been imposed, so it is not unreasonable to think that the readers of the first articles still think that there is such a ban in place.

Anyone who knows how EU legislation is passed would also have known from the start that the amendment would never stand a chance of passing the council. As long as some EU countries think that bullfighting is an important feature of their national culture, there will be no EU action to stop it. It is not in the other EU countries' interests to annoy the bullfighting countries. Neither is it in their interest to add new, more detailed rules about what EU farm subsidies can be used for.

When you write about parliament amendments to legislation that it decides together with the council, you should include a passage about what the chances are that these will actually be accepted by the council. If you know that the chances are nil – and when it comes to a bullfighting ban, they are – then don't write about it at all. Or, if you must, frame the parliament decision as the parliament's opinion, not as a first step to new rules.

Committees, expert groups, working groups…

It is important to understand and communicate in your text the role of the three main EU institutions and not just refer to 'the EU' without clarifying what EU institution it is about.

It is reasonably easy to differentiate the European Commission, the Council of Ministers and the European Parliament. However, even quite experienced journalists may mix them up, because each of them has sub-institutions or sub-groups that have irritatingly similar names. These sub-groups may have names that contain the terms 'expert group', 'working group', 'expert panel', 'authority', 'committee', 'council', etc. Confusing the issue further is the large number of organizations and think tanks that play with the same words in their names.

Never write 'EU committee' or 'EU working group' because it means nothing – you have to know and tell the reader if it is a committee/working group under the commission, council, parliament or some other EU institution, or no EU institution at all. Just google the name of the group to find out.

It is also not sufficient to just write the full name of the group. It may be correct in technical terms, but only a minuscule fraction of your readers will be helped by the information. For the rest it just sounds like gibberish and adds on the feeling that 'the EU is too complicated for me'.

Fact box: Example of EU institutions' sub-groups with similar names

The Expert Group on Animal Health is a European Commission expert group. It is a permanent group of EU country officials, who advise the commission when the commission prepares new animal health legislation and when it implements existing EU legislation.

The sub-group *Animal Health* of the *Working Party of Veterinary Experts* is a working group in the Council of Ministers. It consists of national officials who serve their ministers of agriculture. This working group prepares decisions and legislation on animal health issues in the council to facilitate and smooth the decision process of the EU agriculture ministers.

The *Standing Committee on Plants, Animals, Food and Feed – Section: 'Animal Health and Animal Welfare'* is a 'comitology committee' within the European Commission. The group comprises national officials from all the EU countries. Their job is to control the commission's decisions when the commission implements EU policy in the field of animal health.

All three groups have similar names and they may even have the same people in them, as they are made up of the EU countries' officials who are experts in animal health. However, their functions differ from one another.

'The EU wants to privatize all water': mistakes due to translation

Not infrequently, there are spectacular EU news reports that stem from misunderstandings based on poor translation. This is especially the case for media in countries whose EU information has been written in another language – that is, everyone except those who speak English, French and German. Most EU information that reaches other EU journalists has been written in a foreign language and then translated – by the EU institutions' translators or by journalists themselves. The EU jargon has, as we will see in chapter 20, also developed into a language of its own, so even native English speakers sometimes misunderstand EU English.

Sometimes articles about how the EU institutions want to 'monitor the media' pop up. This horror scenario occurs when a reporter finds a commission budget line for 'media monitoring', which actually is only fancier wording for reading newspapers and cutting out articles – something that most organizations do to keep track of what others are saying about them.

An EU myth that was widely spread in 2012 was that the European Commission planned to privatize all water in the EU. In Germany in particular, this led to a storm of opinion and eventually fed into the citizens' initiative 'Wasser ist Menschenrecht – Right 2 Water', which collected over a million signatures to stop the privatization plans.

The whole affair was about the so-called concessions directive, a typical case of EU internal-market legislation. In brief, the directive sets out rules to ensure transparency and competition in cases in which public authorities contract private suppliers to deliver public services. The directive says nothing about who should manage the water. Where water management is done by public providers, the directive does not apply. When authorities contract private providers, the rules on transparency and competition apply.

In the above case, it seems that a combination of the words 'private' and 'water' was all it took for all critical distance to be thrown overboard.

How to avoid this? Well, again, read the actual proposal. Never re-write EU articles without calling someone from the actual EU institution that you are writing about. And never assume that one million people can't be wrong – this unfortunately is not the case when it comes to the EU.

Who is the critic?

The EU institutions and member countries share some of the blame for frequent errors in articles about the EU. The European Commission uses easily misunderstood jargon and actually suggests very strange laws sometimes. The European Parliament spends a lot of time communicating opinions on matters on which it does not have any legal say. And of course the EU countries' governments confuse journalists by taking credit for popular EU actions and blaming unpopular ones on 'the EU'.

However, it is not only poor communication at play. Quite often the journalist is aided in misinterpretation by someone who has an interest in portraying the EU in this particular manner. In the example with water above, many politicians do not want the concessions directive and would rather play on privatization fears than debate the policy itself.

Two classic objections that can be applied to almost any EU proposal are that it could lead to increased administration and costs (red tape) or that it leads to privatization of a public utility. Usually right-wing politicians say the former and left-wing politicians say the latter. So think about who the critics of EU proposals are.

During the 2009–2014 parliament mandate, the Swedish Pirate Party was behind many of the stories in the Swedish press about the EU threatening individual freedoms, for example with the ban on porn. The Pirate Party MEPs were elected on promises to defend individual freedoms and had an interest in portraying the EU as being on the verge of shutting down the internet.

Of course, political parties and organizations with a clear Eurosceptic approach tend to exaggerate the negative sides of the EU. The EU institutions' own stories can seem more neutral, but they also come from a certain angle. The European Commission and the European Parliament, as a whole, believe in the principle that the more power the EU has, the better, even if there are many individual exceptions. Many people in the institutions who are pro-EU confuse reporters' critical questions with pushing a political agenda. In the EU institutions, 'Eurosceptic' is a dirty word.

'The EU wants to ban snus': When the countries' national treasures are threatened

One of the EU's fundamental traits is its consensus culture. In the institutions, everything is discussed and discussed and discussed until everyone is on board. In the Council of Ministers, it is extremely rare for a particular country's objections to be completely ignored, even though it sometimes happens.

The EU countries in the council should strive for unanimity if there are extremely important interests at stake for one or more countries, even if technically only a qualified majority is needed. This is called the Luxembourg compromise. It is not a legal obligation but it is an underlying principle that to a large degree governs the council's decision-making.

Forcing an EU country to adopt new rules it does not want is very rare. It happens when legislation is urgent, when there are no other solutions and when the alternative is unacceptable to the other EU countries. The 2015 decision to relocate 120,000 refugees from Greece and Italy to all other EU countries, which was adopted by qualified majority voting in the council in the midst of the refugee crisis and in the face of hard opposition from the four Visegrad countries, was a case in point.

If a country has some strange custom that does not affect the other EU countries, it is fair to say that the EU *never* forces the country in question to change that. There is no point in irritating a whole country if it is not absolutely necessary. Culture and tradition are important arguments in Brussels. Every EU country has some national treasure that needs to be protected from the free market, and some tradition that probably violates animal welfare rules, or environmental or health rules. Swedish fermented herring, for example, has dioxin levels that exceed the permitted EU limits. But since fermented herring is a cherished tradition in some parts of Sweden, Swedes are allowed to sell and eat the fish, as long as they only poison themselves and do not export it to the rest of the EU.

EU rules that were in place before a country joined the EU, however, might cause some headaches. Every new EU country will find some rules that were decided without its involvement and that just don't work for it. For Swedes, the prime example of this was that fine-ground tobacco – snuff, or *snus* in Swedish – was already illegal in the rest of the EU when Sweden joined.

During membership negotiations, the would-be member country and the EU usually agree on a couple of exemptions (opt-outs) from some EU rules, just for that country. Take the Czech Republic. The beautiful old houses in the centre of Prague were, at the moment of the Czech Republic's EU entry, expensive for Czechs but clearly affordable for western Europeans. An EU country cannot normally discriminate against other EU citizens in terms of where they can buy houses, but if the Czech market had opened up so soon, the whole of central Prague would have ended up being inhabited by Germans and Italians. Therefore, the Czech Republic was exempted from the rule and non-Czechs were not allowed to buy real estate in the Czech Republic for five years after the country joined the EU. Tiny island Malta, which joined the EU at the same time, has a permanent exemption. It can restrict other EU nationals, apart from those who have been residing on the island for over five years, from buying a second home on Malta.

When Sweden joined the EU, it got an exemption from the snus ban, but the ban is still in place in the other countries. Swedes can use snus all they want but cannot export the tobacco product to other EU countries – the same principle as with the fermented herring.

The Tobacco Products Directive, proposed by the commission in 2012, was intended to tighten the rules for all tobacco products. The directive did not change the principle that Sweden can produce and consume snus but not export it to other EU countries. The directive however set out to ban flavoured tobacco products, such as menthol cigarettes. In Sweden, some interpreted this to mean that *all* snus would be forbidden, because all snus, unlike cigarettes, contains flavourings. Snus would be collateral damage in the legislator's plan to prevent teenage girls from starting to smoke by prohibiting strawberry flavoured cigarettes.

When the tobacco directive was presented, endless articles were written in the Swedish media. They were often very biased and with a clear us-versus-them angle. EU representatives did not get to explain themselves; instead the tobacco company Swedish Match was given space to explain – often unchallenged – the political negotiations as if it were the Swedish 'national snus authority'.

'The EU' does not have any interest in sneakily changing Swedes' snus habits. And 'the EU' does not ban a product by accident. There are many Swedish gatekeepers within the EU who would ring the alarm bell if that were about to happen. The Council of Ministers and the European Parliament amended and adopted the directive, so both the Swedish government and Swedish MEPs amended the draft law. Other member states had no interest in forcing on Sweden stricter snus rules that do not affect them. Next time it could be a German or Belgian tradition that needs to be exempted from EU rules, and they would not want to anger their Swedish allies.

When journalists mistake the Council of Europe for the EU

Sometimes journalists believe that the Council of Europe is an EU institution. This is not very surprising. The name Council of Europe is similar to the name of two EU institutions: the European Council (EU summit) and the Council of the European Union (Council of Ministers). Actually, on rue Wiertz – the Brussels street that separates the European Parliament's two buildings – there is a street sign showing the directions to the different EU institutions. On one of the arrows it is written 'Conseil de l'Europe – Juste Lipse', referring to the Council of Ministers' Justus Lipsius building, but accidentally saying Council of Europe.

To complicate matters further, the blue flag with the 12 golden stars is a symbol for *both* the Council of Europe and the EU. The Council of Europe had the flag first and the EU copied it. Even geography contributes to the confusion. The Council of Europe and its court, the European Court of Human Rights, are based in Strasbourg, France, where the European Parliament also spends a week every month, in the same neighbourhood as the Council of Europe.

The Council of Europe is a European organization that promotes democracy and human rights. There are 47 member states, including Russia and Turkey. Yes, all countries on the European continent are members of the Council of Europe except Belarus, which does not yet meet the basic democracy requirements. The member countries have signed the European Charter on Human Rights. If the state violates an individual's fundamental rights, under this convention, the individual can refer the case to the European Court of Human Rights.

The Council of Europe and the EU were created at about the same time and in the same spirit, the nascent European Movement in the wake of the Second World War. But while the Council of Europe remained an intergovernmental organization, the European Union evolved into a supranational organization. The Council of Europe can make recommendations, but the EU can force the countries to take measures.

The Council of Europe, like all other intergovernmental organizations, is only effective when all the member countries push in the same direction. The European Court of Human Rights' rulings are binding, but it has no way of enforcing them. If the member countries ignore the judgement – and they often do – the court has no way to force them to comply. In the EU, however, the EU court can impose fines and the member states do follow the court's rulings.

But it is not necessarily accurate to say that the two organizations are completely separate from each other. Even if the EU and the Council of Europe are two different organizations, the EU institutions sometimes use the Council of Europe for things that the EU cannot do itself or does not have the necessary expertise for, such as monitoring human rights violations.

When the European Commission, once a year, publishes its reports on the development in the countries that are negotiating to one day become part of the EU, the analysis is often based on the Council of Europe's findings and decisions. The countries in line to join the EU are all members of the Council of Europe, and as such are being monitored with regards to human rights.

The EU can make compliance with Council of Europe rulings a condition for some deals. For example, in 2008 the EU and Bosnia signed a stabilization and association agreement. A year later, the EU suspended that agreement, because Bosnia had not complied with a ruling from the European Court of Human Rights. The ECHR had ruled that Bosnia should change a clause in its constitution that bars Bosnians from communities other than Bosnian Muslims, Serbs and Croats from standing for election to some high political positions.[10]

Writing about the Council of Europe

Journalists tend to report on the Council of Europe when their country has received a judgement from the human rights court or when one of the many monitoring bodies has published a report that includes praise or criticism, for example criticism of the UK for not allowing its prisoners to vote, of Ireland because of abortion restrictions and corporal punishment, or Belgium and France because of the living conditions in overcrowded prisons.

See **upcoming events** from the Council of Europe on its site and make sure that you are on their press mailing list. National authorities and big NGOs will have been consulted in the monitoring process and will be in the loop about upcoming reports or rulings.

When there has been a decision by a monitoring body, use the word 'recommend'. For instance, AP writes: 'Germany should do away with the practice of surgical castration of sex offenders, the Council of Europe's anti-torture committee recommended Wednesday, calling the procedure degrading to the convicted criminals'.[11]

Writing about the same recommendation, tabloid *Daily Mail* clearly confuses the Council of Europe with the EU: 'Germany is rejecting demands from an EU body that it should stop surgically castrating sex criminals [...] Defying Brussels, the German government said it intends to carry on with the practice [...]'.[12]

Even if you yourself do not mistake the Council of Europe for the EU, you can be sure that some of your readers will. Check the comment section below any article about a Council of Europe ruling or recommendation and this will be clear. You should make a point that the Council of Europe is not the EU. Call it a regional intergovernmental organization that promotes democracy, human rights and the rule of law in its member states, or 'the 47-nation Council of Europe' or something along those lines.

Many of the Council of Europe institutions sound similar to the EU institutions. If you mention the Council of Europe's commissioner for human rights in an article, you need to point out that he is working for the Council of Europe, not the EU, so that there is no confusion between him and EU commissioners, who are better known.

Fact box: Checklist – the EU and the Council of Europe

This is the EU:

European Council (EU summit)
Council of the European Union (Council of Ministers)
European Commission
European Parliament
Court of Justice of the European Union
Committee of the Regions

This is the Council of Europe:

Council of Europe
Committee of Ministers
Commissioner for Human Rights
Venice Commission (The European Commission for Democracy through Law)
Parliamentary Assembly
European Court of Human Rights
Congress of Local and Regional Authorities

Links

Upcoming events in the Council of Europe
www.coe.int/en/web/portal/events

Notes

1 *The Sun*, Barmaids in Save Our Jugs, 3 August 2007
2 Directive on the minimum health and safety from exposure to the risks arising from physical agents (artificial optical radiation) (19th individual Directive within the meaning of Article 16.1 of Directive 89/391/EEC)
3 European Commission in the UK, Brussels bans barmaids from baring chests [blog post], Euromyth site, https://blogs.ec.europa.eu/ECintheUK/brussels-bans-barmaids-from-baring-chests
4 An inquiry into the culture, practices and ethics of the press: report [Leveson] Volume 2, No 0780 2012–13, 29 November 2012
5 *Daily Express*, EU wants to merge UK with France, 2 May 2011
6 For example *Dagens Nyheter*, EU: Öland är ingen ö, 11 March 2013
7 European Parliament, Report on eliminating gender stereotypes in the EU, Article 17, 6 December 2012 (2012/2116(INI))
8 European Parliament resolution of 28 October 2015 on the Council position on the draft general budget of the European Union for the financial year 2016
9 For example, *Expressen – Allt om resor*, EU stryper bidrag som går till tjurfäktning, 29 October 2015
10 *European Voice*, EU gives green light to Bosnian deal, 17 March 2015
11 Associated Press, *Germany criticized for castration of sex offenders*, 22 February 2012
12 The *Daily Mail*, Germany rejects demand to stop castrating sex criminals as part of their punishment, 23 February 2012

18 Investigative EU reporting

What investigative reporting is done about the EU? What are the rules on source protection and the protection of whistleblowers in the EU? How can I check how EU money is spent? How do I investigate how lobbyists influence EU policy? How do I make freedom-of-information requests to the EU institutions?

Considering how much power the EU has over our lives and how much money is channelled through the EU, it is remarkable how little we reporters actually dig into Brussels business. The reasons reporters give for this are that it is complicated and costly, and difficult to sell to the readers. But there are some simple tools that can be used for EU investigations and some good examples to be inspired by.

The state of investigative EU reporting

There is very little investigative EU reporting going on. This is the conclusion from a 2012 study about investigative journalism into misused EU money and fraud involving EU funds.[1] For the report, which was commissioned by the European Parliament, Margo Smit, the president of the Dutch investigative journalists' organization, together with some European national journalists' organizations, searched through around a thousand investigative EU articles/features published between 2005 and 2012.

The study shows that investigative EU reporting is very unevenly distributed between the EU countries. British media clearly dominate, with over a third of the total number of articles. No other national media seems to have any continuous investigative approach towards the EU.

The few EU investigations that exist are almost always done from outside Brussels, rather than by Brussels-based correspondents. Some journalists interviewed for the 2012 study believed that this was because Brussels correspondents are too close to the EU institutions and the people who work there. They drink at the same bars after work, their children go to the same schools and they swap jobs with each other after a few years. Truly critical reporting from inside the

Brussels bubble becomes difficult. Others say the lack of digging is a consequence of Brussels correspondents actually knowing how the EU works, and therefore not jumping at what looks like a revelation, but in fact does not hold up to scrutiny.

There is probably some truth in both statements. The lack of investigative reporting by the Brussels press corps is likely just because of a lack of time. The correspondents are often the only representatives of their media and are expected to keep track constantly of all EU news (and often the rest of Europe too). They simply never have the time to dig deep into one topic.

The Smit report showed that EU investigations tend to have a national angle, focus on individuals or companies and demonstrate something absurd about the EU. A case in point was an article that revealed that the British royal family receives large farm subsidies from the EU budget.

The investigations focus on irregular payments in the journalists' own countries or in Brussels, while the EU money spent elsewhere is off the radar. For example, there were almost none into how EU money is spent on foreign aid or on projects in the EU's neighbouring countries.

Two major themes stand out in terms of the number of investigative articles/features: farm subsidies and regional aid. These are also the two main expenditure items in the EU budget, so it is perfectly normal that many reporters want to investigate where this money is spent. To a great extent the many investigations in these areas are spin-offs from two major individual journalistic projects that created databases of agricultural and regional payments, as we will see later in this chapter.

Trends in investigative journalism: data journalism, cross-border cooperation and not-for-profit journalism

Much investigative EU reporting is today done by networks of journalists who piece together information from various sources and create databases that other journalists can use for local and national investigations.

Sometimes this is done by scraping data from public websites (that is, writing computer programs that automatically download the data on a regular basis). Sometimes the data is gathered through coordinated freedom-of-information (FOI) requests. When journalists have been refused access to documents and information about EU funding, it has led to cases in national courts and in the EU court, which have helped to broaden the definition of exactly what kinds of documents should be considered public and free to use, both in EU countries and the EU institutions. Sometimes the investigations are based on big leaks, like Lux Leaks and Swiss Leaks.

Big data journalism projects are based on collaboration between journalists and programmers, to access the data, and between journalists from different countries, to interpret the data. To find the interesting angles, you need local knowledge.

Centres for investigative journalism

In traditional media worldwide, investigative journalism is under pressure. Hardly any media has enough money or staff to let a reporter off the daily news routine so that he or she can concentrate on a month-long digging project. In some places, non-profit centres for investigative journalism have taken over the role that publishers used to have, to produce high quality investigative journalism.

There are several such centres in the United States, which has a long tradition of private donations. The flagship ProPublica started in 2008 and has already won a handful of Pulitzer prizes. In central and eastern Europe these types of investigative organizations, often financed by foreign donations, are playing a larger and larger role, looking into border-less phenomena such as corruption and organized crime.

Similar centres are becoming increasingly important in Western Europe, for example in the UK, Italy, Germany and Denmark. The UK Bureau of Investigative Journalism (BIJ), for example, has done some digging into the EU that traditional media did not have money for. One example was the project 'Europe's hidden millions' which BIJ did jointly with the *Financial Times*. BIJ invested nine months to create a database with all the payments from the EU's structural funds. Such an investment is impossible for traditional media today.

Investigative collaboration across borders

There are no borders within the EU. That means no borders for asylum seekers or victims of trafficking, and no borders for horse meat that is bought in Romania, re-packaged in France and ends up in a Swedish frozen lasagne. There are also no borders for the money of the ultra-rich. Despite this, the EU countries' media is still mainly national or local.

Major EU stories will often branch out from Brussels and your capital. EU investigations might require travelling to several countries, translations, international calls – stuff that editors find it increasingly difficult to pay for today. For this you can apply for money from **the Journalismfund**.

Journalismfund provides grants for European cross-border journalism and investigative European journalism. The criterion for getting money is that the project would not have been able to get off the ground within the usual journalistic frameworks, because it requires the involvement of more countries, or is too costly.

The project must be a collaboration with colleagues from at least one other EU country and the article/feature must be published in at least two European media outlets. There is no set grant amount and applications can be submitted at any time.

Journalismfund receives most of its funds for European projects from the Dutch Adessium Foundation and from the Open Society Foundation, an American organization founded by the famous multi-billionaire George Soros.

Interview: Brigitte Alfter, journalist, Editor Europe for Journalismfund

How do you get started with European cross-border journalism?
Basically you start by building a network or you develop an idea – both are good starting points. You build a research team, develop a research plan, you do the actual research and then you publish. And there is a follow up: you go to journalism conferences and present your findings and share your methods with other journalists. By doing so, you are back to networking.

What would be good themes for cross-border EU reporting?
Look at the EU competences. Everything where the EU has a competence or co-competence is a European cross-border challenge.

But if you are a local journalist, who does not really know how the EU works, how would you start?
Start with what is in front of you. You have to follow your curiosity and go to the source of the rules. Local journalists should think of where a problem really lies, regardless of whether it's next door or in Brussels.

And don't be afraid of sounding like a fool when you speak airport English. We all speak airport English.

An example of a cross-border story is water quality. Sometimes in the summer in Denmark, when there is little wind, the flow through the fjords is so low that the water turns bad and the fish die and become very smelly. Why is that? Because there is too much fertilizer and the algae in the water is growing.

You could say that this is a local story. But who regulates water quality? There are various EU laws on agriculture, water quality, control of fertilizers. In Denmark, the fact that the fish die could be because Denmark does not fulfil the EU water quality legislation. So, there you already have a story: Denmark is in breach of EU law.

Then the Danish farmers will say: but the German farmers are not following the directive either. That would be a competitive disadvantage for Danish farmers if they had to follow the rules, while the German farmers are allowed to break them. At this stage, you try to find a German colleague, who you like and who also speaks airport English. You drink some coffee or beer and you start looking together into water quality in both Germany and Denmark.

Which are the other big agriculture countries? Netherlands, Poland, France? Now you drink some more coffee or wine or whatever with journalists from these countries too, and then you have a story.

If you have four countries in breach of EU regulation, then your story can put the matter on the EU's agenda. If it is only Denmark, it is seen as a regional problem.

> Even if media are cutting back, there are still correspondents in Brussels who report news about what goes on in the EU institutions. There is decent reporting from Brussels to the member states, but there is very little coordinated reporting from the member states, where the EU legislation is in force, back to the decision-makers in Brussels. It has to be a huge thing if it is to get onto the Brussels agenda.

Data Harvest Conference

Since 2011, the Data Harvest Conference has been held in Brussels every spring. The conference is a networking event for investigative and data journalists across Europe.

Its workshops range from what you typically find at conferences about investigative journalism, such as how to use different Facebook profiles when investigating closed circles, to the very nerdy EU-focused themes, such as a workshop at the 2016 conference on how to get climate data collected by satellites from the European Space Agency.

Investigating EU spending

First, a few introductory words about the EU budget for those who want to start digging into it. The EU spending ceiling (MFF) for the years 2014–2020 is 1,083 billion euros.

The EU budget for 2015 amounted to 162 billion euros. That is roughly the size of Romania's economy and a tenth of Italy's. But it does not really make sense to compare the EU budget to a national budget. The EU does not have any costs for schools, hospitals and unemployment benefits, for example. But in a few selected areas such as agriculture and regional policy, the EU has a re-distributional policy and therefore high costs.

Farm support is entirely an EU matter, while foreign aid is only in part channelled through the EU budget and is for the most part paid for by the EU countries' national budgets. So you need to be careful when comparing the EU budget items. If you just compare different items of expenditure at EU level without looking at how much is spent via national budgets, you will be comparing apples with pears.

Direct aid to farmers and money for rural development account for around 40 per cent of the total EU budget. The sums are huge and that is because *all* agricultural support to EU farms comes from the Brussels coffers, and not a cent from national coffers. If EU farm subsidies were scrapped, which some politicians want, it would mean that some EU countries would have to pay the same amount or more to their farmers via their national budgets, while other countries would choose not to and would instead see parts of their farm sectors disappear.

The other big chunk of EU spending is regional support. The aim is to level the playing field for the EU's 276 regions. This is done through a myriad of projects that are co-financed by the EU budget and countries' national budgets. Most money goes to the poorest regions, in the poorest countries. It is often used for infrastructure projects, such as building new roads. Regions in rich countries also get EU money, but this money is more often used to develop tourism or to test new innovations.

All in all, EU farm and regional spending together make up three-quarters of all EU money spent.[2] The rest is everything else: research grants, Erasmus grants, developing transport networks across the continent and the European satellite navigation system that is supposed to be an alternative to the American GPS, democracy-building projects in the EU's neighbourhood countries and much more. Around six per cent of the budget goes to the EU's own administration, i.e. civil servants' salaries, building leases and office equipment.

Now, let us take a closer look at investigative journalism that deals with EU spending, and first and foremost the biggest budget item: farm subsidies.

Farm support

EU agricultural support is not only the EU's largest expenditure item; it is also the most criticized. Over time, agricultural aid as a percentage of the total EU budget has fallen continuously and the policy has been reformed: from production-based aid, which led to the much-criticized butter mountains and milk lakes, to support based on acreage. The farm aid now looks more like employment grants/conversion premiums for farmers.

No one really knew exactly where the money went and who the main recipients were before **Farmsubsidy.org** began their investigation. By the time they finished, they had found that most of the aid ended up in the pockets of large corporations and landowners – not the struggling family farmers that many Europeans would be willing to subsidize through their taxes.

The Farmsubsidy.org project began when a group of Danish investigative journalists requested the data about Danish recipients of agricultural subsidies. In 2004, Denmark became the first EU country to hand over this data. The journalists set up a structure for requesting the same information from other EU countries and built a database with all the payment information. In many countries, the journalists had to go to court to get the information.

The story of Farmsubsidy.org runs parallel with the story of openness in the EU. Work with the database has pushed new rules on access to documents in the EU and in a number of EU member countries. In 2009, the European Commission decided that all EU countries should publish information about who receives farm subsidies and how much they get. But the quality of this information varies a great deal between the countries. Farmsubsidy.org ranks EU countries according to how transparent their authorities are with agricultural data.

Fishing support

Farmsubsidy.org gave rise to numerous articles and features and also inspired the little sister Fishsubsidy.org – a database with payments from the EU's Common Fisheries Policy, launched in 2009. EU aid to the fishing sector is a drop in the ocean compared to agricultural subsidies. But the EU's fisheries policy has been strongly criticized for giving financial support to fishermen that helps maintain overcapacity in the fishing industry and thereby overfishing in European and other waters.

Data from Fishsubsidy.org was the basis for several large journalistic investigations into the fishing sector. Among other things, it was used in a major investigative project, 'Looting the Seas II', carried out by the International Consortium of Investigative Journalists (ICIJ), an American non-profit organization. ICIJ collaborated with two Spanish reporters and a Spanish programmer. The investigation revealed how much money the Spanish fishing industry received overall from various EU funds – a summary of the facts that had until then been lacking.

Regional support

In autumn 2010, the *Financial Times* published a series of articles that amounted to one of the largest EU investigations. A group of *FT* journalists, together with the British non-profit investigative centre The Bureau of Investigative Journalism, had compiled **a database of all the EU's regional aid**. As with Farmsubsidy.org and Fishsubsidy.org, it was the first time that someone got an overview of where all that money actually went.

The timing of the publication was really unlucky because, at almost exactly the same time, WikiLeaks released the leaked diplomatic cables. The EU investigation was crowded out and the sensational data did not get the attention it deserved.

Among the revelations were that multinational companies were among the main recipients of regional aid, which is supposed to go to small and medium-sized companies. Spanish hotels had received grants for building in a nature reserve. And the Italian mafia organization, the 'Ndrangheta, had systematically applied for EU grants and had managed to get their hands on significant sums. A picture emerged of widespread fraud involving regional support money and of the European Commission not really having an overview of where the money ended up.

Work on the database resulted in plenty of articles over five days in the *Financial Times*, but also Al Jazeera, the BBC and France 2. The European Commission was critical of the reporting, which it said had given a distorted picture.

How do you dig in the EU's agriculture, fish and structural funds?

The big story in the three cases was that the reporters, through gigantic databases, for the first time could show the big picture: prove that money went to things other than what the politicians said. That story has now been done and the appetite for piecing together huge databases with EU funding is smaller today. But there are many other stories you can pursue by looking at these three big chunks of EU spending.

Anyone who would like to review the EU's agricultural subsidies can use Farmsubsidy.org. The website includes data from 2000 onwards. For most EU countries, there is missing data for some years.

Use the website for inspiration based on what other journalists are looking into. And download the data from your country to do your own searches. Perhaps you want to look at a list of all recipients of agricultural support in your municipality to see if something weird pops up? Or map the sugar producers in your country? Or all local youth organizations that have received support? The angles are endless.

The British royal family is among the main recipients in the UK because they own so much land. What about your country's royal family, if there is one? Or other rich and famous people? In some countries, politicians or politicians' relatives have been listed as beneficiaries of EU farm subsidies. Might there be a conflict of interest there?

A typical local angle is to check if there are any surprising recipients of farm aid in your particular municipality or city. There tend to be, so it is an easy way to get started on using the database. A simple search for the municipality where my family has a summer house showed that the small local golf course is a recipient of EU farm support …

As with all statistics, do not publish without checking and letting the people or companies involved respond. The data can contain errors and there might be legitimate explanations for payments that look strange.

Unlike Farmsubsidy.org, the regional database and the fish database were one-offs. The regional database has not been updated since 2010, but it remains on the *FT*'s website, and can still be searched. The fish subsidy database can be accessed by directly contacting the people who managed it.

The European Commission's Directorate-General for Regional and Urban Policy is in charge of everything that concerns regional funds, and the Directorate-General for Agriculture and Rural Development is in charge of everything that concerns farm aid. From them, you can find out the rules and eligibility criteria for the different funds.

To see exactly who is getting how much money from what fund, you need to consult the agency in your country that is in charge of the national payments. Since 2009, they have been required to publish who gets what, above a certain threshold. Individuals who receive little money will not be public, but companies and larger individual recipients are. Again, the information that is accessible from the countries' authorities varies widely.

For the farm funds and the fish funds, it is the country's agriculture ministry that is in charge. So contact it for information about recipients. When it comes to regional aid, you can find out which national authority is in charge from the European Commission's **designated website**.

Where does the rest of the EU money go?

Three-quarters of the EU budget goes to farmers and fishermen, and to regional projects. That money is paid to the EU countries' authorities and they hand it out to projects and people. The rest of the EU money is paid out by the European Commission's directorates-general or by the executive EU agencies.

All this expenditure has been, since 2007, available via the European Commission's database **the Financial Transparency System** (FTS). Since 2009, the database also has included information about European Commission salaries, public procurement and administrative costs. If you are looking into public procurement by the EU institutions, you can combine the FTS database with the database for public procurement, TED (see below).

The following information can be found in the FTS: recipients, countries and postcodes of recipients, the amounts of money paid, which commission DGs or implementing agencies have handed out the money and which part of the EU budget payments came from.

Public procurement in the EU countries and the EU institutions

Public procurement represents a very large part of the economies of EU countries. It ranges from municipalities buying new parking meters or school meals for schools, to regions buying X-ray machines for hospitals, for example. All public tenders above 200,000 euros are subject to EU rules. And all these tenders can be found in the EU database for public procurement, **Tenders Electronic Daily** (TED).

The EU institutions' own tenders are also listed in the database if they exceed 200,000 euros, and they are often the stuff of investigative articles on wasteful spending.

The EU institutions buy a great amount of goods and services. The commission procures the most. These procurements are managed by the various EU institutions; there is no central EU unit. The procurements are governed by Regulation 966/2012 on the financial rules applicable to the general budget of the Union. Check it out on EUR-Lex, for example.

TED is a fantastic tool for any European investigative journalist, not only those writing about the EU. You can get reminders via email and set how often you want to receive messages: daily, weekly, biweekly or monthly. Set your profile so that you are notified, for example, every time a public procurement concerning your city comes up. Here you find more details than the authorities themselves might decide to make public – a candy store for local journalists. For example, German reporter Sebastian Heiser in *Die Tageszeitung* used the TED database to show that Angela Merkel's office had bought cheap electricity, causing higher carbon dioxide emissions than the average.[3]

Investigating lobbying, conflicts of interests and corruption in the EU

Whose interests are the EU politicians representing? Who has influenced this EU law? Who benefits the most from this piece of legislation? Whatever

246 Investigative EU reporting

EU initiative you are reporting on, you could, and should, always ask yourself these questions.

EU institutions and lobbying transparency

Since December 2015, the commissioners, their cabinets and the directors general (the highest civil servants) – in total, just over 240 people in the commission – have had to publish information about all their meetings with lobbyists.[4] The information they have to provide includes the date of the meeting, the location, the name of the organization (not the name of the actual person representing the organization) and the topic of discussion.

You can find the information about lobbying meetings on the commissioners' respective websites. For example, look at Jyrki Katainen's homepage. Under the heading 'Agenda', you will find 'information on meetings held by Vice President Katainen' and 'information on meetings held by the Vice President's Cabinet'. The same goes for the directors general of the commission DGs. Go to the director general's homepage, on the DG's website. Somewhere on the site you will see 'Information on meetings'. If not, contact the DG and ask where the information is.

When Transparency International analyzed all the commission's lobbying meetings between December 2014 and December 2015, 75 per cent of the 7,000 plus meetings were with corporate lobbyists. For the financial markets, digital economy and trade policy portfolios, corporate lobbying accounted for more than 80 per cent of the commission's meetings. Within health and environment policy, the shares of corporate lobbying and NGOs were 50–50.[5]

The commission has pledged to meet only with lobbyists who are registered in the transparency register (see chapter 13). This is leading to a push for lobbyists to register – there were 4,000 new registrations in the 12 months that followed the commission's announcement.[6] You also need to be on the commission-parliament register to get a badge to enter the European Parliament, which also creates a push for organizations to actually register.

The much-criticized lobbyists' register is currently being reformed. Whether it will become mandatory or not is, as of September 2016, not known.

Representation and lobbying in the European Commission's expert groups

The European Commission works closely with expert groups when it develops new initiatives. Though the expert groups' recommendations are not binding, they often provide a basis for the commission's actions. Therefore, there has been significant pressure on the commission to publish information about the expert groups. Since 2009, there has been an **online register**.

As a journalist, it is interesting to investigate the representation of various interests in the expert groups that have some say in forthcoming EU legislation. It is less interesting for expert groups with a vague mandate.

Two-thirds of all expert groups are exclusively made up of representatives from EU countries' public authorities. But in a third of the expert groups, there are also persons representing trade associations, corporations, unions and non-profit organizations. Sometimes there are also people who are experts in a personal capacity, such as academics.

The expert groups should be 'balanced', according to the European Commission. The idea is to weigh the interests of different stakeholders against each other. But the lobbying watchdog organization Alter-EU has shown that many of the expert groups convened by the commission's industry and agriculture DGs have a clear preponderance of representatives from large companies and the food industry, at the expense of small and medium-sized enterprises/farmers, trade unions and NGOs.

When the commission looks for 'stakeholders', the focus tends to be on those who have a financial interest in a matter – say a European association for tyre manufacturers – rather than the more difficult to define general interest – for example, all people in the EU who want to breathe air without micro particles. Those who have a financial interest in a particular issue also tend to invest money in building up their own expertise and thereby become valuable to the commission.

Another interesting journalistic question is what the members of expert groups use their access for. *Euractiv* has shown that experts invited to give their opinion on one issue used the access to lobby for something different. For example, Bavarian politician Edmund Stoiber participated in the High Level Group on Administrative Burdens, a commission expert group. During a meeting with then-health commissioner John Dalli, Stoiber, according to *Euractiv*'s sources, took the opportunity to express the opinions of a Bavarian tobacco company on the Tobacco Products Directive, which was then being drafted by the European Commission. Stoiber was thus lobbying for a tobacco company to influence legislation in the making, completely outside his mandate in the expert group, which was about reviewing existing EU rules.[7] This is probably not unusual, and shows what influence you can have when you sit in an expert group – you can come very close to those in power.

The expert group register: a tool for checking the expert groups

Say you are writing about a controversial proposal that the commission has just presented and you want to look into the expert group that was advising the commission. Start by looking in the impact assessment, which is always published along with the commission's proposal. In the impact assessment, it will say if an expert group has been consulted. Check the expert group in the expert group registry.

If you cannot find the group in the registry, it might be because it has already been dissolved. Call the responsible DG and ask.

The following information can be obtained from the registry:

- Who the members of the expert group are. Those who are there in a personal capacity are mentioned by name; otherwise, the names of the institutions or organizations that are represented are given.

- The responsible DG ('lead DG'). This is needed to be able to go ahead and look up the information that you want but cannot find in the registry.
- What the mandate of the expert group is. Look under 'mission'. The mandate may be vague or clear, which is important when you value the news.
- There is often information about when and where the meetings were held, and sometimes what has been discussed.

Sometimes the expert group uploads documents or a link to a website with the group's meeting minutes, recommendations and opinions. If there are no such documents in the registry, try googling the expert group's name or contact the responsible DG and ask where these documents are.

If you get stuck with the registry search, there is a contact form on the website. But if like me you are allergic to anonymous online forms, you can instead call the commission's Secretariat General, and ask for someone who is working with the registry. There are a few people who do.

The 'Cash for Amendments' investigation

One of the biggest EU lobbying stories was the exposure by Britain's *Sunday Times* of some MEPs with their hands deep in the cookie jar. *Sunday Times* reporters posed as lobbyists and offered to pay money to Ernst Strasser, an MEP and former interior minister of Austria. In return, he would put forward their amendments as his own, on a legislative report on the protection of savings in troubled banks. Strasser asked for 100,000 euros as a 'consulting fee' to deliver on the fake lobbyists' requests. In talks with the reporters, which were filmed with a hidden camera, Strasser admitted that he already had five similar projects on the side. In January 2013, a Vienna court sentenced Ernst Strasser to four years in prison for corruption.

The *Sunday Times* investigative team had contacted some 60 MEPs, of whom 14 agreed to a meeting; three were captured on film offering to sell their services to lobbyists. Besides Strasser, the two others were Slovenian Zoran Thaler and Romanian Adrian Severin. Both had previously been foreign ministers in their home countries. Strasser and Thaler left the European Parliament in the wake of the exposé, but Severin remained, even though his party group, the S&D, excluded him. All three claimed that they had not done anything wrong.

It is impossible to say whether three corrupt MEPs out of 60 is representative of the whole European Parliament. But the fact that Strasser stated that he already had several such jobs on the side, and that none of these three MEPs seemed surprised by the offer, says something about how widespread the problem might be.

EU legislation affects a market of 500 million consumers. A small paragraph in a law can mean that a company wins or loses millions. This is why huge companies lobby the EU more than they lobby our politicians at home. The combination of major economic interests and almost non-existent media scrutiny also contribute to potential corruption.

The EU Integrity Watch

The Cash for Amendments scandal led to one good thing. Since then, all MEPs must fill out a form about their other income and side-jobs, a 'declaration of financial interests'.

The information that MEPs put in their declarations is, however, hardly checked at all by the European Parliament. But in 2014, Transparency International launched an online tool called the **EU Integrity Watch**. The compilation shows for example that 50 per cent of all MEPs have jobs on the side.[8] Look up the MEPs from your country in the database and see if there is something that seems worth digging into.

Investigating lobbying in the European Parliament

'Follow the money' is a classic journalistic motto. For journalists who want to track lobbying influence in the European Parliament, 'follow the amendment' is another motto. It means follow the amendments to legislative reports that individual MEPs or political groups propose and that committees or plenary vote on.

A common way of lobbying MEPs is for companies and organizations to deliver their wish-lists in the form of ready-made amendments. These can easily slip into the report that the MEP in question is working on.

During winter/spring 2013, the European Parliament treated a proposal for a data protection regulation, which was eventually adopted by the EU lawmakers in April 2016. An Austrian law student, Max Schrems, followed the regulation's long and winding road through the European Parliament.

Schrems has become a well-known activist after having filed several privacy complaints against Facebook in Ireland, where the company's European headquarters were, and started the organization Europe v. Facebook. (In 2013, Schrems filed a complaint to the EU court, asking the Irish Data Protection Commissioner to stop Facebook from transferring data to US servers, in light of Edward Snowden's revelations about the US government's snooping, through the Prism programme. The EU court invalidated the EU–US framework for data transfers, Safe Harbour, in October 2015.)

Max Schrems was preparing for a meeting with MEPs about the data protection regulation, when he read through the amendments tabled by one MEP and realized that he recognized the exact phrases, word by word, from a lobbyist's position paper he had read earlier. Amazon, eBay and the US Chamber of Commerce were among the sources that the MEP had used, without naming them, when drafting his amendments.

After Schrems discovered how many of the amendments proposed to the data protection regulation had been cut and pasted from lobbyists, transparency organizations and media got onto the story. The London-based organization Privacy International showed in a report that a quarter of all amendments tabled by British Conservative MEP Malcolm Harbour, who was chairman of the internal market committee and shadow rapporteur on the data protection report, had been cut and pasted from lobbyists' texts.[9]

As a result of Schrems' disclosures, a group of German journalists and internet activists started the website **LobbyPlag**. They tried to trace the influence of lobbyists over regulation by comparing lobbyists' position texts and MEPs' amendments. The texts were sent to them by journalists, MEPs themselves and transparency organizations. Some were scraped from the internet. They put all the information into a computer program and let it search for similarities.

LobbyPlag only reviewed the data protection regulation, but the method can be used to look at how lobbyists influence MEPs on *any* issue. Do it with the topics that interest you. You do not need to know how to do computer programming to compare two texts; you can do that manually. Max Schrems discovered the cutting and pasting simply by reading the texts. You can also google suspicious sounding amendments to see if you get an interesting match. You can find the amendments on the European Parliament's homepage.

You probably have an idea of who has an interest in lobbying to change a proposal. If not, check the register of lobbyists, the expert group registry and the commission's consultations to identify the stakeholders. Check their websites. Lobbying texts are not at all secret. They are probably on the company's or organization's website. Or ask the MEPs who are members of the relevant committee to forward emails they get from lobbyists.

It is interesting to see who the MEPs are listening to, and it is important to reveal who is influencing EU legislation. But the fact that MEPs cut and paste from the position papers of business organizations is not news to anyone who works on EU politics. This is the way it has been for a long time.

And is it really wrong? The MEPs in the case of the data protection report did not think that they had done anything wrong. They had nothing to hide; they had only listened to the different arguments and drawn inspiration from the best, they said. MEPs from the other side – those who wanted more protection for individuals' personal data – had also cut and pasted, but from organizations that shared their views on the issue.

The question is perhaps rather how open MEPs should be about their meetings with lobbyists. More and more, one hears demands for a 'legislative footprint' – that MEPs should list all the organizations and businesses they have had meetings with. This is something that individual MEPs and some national delegation and party groups have begun to do, but there is no obligation for the whole European Parliament.

Misused money in the European Parliament

In 2004–2005, I was an exchange student in Strasbourg. A fellow student had managed to get an internship with an MEP from her country, one week a month. But my friend was only an intern on the paper so it would look good on her résumé. The MEP was a family acquaintance and was doing her a favour.

Investigative EU reporting 251

His real assistant, however, came with him on these Strasbourg trips, but the MEP did not pay for her hotel. She was expected to do that herself, which was impossible with her meagre salary. Instead, she slept on my friend's floor.

A few years later it came to light that several MEPs had cheated with their assistants' salaries, and were putting them in their own pockets.

Today, the rules have been tightened. Assistants are employed by MEPs, but their salaries are paid by the European Parliament, not by MEPs themselves. MEPs may not hire family members. That sounds like a no-brainer for people in some EU countries, but this new rule is a bit strange in other places where the whole family is often involved in a political career, a bit like how American presidents are expected to stand arm-in-arm with their first lady.

When you read the European Parliament's set of rules, it is obvious that some rules have been added where warranted. And that serves as a reminder that the media should always examine how elected politicians use taxpayers' money.

MEPs' salaries and allowances. This applies as of 1 July 2015

- An MEP's monthly salary is 8,213.02 euros, representing 38.5 per cent of the salary of a judge at the European Court of Justice (the best paid EU job, and on the basis of which all the other EU salaries are calculated).
  MEPs pay an EU tax on their salary, not Belgian or French taxes. This money goes into the EU budget. After the EU tax, their net monthly salary is 6,400.04 euros.
- Each month, MEPs get a lump sum called 'general expenditure allowance', at 4,320 euros per month. This money should cover mobile phones, computers and other office supplies. Above all, it should cover the costs of an office in their constituency. Now, not all MEPs actually have a constituency office, but the money is paid whether the MEP needs it or not. MEPs do not hand in any receipts for this. Now and then, this scheme is contested and debated in the European Parliament, in terms of both the level of compensation and the lack of controls.
  Individual members have sometimes chosen to publish what they use the money for, and others have paid back the money that they do not use in the job. But this is up to the individual MEP and they are not required to do this. An MEP can, if he or she wants, cash in an extra 4,320 euros per month on top of their basic salary.
  The lump sum is halved if a member has been absent from half of the plenary sessions without a valid reason.
- Travel expenses.
  MEPs are reimbursed for the actual cost of travel to and from the constituency at home and Brussels and Strasbourg. Receipts must be submitted to the parliament's administration, but they do not hand them out to journalists.
- There is an annual travel allowance of up to 4,264 euros for all other trips, such as if an MEP travels to the US to attend a conference or similar.

Receipts have to be submitted and it is only the actual cost that is reimbursed. Journalists do not get to see these receipts.
- A subsistence allowance of 306 euros per day is paid for every day the MEPs are at work in Brussels or Strasbourg. This may sound strange, but the idea behind this is that MEPs live at home in their constituencies and go to Brussels and Strasbourg for work. Working trips come with additional costs, such as hotel and restaurant visits, and the daily subsistence allowance should cover this. There is however no checking if the MEP is actually staying at a hotel. No receipts need to be submitted.

However, MEPs have to prove that they are present at the meetings, in the plenary sitting in Strasbourg and at committee and political group meetings in Brussels, to get this subsistence allowance.

These stricter rules are also the result of an embarrassing scandal. You might remember the painful-to-watch TV feature that became a YouTube hit, showing MEPs trying to hide from the camera? They had just been exposed signing an attendance list in Strasbourg, travel bag in hand, on the way back to the airport, giving them a week's per diem.

Access to documents in the EU

'Any citizen of the Union, and any natural or legal person residing or having his registered office in a Member State, has a right of access to documents of the institutions, subject to the principles, conditions and limits defined in this Regulation.'

So reads article 2 § 1 of Regulation 1049/2001, the transparency regulation. These are the EU's rules about public access to documents held by the commission, parliament and council. It is this text that journalists refer to when they request documents from the EU institutions. Check the fact box to see which sections and articles you should invoke when you request a document.

The European project was initially based more on intergovernmental cooperation than it is today. Traditionally in intergovernmental diplomacy, secrecy is the norm. But as the EU has developed into a supranational organization, there is a constant demand for more transparency.

'When, as a Brussels-based journalist I first started campaigning during the 1970s for meetings of the Council of Ministers to be held in public and for the public's right to know what was happening behind closed doors, the official response was a mixture of bewilderment and alarm', wrote John Palmer, former European editor of Britain's *The Guardian* and later a founder of the think tank the European Policy Centre.[10]

In the 1990s, when Sweden and Finland joined the EU, the EU institutions' official position started to change and transparency began to be considered something positive and desirable. In the negotiations for Swedish EU membership, the principle of openness was one of the main hurdles.

According to the transparency regulation, the public shall have access to documents from the EU institutions. For citizens to be able to exercise this right, the institutions are obliged to set up document registers. The Council of Ministers set up its register in 1999, the European Parliament and the European Commission in 2001.

When you request a document from an EU institution, you should get a response within three weeks (15 working days). The institution can extend it for a further three weeks.

Every year, the three institutions are required to publish a report stating how many FOI requests they have received, how many they have denied and the reasons for the denial. In this annual report, there is also information about how many 'sensitive documents' there are – documents that have not been recorded in the register. This report can be found on the website for respective institutions' document registers.

The transparency regulation has been challenged in the EU court on several occasions. For example, the EU court has ruled that the public has a right to the opinions from the Council of Ministers' legal service, i.e. the lawyers who review the decisions taken and say if they are compatible with the EU treaties or not. These documents should therefore in principle be public, but journalists who request them from the legal service do not always get them.

In 2015, 29 journalists from all EU countries launched a complaint to the European Court of Justice over the European Parliament not handing out information of how MEPs spend the allowances that they get on top of their salaries.

In 2008, the European Commission presented a proposal to reform the transparency regulation. The proposal introduced more exceptions from the principle of transparency and a narrower definition of what a public document is. The negotiations on the proposal soon became stranded. The proposal was a matter for the ordinary legislative procedure, i.e. both the Council of Ministers and the European Parliament decide, and the two institutions are currently extremely far apart.

In the council, most countries want more areas to automatically be excluded from the principle of transparency, without examination, for example competition cases and infringement procedures. In the European Parliament, a broad centre-left majority adopted the 'Cashman report', named after MEP Michael Cashman, which would have increased transparency. The positions of the two lawmakers remain locked nearly ten years on. In the meantime, Regulation 1049/2001 still applies.

Fact box: Regulation 1049/2001 – 'the transparency regulation'

Article 1 of the regulation states that the purpose of the regulation is to ensure 'the widest possible access to documents'.

The regulation applies to 'all documents held by an institution, that is to say, documents drawn up or received by it and in its possession, in all areas of activity of the European Union' (Article 2.3).

Documents are defined as 'any content whatever its medium (written on paper or stored in electronic form or as a sound, visual or audiovisual recording) concerning a matter relating to the policies, activities and decisions falling within the institution's sphere of responsibility' (Article 3.a).

Thus far the principle. Now the exceptions:

First there are the typical exceptions from the principle of public access to documents, such as documents that may pose a security risk if they become public.

The institutions *shall* refuse access to a document if 'disclosure would undermine the protection of the public interest as regards public security, defence and military matters, international relations, the financial, monetary or economic policy of the Community or a Member State' (Article 4.1.a).

The institutions *shall* also refuse access to a document if the document would undermine the 'privacy and the integrity of the individual, in particular in accordance with Community legislation regarding the protection of personal data' (4.1.b).

These exceptions to the principle of access to documents are broad and could cover many documents. If an EU institution does not grant you access to a document on these grounds, you can question its interpretation of these articles, i.e. argue that the release of the document *does not* pose a security threat, for example.

You can also always ask the institution to delete the sensitive parts of the document and release the rest. Article 4.6 states that 'if only parts of the requested document are covered by any of the exceptions, the remaining parts of the document shall be released'.

Documents relating to commercial interests, court proceedings and legal advice, as well as the purpose of inspections, investigations and audits, are also exempt from the principle of public access to documents. On these grounds too, the institutions *shall* refuse access to a document. But unlike documents concerning security and defence, there is a clause: 'unless there is an overriding public interest in disclosure' (Article 4.2). When it comes to access to these documents, you have another argument in your toolbox: the overriding public interest.

The exception to the principle of public access to documents also applies to documents that are intended for 'internal use' or when the institution has not yet made a decision. Access to such documents 'shall be refused if disclosure of the document would seriously undermine the institution's decision-making process', again with the clause 'unless there is an overriding public interest in disclosure' (Article 4.3).

The fact that a document is for 'internal use' or is a 'working document' is not argument enough for an EU institution to refuse access to it; the institution needs to argue that releasing the document would 'seriously undermine its decision-making process'. Even so, you can still argue that the public interest weighs more heavily.

Exceptions to the principle of access to documents also apply to documents that come from 'third parties'. 'Third party' is defined, in Article 3.b, as EU member states, other EU institutions as well as other countries, institutions and individuals. According to Article 4.4, the EU institution in question shall 'consult the third party' whether to release the document or not. Article 4.5 specifies that an EU country may request that the EU institution not disclose a document that originates from that country, without its agreement.

Clause 6 in the preamble to the regulation states that 'wider access should be granted to documents in cases where the institutions are acting in their legislative capacity'.

This means that you can argue that documents relating to legislation that will become binding for EU countries should be made public. The bar to restrict those documents is higher than for other documents.

Requesting documents from the EU institutions

The European Commission, the European Parliament and the Council of Ministers each has an online **documents register**. These registers, however, leave much to be desired. What is most important is that you can often see what documents exist, and what you can thus request, even if they are not made public. When you search the registers, make sure that you use either English or French. If you use other languages, you risk missing many documents.

If the document is public, it will be in full text in the register, often as a PDF file. Then just click on that and read. In other cases, you can request the document by filling in an electronic form, which automatically opens when you click on a document that has not been made public in the register. You can also email the institution that has the document you want and request it.

Before requesting a document – which often entails a wait of at least three weeks – it is worth checking the EU institutions' databases and websites, and of course googling it. Though the institutions have not made the document available in the register, it could still exist somewhere else and the institution might give it to you.

Also remember that there are many organizations, companies and national authorities involved early on in the legislative process. Think about who might have access to the documents you are interested in, and who has an interest in having them leaked. Call them.

The EU institutions are full of interns and they do not always know what they can and cannot hand out. If, for example, you ask the European Parliament's press service for some information and they will not give it to you, you can always try emailing the General Secretariat and, with an authoritative tone, urging them to send the information, hoping that the person checking the inbox is working his or her first week.

See how other journalists do it

Ask the EU is a great website that can help you make FOI requests to the EU institutions. Fill in a form on the organization's website and it will send the email to the appropriate EU institution. When the institution has answered, **Ask the EU** emails you back, and publishes the whole correspondence on its website. It is a transparency project; if you do not want to reveal to the rest of the world which documents you are looking for – maybe you have a scoop – then Ask the EU is not for you.

But it is worth having a look just to see how other people phrase their FOI requests and what documents they were able to get. Here you can see that reporters ask for things like 'all documents that concern the relationship between tobacco lobbyists and health commissioner John Dalli' and the like. Your request does not have to include precise reference numbers, although the more precise you are, the better your chances of getting the document quickly.

You can also browse the website by EU institution or EU body, which can give ideas for topics for investigations. For example, see all the requests to DG Competition, the European Support Office on Asylum, or to the European Council.

Between its launch in 2011 and September 2016, some 3,200 requests have been made through the site. Out of these, about 1,400 requests were partially or completely successful in getting the documents requested. About 550 were unsuccessful, because the request was refused or because the document requested was not held by the institution. The other requests were ongoing or overdue.

The website is run by the Madrid-based transparency organization Access Info Europe. The site is run by volunteers and the start-up capital came from the private Open Society Foundation.

Request EU documents in your own country

For European Commission or European Parliament documents, you need to ask those institutions directly. But documents relating to whatever the Council of Ministers is working on are as much French as German or Slovak, and you can request them from the relevant government ministries or agencies in your home country. Remember, the council is nothing more than the 28 countries' governments and a small secretariat.

Check the Council of Ministers' register to get an idea of what documents exist. Then ask for them in your country. The other countries' positions in the deliberations will probably be redacted, but, depending on your country's transparency tradition, your own country's position will sometimes be visible.

Investigative EU reporting 257

Shop around among EU countries

According to the founder and director of the organization Access Info Europe, Helen Darbishire, the EU institutions are actually better when it comes to access to documents than many EU countries' administrations. Some EU countries completely lack fully statutory rights to information; in these cases, the EU has a higher standard.

Darbishire says that she once requested correspondence between the Spanish government and the European Commission, and received it from Brussels, not from Madrid. The German data journalist and activist Friedrich Lindenberg requested the entire EU budget in electronic format via the website Ask the EU. Once he got it, he used it as an argument when requesting the German Federal budget in electronic format from Berlin.

When the Ask the EU activists requested all the documents that had to do with the negotiations on the reformed transparency regulation from the Council of Ministers, the council secretariat told them to request the documents directly from the member states. So they did. They got the documents from the UK, the Netherlands, Sweden, Finland, Denmark and Estonia. This is a fairly accurate shortlist of the most transparent EU countries when it comes to access to documents. If you are not from one of these countries, use them anyway to get EU information that you want.

But it is not always these countries that are the most transparent. If an issue is especially sensitive for a country, access might still be blocked. Ask the EU requested an EU document that had to do with the illegal renditions that took place in the aftermath of the 9/11 attacks. Some EU countries abducted and transferred alleged terrorists to other countries where they were interrogated, at the request of the CIA. Sweden was exposed as one of the EU countries taking part in this shameful exercise and Stockholm refused the document request from Ask the EU. Instead, the document in question was obtained from Portugal.

Therefore, it is advisable to shop around in the different EU countries. Ask your European colleagues for help. You can find what FOI legislation is in force in the specific EU countries on the website **Wobbing** – a Dutch slang word for getting documents through FOI legislation.

Use Sweden as a shortcut

The Swedish constitution states that every Swedish citizen has the right to access public documents. The definition of a public document is very wide, wider than in most other EU countries and the EU institutions. The exceptions to the principle of public access are few and precise, such as protecting national security.

This principle also applies to foreigners, according to the constitution. There is no difference in right to access to documents between Swedes and non-Swedes. Since Sweden has possibly the widest definition of a public document within the EU, and since basically every state employee speaks English to a minimum level, any EU reporter could try to request the common EU documents from Stockholm.

You have the right to request and receive public documents, except those subject to confidentiality, and you do not have to explain who you are and why you want the document. It is actually illegal for the authority in question to ask you what you want the information for.

Fact box: Step-by-step guide to getting your EU document

- Start by googling the document. It might actually not be difficult to get hold of it at all. Check Ask the EU to see if someone else has already asked for the information you want.
- Make a request to the EU institution that holds the document. If it is the Council of Ministers, you could also make a request to your country or to another EU country. Check Ask the EU for inspiration on how to phrase your request.
- You do not have to know the exact name or reference number of a document to request it. For example, you can ask for all documents related to a particular issue.
- If you have time, you can proceed as follows: first request a list of the month's meetings of, say, your country's commissioner. When you have the list and see a meeting you are interested in, you can request the minutes, the agenda and all documents that were dealt with in the meeting. And so on.

If they turn you down, turn to the European Ombudsman

Are the institutions withholding documents that you believe should be public? Then you should turn to the European Ombudsman, at the moment Irish former journalist Emily O'Reilly. She does not have any legal power to force an EU institution to disclose a document, but her words weigh heavily.

In 2015, lack of transparency – for example EU institutions' refusals to give access to documents or information – was the top complaint to the European Ombudsman. It accounted for 22 per cent of all complaints.[11]

Ultimately, it is only the European Court of Justice that can rule whether or not the EU institution has the right to deny you a document, but that is of course a long and costly road to take.

By the way, the European Ombudsman can also be a source for finding stories about 'the little person against the big EU', just like the European Parliament's petitions committee (see chapter 5). Check the annual report from the Ombudsman (typically out sometime in spring), which analyzes the previous year's complaints and investigations, to see what the complaints are against the EU institutions and to get ideas for things to look into.

In 2015, the Ombudsman opened 261 inquiries, 249 of which were based on a complaint. Often the complaints are about an unfair recruitment process or that the European Commission has not lived up to its role of 'guardian of the treaties', i.e. has not monitored and sanctioned EU countries that do not follow the EU rules.[12]

Whistleblowers

Apart from a few designated spokespersons, EU officials only speak on background and refuse to be quoted. The hush-hush culture can be very irritating for reporters. But you need to know that most of them are actually prohibited by their employers from speaking to the press, and are expected to refer journalists to the press people. If they write an opinion piece, for example, the article must first be submitted to their superiors for review. Their freedom of speech is subordinate to the duty of loyalty to their employer. This is also the case for national officials in some EU countries, so it will come as no surprise, but it feels very strange for reporters from countries where civil servants can speak freely to the press and the employer is not allowed to look for the source. The EU institutions both can and do look for the source.

This means that you need to be very careful and make sure you protect your sources. First, you should always know if the civil servant that you are talking to is employed directly by the EU institution or if he or she has been seconded to the institution but is employed by a national institution. Depending on the case, their protection can look different.

Helle Larssen's book *Tystnadens Europa* ('The Silent Europe', 2012) was based on interviews with a dozen whistleblowers within the EU administration. They were officials who had revealed corruption or other irregularities in their workplaces. They had first told their superiors about their suspicions. When that did not lead to any action, they went public with the information, often through the European Parliament.

Larssen's review showed that whistleblowers were treated roughly the same way: they were ostracized in the workplace and punished through being demoted or assigned duties that were not consistent with their competence. Most of them eventually went on sick leave. Finally, they were dismissed or went into early retirement, and as such they continue being paid by the EU for many years, even though they would want to work.[13]

The experiences of these ten or so whistleblowers might not be representative, but it is no exaggeration that whistleblowers are not liked by the EU administration. According to Larssen, the situation is aggravated because EU officials have extremely favourable working conditions. An EU official with a permanent contract – a *fonctionnaire* – is not only dependent on his or her employer for wages, like all employees are, but also for the entire social safety net for the family. That can include the husband/wife's parental leave, unemployment benefits and health insurance, and the children's schooling at Brussels' special EU elite schools. A single civil servant has much to lose by making him- or herself an enemy within the workplace.

It can therefore be difficult to find sources in the administration. One way to get around this is to talk to those who are protected by their popular mandate: the MEPs. Some MEPs have made it their duty to examine the European Commission and the other EU institutions. The parliament welcomes leaks and gladly holds hearings where they confront the commission with leaked information, for example. Several of the best known EU whistleblowers have, since they stopped working as civil servants, instead made careers as MEPs.

The Tillack case

The protection of journalists' sources varies considerably in different EU countries. In some countries, there is strong source protection, enshrined in the constitution. It can be a criminal offence for a journalist to reveal his or her source. In some other EU countries, source protection is in the common law, and in still others, there is no legal protection of journalistic sources.

Belgium, for example, did not have any statutory protection for journalistic sources before the Tillack case. Hans-Martin Tillack, EU correspondent for the German weekly magazine *Stern*, in 2002 published a series of articles based on a secret report from the anti-corruption agency OLAF. The report focused, among other things, on irregularities in the statistics office Eurostat. When Tillack published the articles, OLAF immediately began looking for the leak.

An anonymous official accused Tillack of having paid 8,000 euros for the confidential information. OLAF was never able to identify the source, but the Belgian police began to investigate Tillack for bribery. In 2004, Belgian police knocked on the door of his office and confiscated Tillack's computers and notebooks. The Belgian Supreme Court ruled that the police had acted correctly and that it was a legitimate investigation.

There followed a long, drawn-out legal process. Tillack questioned the legality of OLAF passing on information to the Belgian police and brought the case to the EU court in Luxembourg, without success. Tillack also brought the case before the European Court of Human Rights in Strasbourg. There, the issue was whether Belgian authorities had violated the protection of sources.

In 2007, Tillack won his case against Belgium in the European Court of Human Rights. The ECHR concluded that the Belgian police had violated Article 10 of the European Convention on Human Rights. The court concluded that the right to information must be protected carefully and in the Tillack case, the bribery allegations against him were based only on a rumour, nothing else. In 2009, the Belgian police ended its investigation into Tillack and soon after OLAF also stopped its investigation.

As a result of the Tillack case, Belgium adopted a law that provides wide-ranging source protection. The protection of sources can be overridden only by a court and only in cases of serious threat to a person, and provided that the information cannot be obtained otherwise. This law affects all reporters working with EU sources in Brussels.

Links

Journalismfund
www.journalismfund.eu

Farmsubsidy.org
farmsubsidy.openspending.org

Financial Times' database of EU regional spending
eufunds.ftdata.co.uk

Finding the managing authorities for EU regional funds in different EU countries
ec.europa.eu/regional_policy/en/atlas/managing-authorities

Beneficiaries of EU regional funds
ec.europa.eu/regional_policy/en/atlas/beneficiaries

Beneficiaries and finding the managing authorities in my country for agriculture funds
ec.europa.eu/agriculture/cap-funding/beneficiaries/shared/index_en.htm

European Commission Database Financial Transparency System (FTS)
ec.europa.eu/budget/fts/index_en.htm

The TED (Tender Electronic Daily) registry
ted.europa.eu

Register of European Commission expert groups
ec.europa.eu/transparency/regexpert

Integrity Watch
www.integritywatch.eu

European Commission document register
ec.europa.eu/transparency/access_documents/registers_of_documents_en.htm

European Parliament document register
www.europarl.europa.eu/RegistreWeb/search/simple.htm;jsessionid=10995C292 1570FADD322BE927A1236AB?LanguageEN (or google 'European Parliament', 'register' and 'document')

Council of Ministers document register
www.consilium.europa.eu/en/documents-publications

Ask the EU
www.asktheeu.org

Wobbing
www.wobbing.eu

The European Ombudsman
www.ombudsman.europa.eu

The EU budget
Interactive charts, EU expenditure and revenue 2014–2020, European Commission
ec.europa.eu/budget/figures/interactive/index_en.cfm

Notes

1 Smit, Margo, *Deterrence of fraud with EU funds through investigative journalism in EU-27*, 2012, European Parliament, Directorate-General for Internal Policies, policy department D: budgetary affairs
2 In the Multiannual Financial Framework 2014–2020, 39 per cent goes to 'sustainable growth: natural resources', which mainly is direct payments to farmers, and 34 per cent to 'economic, social and territorial cohesion'.
3 Heiser, Sebastian, Ausschreibung offenbart, dass Merkel Klimakillerstrom bezieht [blog post], *Journalismus & Recherche*, http://recherche-info.de, 17 December 2009
4 Transparency International EU, *7000 and counting – Lobby meetings of the European Commission*, 1 December 2015
5 Transparency International EU, *7000 and counting*
6 *Politico*, Brussels Playbook [newsletter], 7 September 2016
7 *Euractiv*, Tobacco lobby focus switches from Dalli to Stoiber, 26 October 2012
8 Transparency International EU, *7000 and counting*
9 *EUobserver*, MEPs copy-pasting amendments from US lobbyists, 12 February 2013
10 Palmer, John, *Openness and Transparency – the state of the debate in the European Union*, European Information no 6, April 1999
11 European Ombudsman Annual Report 2015, 3 May 2016
12 European Ombudsman Annual Report 2015
13 Larssen, Helle, *Tystnadens Europa*, Celanders förlag, 2012

19 Practical help in Brussels

Where do I turn if I have problems with the EU institutions? Are there EU seminars and scholarships? How can I get accreditation to the EU institutions? From where can I work when I am in Brussels?

Accreditation to the European institutions

Permanent accreditation

The yellow press card marked 'laissez-passer' is the key to all the EU institutions. The European Commission's Directorate-General for Communication handles requests for **general accreditation** to the commission, parliament and council. The press card is valid for one year and must then be renewed. There is also an annual accreditation just for the **European Parliament**, which is slightly easier to get, but that only gives you access to that institution.

To be permanently accredited to all the EU institutions you must provide:

- Proof that you live in Brussels or nearby: evidence of residence or a Belgian identity card.
- Proof of professional activity: published articles/radio or TV features, and proof of payment.
- A letter from an editor stating that you are their correspondent in Brussels. This media organization must be demonstrably independent.

Start by contacting the commission accreditation office. Even if you cannot provide all the required documents directly, it is worth giving them a call. They can give a temporary accreditation for a couple of months, to give you time to prove that you are working as an EU reporter.

In a media landscape in which more and more journalists are freelance or part-time reporters and part-time something else, these requirements are sometimes difficult to meet. Quite a few Brussels-based reporters cannot put the above-mentioned documents on the table. It goes without saying that it is difficult to earn a steady income if you cannot enter the buildings of the institutions that you are setting out to cover. This issue will probably grow in importance as the ratio of freelancer to permanent correspondents shifts.

It is so difficult to get into the institutions – particularly the European Commission – because there are so many lobbyists who would like to use the press room, where they can get very close to the people in power. In Brussels, the gap between a journalist and lobbyist is not wide. Some reporters change jobs during the year and save their press cards for use in their new lobbying jobs.

But the excessively harsh accreditation requirements are also the fault of the journalists' own representatives, the International Press Association (API). In the committee that sets the rules for journalists in the EU institutions, API speaks for the Brussels journalists and API's approach to media is, or at least has been in the past, quite protectionist. API was, for example, opposed to the EU institutions' TV channel EbS online streaming of the commission's daily press conferences, because Brussels correspondents would then not have a monopoly on quotes and the latest information.

Short-term accreditation

If you are just coming to Brussels for one or a few days, you need to contact **the respective institutions individually for accreditation**. You are required to show a copy of your passport and national press card. Not all EU countries' journalists have national press cards, so if you do not, write that this is not a requirement in your country and send a letter from your editor certifying that you work for him or her. If you are freelance, explain that in the email.

Email your documents 24 hours in advance to the:

- European Commission: comm-pressroom-team@ec.europa.eu
- Council of Ministers: press.centre@consilium.europa.eu
- European Parliament: media.accreditation@ep.europa.eu

Do not forget to bring the same documents with you and show them when you pick up your badges in the institutions' receptions.

Accreditation to EU summits

For EU summits it is another story. Even journalists who have a permanent EU accreditation need separate **accreditation for the EU summits**, even though there is now a six-month badge that you can apply for. To obtain accreditation to an EU summit, you can register on the website from a few weeks before the summit up to the last minute. The places are not limited.

The first time you register, you need to fill in some information and send a passport photo, your passport number and press card. If you do not have a press card, write and explain this and instead send a letter from your editor. If you are a freelance journalist, type 'freelancer' in all the mandatory fields about your media, and email the council press centre. They will probably ask you to send some published articles as proof that you work as a journalist. If you have already been to an EU summit, your information remains in the database. Just go in and check that it is still correct.

Pick up the badge in the LEX building, to the right-hand side of the council building. Remember to bring your passport and press card/original letter from the editor with you when you pick up your badge.

When in Brussels

Where to work when you are in Brussels

The three main EU institutions all have press rooms with workplaces, Wi-Fi and cheap coffee in nearby cafeterias. Many EU correspondents choose to work from these places even if they have their own offices.

Close to the council's Justus Lipsius building is the international press centre, the Residence Palace. It houses the Brussels bureaus of many media organizations. In the lobby and the meeting rooms on the ground floor there are often seminars and debates organized by think tanks. There is also a restaurant.

Even if you do not have an office there, the Residence Palace is a nice, neutral place to set up a meeting or conduct an interview. It is right in the EU quarters, it feels more professional than meeting up in a coffee shop and there is plenty of space to sit down and talk undisturbed. There are also two rooms with work spaces for journalists, with free Wi-Fi.

The Brussels Press Club also has an office close to the main EU institutions. There are some designated work spaces for journalists, extremely cheap beer and a lounge that is good for meetings or interviews. You do however need to be a member, which costs 100 euros a year.

European Parliament and European Commission travel grants

The European Parliament's information offices in the EU countries offer travel grants for national journalists to go to Brussels and to the plenary week in Strasbourg. The grant covers travel expenses plus a lump sum to pay for a hotel and food. The number of journalists each office can send, and how often, varies from country to country. Check with your country's office.

Some, but not all, of the European Commission's representations bureaus in the capitals also provide travel grants to Brussels. Check with the office in your country to see if you can participate.

The European Parliament also gives grants to accredited Brussels-based journalists to cover plenary sessions in Strasbourg. The application process is handled by API.

Use radio and television studios in the institutions

All three main EU institutions have radio and television studios that you can use for free. You do not have to be an accredited journalist to reserve a studio.

All institutions also have a team of technicians that can help you and a TV team that you can use for filming.

Go to the respective institution's **audiovisual service** to book the studio and crew. There, you can also see all the necessary technical information.

Journalist organizations

The International Press Association (API)

API was founded in 1975. It brings together journalists who live in Belgium and work for foreign media, both employed and freelance. API is not really a union, but rather an interest group for EU correspondents. API represents foreign journalists to the EU institutions and the Belgian authorities, for example on issues such as access to EU buildings, accreditation or Belgian tax issues.

It sometimes happens at press conferences that a representative from API stands up and protests – for example, against the European Commission having leaked information to a small, selected clique of journalists, against a commission spokesperson who does not respond to a journalist's question or against lobbyists sitting among journalists at the press conference.

If you are not a Brussels correspondent, you cannot become a member of API. But it is API you should contact if any of the EU institutions treat you as a journalist badly in some way. API will take up the complaint directly with the institutions.

European Journalism Centre (EJC)

The EJC is located in Maastricht in the Netherlands and has an office in Brussels. It organizes training for journalists, primarily with a focus on the functioning of the EU. Check out their website for upcoming seminars, press trips or grants.

Often, EU institutions pay for seminars and the EJC manages the practical aspects. A typical example is a two-day seminar on the financial crisis, organized and financed by the European Commission's economic affairs DG. Or the EJC might organize a press trip for young European journalists to the EU institutions in Luxembourg, paid for by the Luxembourg Ministry of Foreign Affairs.

European Federation of Journalists (EFJ)

The EFJ is the European branch of the International Federation of Journalists (IFJ) and has its headquarters in Brussels. The EFJ represents journalist unions and their members – indirectly 300,000 journalists in thirty countries. It lobbies the EU institutions on behalf of its members, our journalist unions, about EU legislation that can affect journalists. Sometimes the EFJ can be a source, for example when writing about press freedom in European countries.

Links

The European Commission's accreditation centre (annual accreditation to all the EU institutions)
ec.europa.eu/dgs/communication/press/accreditation_en.htm#Annual

Accreditation to the European Parliament (annually, daily)
www.europarl.europa.eu/news/en/contacts-and-services/20150617SRV67416/media-accreditation

Accreditation to the European Commission (daily)
ec.europa.eu/dgs/communication/press/accreditation_en.htm#oneday

Accreditation to the Council of Ministers (daily)
www.consilium.europa.eu/en/press/accreditation

Accreditation to an EU summit
www.european-council.europa.eu/media-accreditation

European Parliament's audiovisual service
audiovisual.europarl.europa.eu
Click on 'facilities'

European Commission's audiovisual service
ec.europa.eu/avservices
Click on 'My AV Services'

The Council of Ministers' audiovisual service
www.consilium.europa.eu/en/press/tv-radio-studios

The International Press Association, API
www.api-ipa.org/home

European Journalism Centre, EJC
www.ejc.nl

European Federation of Journalists, EFJ
europeanjournalists.org

20 Writing about the EU

EU jargon

The EU has its own language that is foreign to anyone who does not live in the Brussels bubble. There is of course the lawyers' language – all the technical, legal terms. There is also the EU jargon that politicians, officials and Brussels-based journalists use in their day-to-day communication.

EU jargon is a hodgepodge of the member states' languages and a result of the EU's consensus culture. Difficult political compromises can sometimes be achieved by coming up with a new word for something and everyone reading the word to mean what they want it to. Not infrequently, EU summits generate a new EU term that previously did not exist. It is often a long series of words that includes the word 'union' or 'mechanism'.

During one single background briefing with national officials from one EU country, I noted the following words and expressions, which are good examples of how impenetrable typical EU-speak can be: 'decision on whether CETA will be a mixed agreement or not', 'German non-paper', 'Five Presidents' Report', 'portability regulation', 'commission communication about the security union', 'smart borders', 'instrument of ratification', and 'partnership framework with third countries'.

All official EU terms exist in all official EU languages, but the jargon does not. As English and French are the main EU languages, the EU jargon is often closer to the way normal people talk in English or in French, but will sound more foreign in other languages. People from small countries working in the EU institutions tend to use the English jargon, which makes it difficult for journalists to know what term to use when writing the story.

Sometimes there is no widely understood common term for an EU term. Instead you need to use the correct, bureaucratic term and then explain what this means, which contributes to many EU articles being somewhat dry and educational. It can look something like this, from an article in *EUobserver*: 'The one-page proposal "is a piece of paper, it's not an Ecofin document", he told his colleagues, using the abbreviation for the finance ministers' council'.[1]

Be aware of the jargon when you do interviews. It can happen that, when you listen to the recording, you realize that the sentences are full of words that no outsider understands and you have to discard good quotes. Pressure your interviewees to use normal words and say 'explain this in a way that someone who does not know anything about the EU can understand'.

Another thing to be careful about is using terms like 'Eurozone', 'Schengen countries', 'founding members', 'EU-15' or 'the new member states'. You cannot assume that your readers know which countries you are referring to. If it is important, you might need to spell it out, or put the information in a fact box.

Frenglish

If you are reading an EU text in English and do not understand what it means, it is probably because some of these words do not really exist in the English language outside the EU bubble. It is the EU's made-up language: French disguised as English.

French was for a long time the only working language of the EU institutions. Many typical EU words are from French but are now used in all languages. French is still the working language of the European Court of Justice, but the European Commission now works in English, French and German. In most other EU institutions, English has replaced French as the language that everyone needs to know.

Most Frenglish words are what the French call 'faux amis' – false friends. They are French words that sound similar to English words, but actually mean something else. They have seeped into EU English without anyone noticing. Some are unknown to native English speakers outside the EU institutions, others are real words that have changed meaning and others are used correctly but in a context in which they would never be used by native speakers. A report from the Court of Auditors translation unit sourly notes that the word 'comitology' gets 1,253 hits in the EUR-Lex database, when it is a word that does not exist outside the EU institutions.[2]

'Modality' in the EU context means procedure, process or method. And the word 'third country' is used profusely in all sorts of contexts and can refer to a country not being an EU member state, not being part of the Schengen Area or not belonging to some other EU-related group of countries.

Typical French EU-speak that sometimes finds its way to where it does not belong is the prefix 'euro'. French media often call MEPs 'eurodéputés'. And in French and Spanish media 'Europe' and 'EU' are often used as synonyms. It may be tempting to use 'euro-', to get away from the aesthetically unappealing 'EU'. It works in some languages, but not all. In some languages, 'euro' very clearly connotes the euro currency and could give the reader the wrong impression.

Anglicisms

If the English speakers should watch out for the EU Frenglish, everyone else should be wary of Anglicisms. Even though all formal EU terms exist in all official languages, you can often see the English term – for example the name of a European Parliament's committee – in articles written in other languages. This is often because the journalist re-wrote the story from English media or took it from a press release in English, and did not know that the term exists in his or her language or where to find it. It is ugly and unnecessary to mix languages in a journalistic text, and it contributes to the reader feeling that the EU is something foreign.

Another danger with copy-pasting from English for non-English speakers is that names written in Cyrillic or Greek letters are transcribed differently in different languages. For example, the current Bulgarian EU commissioner's surname is transcribed Georgieva in English, Gueorguieva in French and Georgiewa in German and Polish. Beware of this when you write about Bulgarian and Greek EU politicians. Double-check their names with your language rules.

How to find the EU term in your language

For legal, technical terms, start by checking **IATE**, the EU institutions' terminology database, run by the EU translation agency in Luxembourg. The database contains over one million terms in all official languages, and is the tool that the EU translators themselves use to find the right word. It will not pick up the EU jargon though, only the legal terms.

When you look for an EU jargon term in your own language, start by finding an EU institution website or an EU document in English that contains the word. Then change the language settings of that site. If the information exists in other languages, there is a language menu in one of the top corners. If not, try changing the language code in the URL. Personally, I often google whatever term I am looking for in English and limit my searches to the European Parliament site. It is the EU institution that is the most 'language sensitive', where the pressure is greatest not to discriminate between languages. Even if you write about an issue that is not decided by the parliament, there is a chance that someone has discussed the matter there once and thus left a trace on the website.

Prejudices

In all European countries there are plenty of prejudices against neighbouring countries. This is also reflected in EU journalism. For example, during the ongoing euro crisis, some Greek and German newspapers were full of references to the Second World War and lazy Greeks. Many media in rich EU countries casually used the derogatory term PIGS or PIIGS for a group of indebted EU countries (Portugal, Ireland, Italy, Greece, Spain).

Subtler are the terms and stereotypes used about other European people and countries. In countries where the media tends to re-write much EU news from British media, typical British prejudices towards other EU countries tend to tag along. A typical British language bias is the concept of 'Club Med' countries, from the exclusive holiday operator Club Méditerranée. The term is demeaning for southern Europe, alluding to beach holidays and dilapidated economies.[3]

In French, the term 'Anglo-Saxon' is used for most things that one does not like and that come from the UK or the US. 'Ultralibéral' and even 'libéral' are negative terms in France, often used to describe 'Anglo-Saxon' policies, while 'liberal' in most northern EU countries has positive connotations, wherever you find yourself on the political spectrum.

The Second World War is never far away. When one dislikes another EU country's position, military terms usually pop up, such as using the term 'the British front' to refer to the UK's opinion on an EU issue.[4]

Writing about the EU institutions

Instead of writing 'the French president' ten times in the same article, you might replace it with 'Paris' or 'the Elysée palace', after his residence. Similarly, the Kremlin, the Knesset and the White House are used as synonyms for a state power.

The question is whether the EU institutions' buildings are sufficiently well known to be used as synonyms. Maybe it is time to wear them in? In that case, you can use 'Justus Lipsius' as a synonym for the Council of Ministers and 'Berlaymont' for the European Commission. The foreign service EEAS' home is a building called the Triangle Building. The European Parliament buildings, by contrast, have no names.

You should also be careful when using 'Brussels' as a synonym for the EU. In a text about the EU countries' position on something, Brussels could equally be the synonym for Belgium. As for the European Parliament, check where the decision was taken before you call it either 'Brussels' or 'Strasbourg'. 'Strasbourg rejects the budget', wrote Italian *24 Ore*, for example, which was correct, because the vote took place in Strasbourg.[5]

In general, be careful what institution you are writing about. Writing 'the European Commission' instead of 'the Council of Ministers' is as wrong as writing 'government' instead of 'parliament'. Also, there is no 'EU building', 'European headquarters' or 'EU committee'. There is a European Commission headquarters, a council building and many committees in the European Parliament.

As mentioned before, communication from the EU institutions is EU-centric. They are inside the EU and look out. From their perspective it makes sense to talk about 'member states'. For our readers, that does not make any sense. Translate the jargon to 'national governments' instead.

Illustrating EU news

Be careful when your editor is choosing photos to go with your EU articles. Quite often, EU people get frustrated by articles about the European Parliament that are illustrated by a picture of the commission's star-shaped building, and vice versa. Also make sure you do not use a picture from the Brussels parliament when you are illustrating a decision that has just been adopted in plenary session in Strasbourg. This happens on occasion, and is a small mistake that diminishes the credibility of the whole article.

Links

The EU institutions' terminology database, IATE
iate.europa.eu

Notes

1 *EUobserver*, EU financial transaction tax on life support, 8 December 2015
2 Court of Auditors, *Misused English words and expressions in EU publications*, Secretariat General, Translation directorate, May 2013
3 For example, *The Times*, Unifying Europe will bring trouble, not peace, 14 March 2013, and *The Guardian*, 'Club Med' countries have spoiled the eurozone party, 17 July 2011
4 For example, *Le Soir*, Plafonner le bonus des banquiers: shocking!, 1 March 2013
5 *24 Ore*, Strasburgo boccia il budget, 14 March 2013

Glossary

Below is a combined dictionary and thesaurus. The list is far from complete but can hopefully be helpful when you read EU texts.

Some of the examples are taken from the BBC guide to Brussels-speak,[1] the European Commission's guide to jargon alternatives,[2] and from various media.

Absorption capacity A country's ability to use (absorb) money received, for example EU regional aid. A country could have a poor absorption capacity because it lacks skills or staff or because EU funds require co-funding from recipient countries, meaning that very poor countries have difficulty absorbing EU funds.

Accession As in 'accession treaty' or 'accession country'.
Synonyms: membership treaty, country joining the EU.

Accession criteria See Copenhagen criteria.

ACP countries African, Caribbean and Pacific countries – basically the EU countries' former colonies – which the EU has trade and assistance agreements with.

Acquis communautaire 'The Acquis' in Brussels jargon.
Meaning: The entire body of EU law: all EU legislation, all the EU case law and all international agreements. When a new country wants to join the EU, it has to reform its legal system to incorporate all this before it can join, which takes a substantial amount of time.
Synonym: All existing EU laws and rules.

Ad hoc Often used in EU-speak, for example 'ad hoc group' or 'ad hoc committee'. Better to write 'temporary group' or 'committee set up for a specific purpose'.

Advocate General Advisors to the EU judges who give opinions before rulings. This opinion is seen as an indication of how the EU court will rule, but the court does not always follow the opinion.

Agencies Decentralized EU agencies provide EU policymakers with expertise or execute EU policies.

A item An issue that has already been negotiated on a lower level in the Council of Ministers and that will be adopted by the ministers without further debate. Compare it to 'B item'.
Synonyms: non-controversial issue, item that will be approved without discussion, to be formally adopted without debate.

ALDE Liberal party group in the European Parliament.
Synonyms: the liberal political group, liberal MEPs, centrist group.

Article 7 Article 7 of the Treaty on European Union states that an EU country can have its voting rights in the Council of Ministers suspended if it 'seriously and persistently' breaches the EU fundamental values.
Also called 'the suspension clause'.

Article 50 Article 50 of the Treaty on European Union sets out the procedure for when a country wants to leave the EU.
Also called 'the withdrawal clause'.

Association Agreement Agreement between the EU and countries outside the EU for privileged treatment, such as scrapped duties on certain goods. Often the first step to EU membership.

Berlaymont The European Commission's headquarters.

B item A matter that hasn't been resolved at lower levels of the Council of Ministers and that requires discussion by ministers.
Synonyms: Discussion point, crucial issue, outstanding issue, issue to be debated.

Bureau Consists of the European Parliament's president and his 14 vice presidents and five finance officers. They deal with administrative and personnel issues.

BusinessEurope The European federation for industry and commerce, business umbrella organization, the main European business lobby, EU employers.

Cabinet In the EU context, a group of important advisors to the European Commissioner.
Synonyms: advisors, team, the commissioner's closest men and women.

Candidate country A country that is in the process of negotiating to join the EU. 'Potential candidate countries' are recognized as potential members, but there are still no direct talks with Brussels on future membership.
Synonyms: Future EU country, would-be member, country that aspires to join the EU.

CAP/PAC See Common Agricultural Policy. Both the English and French acronyms are often used in EU jargon.

Chapter Negotiating chapters, policy area.
For example: 'Yesterday the EU foreign ministers agreed to open a new chapter in membership negotiations with Turkey' = Yesterday the foreign ministers decided to begin negotiations within a new policy area with Turkey. There are around thirty chapters, e.g. animal rights and company law, when the EU negotiates with candidate countries.
There are also negotiating chapters in trade negotiations, for example the negotiations for the EU–US TTIP trade deal.

Citizen's initiative Meaning: One million EU citizens from seven EU countries can petition the European Commission to propose EU legislation and the commission has to examine the proposal.
Synonyms: EU-wide petition, petitioning system.
Codecision See ordinary legislative procedure. Codecision is the old word, which is still used in EU jargon.
Cohesion As in 'cohesion fund' or 'cohesion policy'.
Meaning: EU redistribution policy through funds for poor regions.
Synonyms: EU support to the poorest regions, regional development funding.
College The 28 commissioners, the group of commissioners.
Comitology Committee procedure, a set of procedures for adopting technical regulations, committees in which national authorities scrutinize how the commission implements EU law, system of national experts overlooking the technical aspects of the implementation of EU laws, delegated decision-making.
Comitology is an old term that is still used in EU jargon. It is however vague. It sometimes refers to implementing acts, which is similar to the old comitology procedure, and sometimes to all delegated decision-making, i.e. both implementing acts and delegated acts.
Committee of the Regions Consultative body representing local and regional authorities, platform for regional interests in the EU.
Common Agricultural Policy (CAP) The EU's agricultural policy.
Synonyms: EU farm policy, farm spending, subsidies for European farmers and landowners, farm support, farmers' aid.
Common Fisheries Policy (CFP) The EU's fisheries policy.
Synonyms: EU fishing policy, subsidies for European fishermen.
Community Often used in EU jargon, for example 'community programme' or 'community action'. Write 'EU programme' or 'EU action' instead.
Community method Old EU term that basically means the ordinary legislative procedure, i.e. the European Commission proposing legislation and the European Parliament and the Council of Ministers (voting with qualified majority) jointly amending and adopting the legislation, as opposed to the 'intergovernmental method'.
Competencies EU jargon. Used in the context of talking about what powers the EU has as opposed to the member states. For example, 'monetary policy is an exclusive EU competence in the euro countries'.
Synonyms: power, obligations.
Conference of Presidents The European Parliament president and the chairmen of the party groups.
The Conference of Presidents organizes the parliament politically, through for example dividing top posts between the political groups. Compare it to the bureau, which decides on administrative matters.
Synonym: party group leaders.

Convention Representatives of EU institutions and EU member states meeting up to work out an important document. For example, the European convention that drafted the EU constitution, which eventually became the Lisbon Treaty.

Convergence criteria Five criteria for national economies in order to be eligible to join the euro, e.g. public debt has to be less than 60 per cent of GDP. Criteria for maintaining similar economic policies for countries wishing to join the single currency.
Synonyms: requirements for joining the euro, euro criteria.

Copenhagen criteria Three main requirements for countries that wish to join the EU: the country must have a market economy, must be capable of taking on all the existing EU laws (the acquis communautaire), and must be a democracy that respects the rule of law and human rights and protects minorities.

Coreper Committee of Permanent Representatives, EU ambassadors.

Coreper I EU deputy ambassadors.

Coreper II EU ambassadors.

Council of Europe European human rights organization that promotes democracy and seeks to protect human rights in its 47 member countries. It is not a part of the EU, although all EU countries and all candidate countries to the EU are members of the Council of Europe.

Council of Ministers The EU institution that represents the national governments. Synonyms: EU governments, EU ministers, representing the member countries, EU member countries.
Instead of 'the transport council', you can write 'meeting of EU transport ministers' or 'EU transport ministers meeting in Brussels'.

Council of the European Union/Council of the EU The formal name for Council of Ministers.

Court of Auditors The EU's external and independent auditor. Reviews the EU institutions' accounting and budget to see if EU money has been spent properly. Synonyms: EU financial watchdog, EU's top auditor.

Court of First Instance Old term. Now called the General Court.

Court of Justice First chamber of the Court of Justice of the European Union. Gives preliminary rulings, hears actions against EU institutions brought by EU countries. Hears appeals against General Court rulings.

Court of Justice of the European Union EU's top court, EU judges, Luxembourg-based European Court of Justice.

Derogation Meaning that a certain EU rule is not binding for a certain EU country.
Synonyms: exception, opt-out.

DG See Directorate-general.

Directive EU law that sets a goal that all EU countries have to achieve, but leaves it up to each country to decide how to live up to the goal. Differs from regulations.
Synonym: EU framework law.

Glossary 277

Directorate-general DG, department of the European Commission, policy department.
Dublin Convention A refugee should ask for asylum in the first EU country that he or she comes to.
Eastern Partnership Cooperation between the EU and six former Soviet republics: Ukraine, Belarus, Moldova, Georgia, Armenia and Azerbaijan. The partnership includes, among other things, visa facilitation, democracy-building projects and money to build efficient administrations.
Ecofin EU governments' finance and economy ministers, EU finance ministers.
Economic and Monetary Union The rules governing the euro.
 Synonyms: the euro, the common (single) currency, the common currency and monetary policy.
ECR Conservative Eurosceptic party group, EU-critical conservatives.
EEA See European Economic Area.
EEAS See European External Action Service.
EFDD Nationalist party group, the political group that gathers populist anti-EU parties.
EMU See Economic and Monetary Union.
ENF Right-wing populist party group in the European Parliament, nationalists and eurosceptics, extreme right EU politicians
Enhanced cooperation A minimum of nine EU countries can move on within an area in which the EU has power, within the EU structures, without the other EU countries being involved. A method used to avoid paralysis when a small group of countries blocks a proposal in the Council of Ministers.
Enlargement EU-centric word. Instead use 'EU expansion' or 'new countries joining the EU'.
EPP EU centre-right group, the right-wing parliament group, the conservative group, group of Christian democrats.
EU The bloc, the union, 28 European countries.
EU-10 The countries that joined the EU in 2004: eight former communist countries of central and eastern Europe, and Cyprus and Malta.
EU-15 The EU countries before 2004, basically Western Europe.
Eurobarometer EU public opinion institute, the EU poll, pan-European poll, European Union public opinion survey.
Eurogroup Forum for the euro countries' finance ministers. Their meetings usually take place the evening before Ecofin meetings, which are meetings of the 28 EU finance ministers.
Europe 2020 The EU's growth strategy.
Europe à la carte EU countries choosing to adhere to some, but not all, EU policies. See also multi-speed Europe and enhanced cooperation.
European Commission The commission, Berlaymont, the EU executive, the institution that manages the daily work of the EU, the EU's executive body, EU's civil service, Eurocrats (disparaging).
European Council EU summit, EU leaders, EU heads of state and government, EU countries' prime ministers and presidents.

European Economic and Social Committee Consultative EU body representing civil society.

European Economic Area (EEA) The free movement of persons, goods, services and capital both within the 28 EU countries (EU's internal market) and between the EU and three out of the four member states of the European Free Trade Association (EFTA).

EFTA member Switzerland has not joined the EEA. Instead it has several bilateral agreements with the EU, allowing it to participate in the EU internal market.

Instead of writing 'EEA countries', spell them out – there are only three: Norway, Iceland and Liechtenstein.

European External Action Service EEAS in short. The EU's diplomatic branch, the EU's foreign policy branch, the EU's foreign ministry, the EU's diplomatic service.

European Parliament Legislature, assembly, parliament, MEPs, elected EU politicians, representing EU citizens.

European semester The EU countries hand in their planned national budgets to the European Commission, which reviews them and makes recommendations. The treatment takes about six months, hence the term 'semester'.

Synonyms: budget review, commission review of national budgets.

Eurorealist Term eurosceptics sometimes use to refer to themselves.

Eurosceptic Person who opposes European integration.

Eurostat EU statistics agency.

Eurozone Eurozone is used in many EU languages, but it is both an Anglicism and EU jargon.

Synonyms: EU countries that have adopted the common currency, euro countries, the countries with the euro as their currency.

The Eurozone countries are (2016): Austria, Belgium, Cyprus, Estonia, Finland, France, Germany, Greece, Ireland, Italy, Latvia, Lithuania, Luxembourg, Malta, the Netherlands, Portugal, Slovakia, Slovenia and Spain.

Excessive deficit procedure The threat of sanctions against euro countries for excessively large government deficits and debt (more than 3 and 60 per cent of GDP respectively). The procedure requires the country to provide a plan and a deadline by when it will act. Ultimately, euro countries that don't follow up on recommendations can be fined.

Four freedoms The free movement of people, goods, services and capital within the EU.

Frontex The EU agency that coordinates external border surveillance.

FTT Financial Transaction Tax.

Tax on financial transactions, finance tax, Tobin tax.

General Court Hears cases filed against EU institutions brought by citizens and sometimes by EU countries. Second chamber of the Court of Justice of the European Union.

Green paper   Discussion paper, the commission suggested referral, consultation document.
Greens-EFA   The Greens, the green parliamentary group, the European Green Party.
GUE-NGL   Left-wing group in the European Parliament, parliamentary group with former communist parties in Europe, the united left political group, left-leaning.
Often only GUE, for example 'Gabi Zimmer, leader of the leftist GUE group, said that …'
Harmonized rules   Standard rules.
Head of cabinet   Commissioners' office manager.
Heads of state and government   EU leaders, prime ministers and presidents.
High Representative of the Union for Foreign Affairs and Security Policy   High representative, high rep, foreign policy chief, the EU foreign chief, EU foreign policy representative, representing the EU's foreign policy, EU external affairs commissioner.
Horizon 2020   The EU's seven-year research programme. For 2014–2020 it has a budget of around 80 billion euros.
Synonym: EU research grants.
Internal market   Common market between the EU countries, one of the EU's main objectives.
Legal services   Legal department. All EU institutions have one.
Like-minded   As in 'like-minded countries'. Countries that have the same view on something. A group of countries that acts together in EU negotiations.
Lisbon strategy/Lisbon agenda   EU competitiveness strategy, EU strategy for growth and jobs. No connection to the Lisbon Treaty.
Lisbon Treaty   The EU's main rulebook, the most recent EU treaty, much like an EU constitution.
Macro-region   Cooperation between some EU countries to achieve economies of scale with existing EU funds. The Baltic Sea region is a macro-region, focusing on environmental cooperation. The Danube region is also a macro-region working on issues as diverse as water purification, counter-corruption and integration of Roma people.
MEP   Member of European Parliament, legislator, elected EU politician.
Multiannual Financial Framework (MFF)   Long-term EU budget. The EU's seven-year budget ceiling, the EU's multiannual budget.
Multi-speed Europe   The term used for the idea of differentiated EU integration, with some countries advancing and others following later. Close to the concept of 'Europe à la carte'. See enhanced cooperation.
Net beneficiary   Country receiving more from the EU budget than it pays in. The relatively poor EU countries.
Net contributor   Country paying more into the EU budget than it receives in grants and support. The relatively rich EU countries.
NI   Non-attached, from non-inscrit (French), MEP who doesn't belong to a political group, maverick.

Non-paper   Proposal from a European institution or a member state that has no official status and is supposed to be confidential, but often finds its way to the press. Journalistically speaking, non-papers can be interesting because they often mark the start of a political debate. For example, 'Ahead of the summit, Germany, France and the Netherlands circulated a non-paper on the long-term budget'.
Synonyms: non-official proposal, a test balloon.

OLAF   The EU counter-corruption agency, the EU's counter-fraud agency, the EU anti-corruption body, the EU's anti-fraud investigator.

Ombudsman   The European Ombudsman acts as a watchdog for the EU institutions. It ensures that they are transparent and accountable. However, its opinions do not carry any legal weight.

Open method of coordination, OMC   A way for member states to co-ordinate their policies in areas in which the EU doesn't have power, such as healthcare and retirement policy.
Synonyms: common goals and comparisons between EU countries, policy coordination by EU governments.

Opinion   A non-binding statement from any of the EU institutions.

Opting out   An EU country can choose not to join a particular EU policy. For example, Denmark has an opt-out from the euro and Poland has an opt-out from the EU Charter of Fundamental Rights.

Ordinary legislative procedure   The European Parliament and the Council of Ministers share decision-making. Both institutions amend and adopt draft proposals from the European Commission. This procedure applies to the vast majority of all EU legislation. The old term, codecision, is still used sometimes.

Outermost regions   The EU has nine outermost regions, for example the Canary Islands, Madeira and French Guiana, which are a part of the EU and are eligible for EU funding from the structural funds.
Synonym: The EU's outlying territories.

Overseas countries and territories (OCTs)   The EU has 25 overseas countries and territories, such as ex-colonies including Greenland, the Falkland Islands and French Polynesia, that have special ties to certain EU countries.

Own resources   There is confusion about the term. The European Commission uses it for all EU revenue, including the member states' contributions to the EU budget. But often, when MEPs talk about 'own resources', they mean an EU-wide tax, money that won't depend on the EU governments.

Permanent representation to the EU   A government's extended arm in Brussels, EU embassy, 'perm rep'.

Permanent representative   Head of the permanent representation.
For example, Denmark's top EU diplomat, Denmark's ambassador to the EU, negotiating for Denmark, Denmark's representative.

Plenary session   When the whole European Parliament meets. Monthly meeting in Strasbourg, the whole chamber.

Rapporteur MEP who is responsible for a draft bill, European Parliament's chief negotiator, main negotiator, responsible MEP, lead MEP, MEP who is steering the bill through parliament.
REACH Regulatory framework for chemicals, EU rules on chemicals.
Reading Treatment in the two legislatures, the European Parliament and the Council of Ministers. First reading = first treatment.
Regulation EU law that is the same in all EU countries and is directly enforceable. Compare to directive.
Right of initiative Only the European Commission can propose new EU legislation. It has exclusive right of initiative.
Schengen The right to travel within the EU without a passport, the passport union, open borders within the EU, rules on open, invisible borders between EU countries, and all citizens' freedom of movement within the union.
Synonyms: border-free area, passport union
The Schengen countries are (2016): EU countries Austria, Belgium, Czech Republic, Denmark, Estonia, Finland, France, Germany, Greece, Hungary, Italy, Latvia, Lithuania, Luxembourg, Malta, the Netherlands, Poland, Portugal, Slovakia, Slovenia, Spain, Sweden; and non-EU countries Iceland, Liechtenstein, Norway, Switzerland.
(Among the EU countries that are not in the Schengen Area, Bulgaria, Croatia, Cyprus and Romania will eventually join when they are ready. Ireland and the United Kingdom have opt-outs.)
S&D The centre-left Progressive Alliance of Socialists & Democrats, the European Parliament's socialist group, European social democrats, labour MEPs, the parliament's second largest group, the socialist bloc.
Social dialogue Negotiations between the social partners within the EU. Meetings between the EU employer organization BusinessEurope and trade union federation ETUC.
Social partners Employers and trade unions.
Stabilization and association agreement (SSA) EU agreement with non-EU country that typically is the first step towards EU membership. It can cover a wide variety of sectors, often free trade and the application of EU standards, along with EU money to help make the necessary reforms.
Synonym: Association agreement, a first step towards EU membership, pre-membership talks.
State aid Government support to the private sector, support from public authorities, government-backed programmes.
Subsidiarity principle The proximity principle, the principle that decisions be taken at the level closest to citizens.
Subsidiarity test National parliaments deciding whether the EU should take some political action, or if it should rather be local or national governments.
Suspension clause See Article 7.
Third countries EU jargon. Depending on the context, it means countries outside the EU or countries outside some other EU cooperation framework.
Synonyms: Non-EU country, from outside the EU, other country.

Transpose As in 'transpose a directive'.
Meaning: incorporating an EU directive into national law.
Synonyms: adopt the necessary laws to follow the directive, translate/transform the directive into national legislation.

Treaty Binding agreement between the EU countries, the EU's rulebook.

Trialogue Negotiations between the commission, parliament and council, direct negotiations between the legislatures, tripartite meeting, behind-closed-doors deal-making process, three-way talks.

Troika Mostly used to refer to (the representatives of) the International Monetary Fund, the European Commission and the European Central Bank, who oversee that the euro countries that have received emergency loans make the economic reforms that were conditions for the loan.

'The troika' is also used in EU jargon for many other threesomes. Before the Lisbon Treaty, which created the post of EU foreign chief, the troika was for example used for the group comprising the foreign minister from the EU country that held the council presidency, the high representative of the common foreign and security policy and the European commissioner for external relations.

Visegrad countries/Visegrad group Poland, Hungary, the Czech Republic and Slovakia.

Weimar Triangle Poland, Germany and France.

White paper Meaning: concrete proposals from the European Commission before the actual draft law is presented.
Synonyms: policy document, policy proposals, plans, blueprint.

Withdrawal clause See Article 50.

Yellow card procedure Formally 'early warning system'.
If a third of the EU countries' national parliaments object to a European Commission proposal, the commission has to withdraw and review it.

Notes

1 BBC News, *A-Z guide to Brussels-speak*, 16 May 2016
2 European Commission, *EU jargon in English and some possible alternatives*, Information providers guide, The EU Internet Handbook. [Website: ec.europa.eu/ipg/content/tips/words-style/jargon-alternatives_en.htm]

Index

References in bold indicate key passages.

A item 110
absolute majority, parliament 30, 140, 145–6
abuse of dominant position 50–1
Access Info Europe 256–7
access to documents 256–9
accreditation, to EU institutions 263–4
Acea 188
ACTA 139
advisory procedure, implementing acts 159
Advocate General 169–70
AGE 189
Agence Europe 203, 206
agencies, decentralized EU 174–8
Agra Europe 203
Agriculture and Fisheries Council 97
ALDE 61–4, 67
Alfter, Brigitte 240–1
amending treaties 153
amendments 74, 78–9, 142, 144–7, 228
Amnesty International 189
Amsterdam Treaty 153
Andriukaitis, Vytenis 34–6
antici 119–20
API *see* International Press Association
Arte 208
Article 7 139
Ashton, Catherine 165
Ask the EU 256–8
assistant, to MEP 58
attendance, MEPs 83
audiovisual archives 183

B item 110
background briefing: commission 46; council 101–2, 105–6
Barroso, José Manuel 135
Bathing Water Directive 174
Berlaymonster 209

Berlusconi, Silvio 121
BEUC *see* European Consumers' Organization
Bologna process 22
Bruegel 198
Brussels Briefing 207
Brussels Playbook 206
Brussels Press Club 265
budget: annual 128–9, **140–1,** 228; investigating journalism into 241–5; long-term 120, 128, 140, 219–20
budget discharge 86–8
Bureau of Investigative Journalism 239, 243
BusinessEurope 118, 187, 221
Buttiglione, Rocco 32

candidate country 16
Carnegie Europe 198–9
cartels 49–51
Cash for Amendments scandal 248
Cashman report 253
Centre for European Policy Studies (CEPS) 198–9
Centre for European Reform (CER) 199
CETA 139
Childers, Nessa 85
citizens' initiative 230
Civil Service Tribunal 169
Climate Action Network 189
codecision *see* ordinary legislative procedure
college of commissioners 29–30; appointment of 30–2; meeting 132–3
comitology *see* delegated acts; implementing acts
comitology committee 159–62, 230
comitology register 159–60
commitments, budget 141
Committee of the Regions 172–3, 215

Committee on Budgetary Control, parliament 86–7
Committee on Petitions, parliament 88–9
committees, parliament 72–5
communications advisors, commissioner's 40–1
competence, EU: exclusive 17–20; shared 17–21
competence catalogue 17, **18–19**
competition policy, EU 49–52
Competitiveness Council 98
concessions directive 230
conciliation committee: budget 140–1; ordinary legislative procedure 146
conclusions, EU summit 120, 127
Concord 190
Conference of Presidents, parliament 60–1
consent procedure 138
constituency week 81
consultation procedure 138–9
coordinator, party group 61, 71, 79, 87
Copa-Cogeca 187
core treaties 153
Coreper **108–9**, 110–12, 143–6
Coulisses de Bruxelles 209
council formations 96–9
Council of Europe 170, 233–5
Council of Ministers 95–116; press service 105–8
Council of the European Union *see* Council of Ministers
Court of Auditors 86–7, **171**
Court of Justice of the European Union 52–4, **168–70**, 213–14, 260
cross-border journalism 238-41

Data Harvest Conference 241
data retention directive 168, 213–14
Debating Europe 208
decision, commission 128
declaration of financial interest, MEPs 58, 249
delegated acts 157, **160, 162**
delegation: EEAS 167; European Parliament 75–6; national within party group 72
Delors, Jacques 25
desk officer 43
DG *see* directorates-general
Dieselgate committee 89–90
Dijsselbloem, Jeroen 103
directive 128
Directive on Optical Radiation 225–6

directorates-general 37, 43–4
document register, EU institutions' 255
doorstep interview 118
Duterte, Rodrigo 92

early warning system *see* subsidiarity test
EbS *see* Europe by Satellite
ECB *see* European Central Bank
ECHR *see* European Court of Human Rights
Economic and Financial Affairs Council (Ecofin) 97
Economist 203, 209
ECR 62, 64, 67
Education, Youth, Culture and Sport Council 99
EEA *see* European Environmental Agency
EEAS *see* European External Action Service
EEB *see* European Environmental Bureau
EFDD 61, 63–4
EFJ *see* European Federation of Journalists
EFSA *see* European Food Safety Authority
EJC *see* European Journalism Centre
elections, European Parliament: political platforms 64–5; turnout 70
electronic voting, parliament 79
embargoed information, commission 47
EMCDDA *see* European Monitoring Centre for Drugs and Drug Addiction
Employment, Social Policy, Health and Consumer Affairs Council 99
ENDS 203
ENF 61, 63–4
enhanced cooperation 96
Environment Council 98
Environmental Noise Directive 25
EP TV 60, 80
EPP 61, 63–4, 67
Epsco *see* Employment, Social Policy, Health and Consumer Affairs Council
Estrela report 68
ETUC *see* European Trade Union Confederation
EU Integrity Watch 249
EUobserver 203, 207
EUR-Lex 154–6
Euractiv 203, 207
Eurobarometer 181–3
Eurofound *see* European Foundation for the Improvement of Living and Working Conditions
Eurogroup 97, 103

Eurojust *see* European Union's Judicial Cooperation Unit
euromyths 204, 225–7
Euronews 202
Europa (council building) 88
Europarties 65–6
Europe by Satellite 8
Europe Daily Bulletin 206
Europe v. Facebook 249
European (magazine) 202
European Affairs committee, national parliaments' 113–14, 123
European Central Bank 97, 138, 170–1
European Centre for International Political Economy 200
European Commission 29–54; national representation offices 10, 40, 265
European Consumers' Organization 189
European Convention on Human Rights 24, 260
European Council on Foreign Relations 199
European Council *see* summit
European Court of Human Rights 170, 233–5, 260
European Economic and Social Committee 172–3
European Environment Agency 87, 174, 176, 178
European Environmental Bureau 189
European External Action Service 165–8
European Federation of Journalists 266
European Food Safety Authority 161, 174, 176
European Foundation for the Improvement of Living and Working Conditions 174, 176
European Journalism Centre 266
European Medicines Agency 174, 176
European Monitoring Centre for Drugs and Drug Addiction 174, 176
European Ombudsman 258–9
European Parliament 56–93; national information office 10, 59, 265; press service 59–60
European parliamentary assembly 56
European Policy Centre 200
European Trade Union Confederation 118, 189, 221
European Union Agency for Fundamental Rights 174, 177
European Union's Judicial Cooperation Unit 174, 177

European Values Study 183
European Voice 206
European Women's Lobby 189
Europolitique 203
Eurostat 180–1
Eurotopics 203, 208
ever closer union 16
examination procedure, implementing acts 159
executive board, European Central Bank 171
executive power, commission 48–52
expert group 131–2, 229
expert group register 131, 246–7

FAC *see* Foreign Affairs Council
Farage, Nigel 70
Farmsubsidy.org 242–4
Financial Times 203, 207, 239, 243
Financial Transparency System 245
first reading 141, **142,** 143, 147
first vice-president, commission 36
Fishsubsidy.org 243
Five Star Movement 63
Flash Eurobarometer 182
FOI requests *see* access to documents
Fondation Robert Schuman 200
FoodDrinkEurope 188
foreign affairs chief 102, 165–8
Foreign Affairs Council **97,** 102, 165–6
foreign policy, EU 165–7
foreign policy, European Parliament 76, **92–3**
four-column-document 144
Freedom Party 63
Friends of Europe 198, 200
Front National 63, 84
FTT 138

General Affairs Council 96–7
General Court 169
general expenditure allowance, MEPs 251
German Marshall Fund of the United States 201
GMOs 161
governing council, ECB 171
green paper 131
Greens/EFA 61–2, 64, 66–7
guardian of the treaties 52
GUE-NGL 61–2, 64, 67
Guéguen, Daniel 192
Gymnich 106

Harbour, Malcolm 249
head of unit 43–4
Heath, Ryan 209
High Representative for Foreign and Security Policy *see* foreign affairs chief

IATE 270
Ilga 190
impact assessment 129
implementing acts 157, 158–60, 161
informal meeting, council 106
infringement procedure 52–4, 89
Integritywatch 58
intergovernmental 15, 96
intergroups, parliament 76
International Herald Tribune 203
International Press Association 264–5, **266**
investigative committees, parliament 89–90

jargon 11, 268–70
Javorčík, Peter 111–12
Jeleva, Rumiana 32
JHA *see* Justice and Home Affairs Council
Journalismfund 239
Juncker, Jean-Claude 31–2, 86, 90, 121
jurisdiction, EU 16–24; *see also* competence; competence catalogue
Justice and Home Affairs Council 97–8
Justus Lipsius 106

Katainen, Jyrki 40–1
Kirkhope, Timothy 149–51

labour summit 118
Le Pen, Marine 70
legal basis 152–3
Legislative Observatory 59, 140, **155–6**, 228
letter of formal notice 53–4
Leveson Report 226
liaison officer, from national parliaments 135
Libération 209
like-minded group 117
Lisbon Treaty 7, 17, 21, 56, 102, 116, 137, 153, 157–8, 160
lobby register 193–4, 197, 246
lobbying 130–2, 150, **185–96;** investigative journalism into 245–50
LobbyPlag 250
Lux leaks committee 89–90
Luxembourg compromise 232

Maastricht Treaty 3, 137, 153
Mates, Neven 138
MEPranking 83
mergers 51
Mersch, Yves 138
midday briefing 45-6
mini-plenary, parliament 80
mixed council 96
MLex 203
Mogherini, Federica 165
More O'Ferrall, Richard 66
Multi-annual Financial Framework *see* budget
multi-speed Europe *see* enhanced cooperation

national implementing measures 154
Navracsics, Tibor 32
New York Times 203
NI *see* non-attached
Nice Treaty 153
non-attached 61, 63, 70
Nordic-Baltic group 117
Notre Europe 200
NUTS 180

O'Reilly, Emily 258
Œil *see* Legislative Observatory
Official Journal 154–5
official languages, EU 9–10
Ohlsson, Birgitta 23–4
OLAF 171–2, 260
on/off the record 37, **44–5**, 59
one-minute speech 78
online newsroom, EU 8
Open days 173
Open Europe 198, 200
orange card 134–5
ordinary legislative procedure 57, 137, **141–9**
own-initiative report, parliament 91–2, 127, 227–8

party groups, parliament 60–72; after Brexit 63–4
Passenger Name Record Directive 149–51
payments, budget 141
permanent representation to the EU 100–2, 107
plenary sessions, parliament 76–80
political dialogue, national parliaments and commission 135
Politico Europe 203, 206, 209

Politikportal.de 209
portfolio, commissioners' 30–1
potential candidate country 16
preliminary ruling 168
presidency, council 78, 102–5, 112
president: commission 127; European Council 102–3, 116–18
press corps, Brussels 204–5
protection of sources 259–61
public consultation, commission 130
public procurement 25, 245

qualified majority, council 112–13
Quatremer, Jean 209
questions to commission 82, **84–5**

radio studio, in EU institutions 265–6
Rapid 46–7
rapporteur 58–9, 71, **74–5,** 79, 143–6, 150–1
reasoned opinion 53–4
regions: Brussels offices 190–1, 215; EU influence over 25
regulation 24, 128
Reinfeldt, Fredrik 121–4
Residence Palace 265
right to initiative, commission 127
road map 128
roll-call voting, parliament **79,** 80–1, 83

S&D 61–4, 67
Safe Harbour 249
Sakharov Prize for Freedom of Thought 93
Salla, Aura 40–1
Santer, Jacques 86–7
Sarvamaa, Petri 87
Schengen agreement 98
Schlyter, Carl 192
Schrems, Max 249–50
Schulz, Martin 78
Schwalba-Hoth, Frank 191
second reading 141, **145–6,** 147
Severin, Adrian 248
shadow rapporteur 58–9, **71,** 73–4, 79
Ship Recycling Regulation 152, 158
single seat, parliament 68, 77
social partners 118
Social Platform 190
Solvit 222–3
Special Committee on Agriculture, council 109
special Eurobarometer 182
special legislative procedures 138–40

Spitzenkandidaten 30–1, 65, 69
spokespersons, commission 37–9, 45–6
Stakeholder 194
Standard Eurobarometer 181–2
state aid 51–2
State of the European Union speech 127–8
Strasser, Ernst 248
Strazdina, Ina 205–6
Stubb, Alexander 56
subsidiarity: principle 134; test 134–5
subsistence allowance, MEPs 252
summit, EU 103, 116–24
Sunday Times 248
supranational 15, 96
Swift agreement 80, 139

Tenders Electronic Daily 245
TEU *see* Treaty on European Union
TFEU *see* Treaty on the Functioning of the European Union
Thaler, Zoran 248
think tank 197–201
third reading 146–7
Thorning-Schmidt, Helle 56
Tillack, Hans-Martin 260
Times 209
Timmermans, Frans 32, 36
Tobacco Products Directive 232–3
Tories 61–2, 64, 67
Transparency International 190
transparency regulation 252-5
Transport, Telecommunications and Energy Council 98
travel grants 265
treaties, EU 16–17, 128, 152, **153**
Treaty of Rome 16, 153
Treaty on European Union 153
Treaty on the Functioning of the European Union 153
trilogue 142–5, 151
TTE *see* Transport, Telecommunications and Energy Council
TTIP 139
Tusk, Donald 103
tv studio, EU institutions 265–6
Twitter 209

UK Independence Party 63-4
unanimity, council 112–13

Van Rompuy, Herman 121
vice-president, commission 33, 36

Visegrad group **117**, 232
vote of no confidence 86
Votewatch 81–3, 115–16
voting calculator, council 115
Voxeurop 203, 208

Waterfield, Bruno 209
weekly calendar, parliament 81
Westlund, Åsa 192
whistleblowers 259–60
white paper 131

Wobbing 257
Wojciechowski, Janusz 138–9
work programme, commission 91, 128
working groups, council 108, **109–10**, 229
WWF 190

yearly calendar, parliament 81
yellow card 134–5
Your Voice in Europe 130
Youreurope 222

For Product Safety Concerns and Information please contact our EU representative GPSR@taylorandfrancis.com
Taylor & Francis Verlag GmbH, Kaufingerstraße 24, 80331 München, Germany

www.ingramcontent.com/pod-product-compliance
Lightning Source LLC
Chambersburg PA
CBHW070747020526
44116CB00032B/1996